ARCO

100 BEST CAREERS

FOR

WRITERS AND

ARTISTS

Shelly Field

MACMILLAN • USA

This book is dedicated to my parents, Ed and Selma, and to my sisters, Jessica and Debbie, for teaching me to have dreams, letting me live the ones I chose, and giving me love and encouragement always.

Macmillan General Reference
A Simon & Schuster Macmillan Company
1633 Broadway New York, NY 10019

Macmillan Publishing books may be purchased for business or sales promotional use. For information please write: Special Markets Department, Macmillan Publishing USA, 1633 Broadway, New York, NY 10019.

An Arco Book

MACMILLAN and colophon is a registered trademark of Macmillan, Inc.
ARCO and colophon is a registered trademark of Simon & Schuster, Inc.

Library of Congress Number: 97-071489
ISBN 0-02-861926-9

Manufactured in the United States of America

10 9 8 7 6 5 4 3 2 1

CONTENTS

PREFACE

This is a comprehensive guide to 100 of the best jobs for writers and artists. It is a valuable resource for those planning careers in these fields, individuals just entering the job market, and those hoping to change careers.

Thousands of people aspire to find good jobs using writing or artistic skills but have no idea how to get a position. They have no concept of what career opportunities are available, where to find them, or what qualifications and training are required. *100 Best Careers for Writers and Artists* is the single most comprehensive source for learning about job opportunities in these fields.

This book was written to help aspiring writers and artists to prepare now for interesting, exciting, fun, glamorous, and high-paying jobs. The industries covered in this book offer vast opportunities. The 100 careers discussed here encompass a multitude of interests and fields.

The job market provides opportunities for a wide range of people with a variety of skills at a number of levels of expertise and experience. The trick to locating the job you want is to promote your skills and use them to enter an industry that will let you utilize your creativity. Once you have your foot in the door, you can climb the career ladder to success.

INFORMATION SOURCES

Information for this book was obtained through interviews, questionnaires, and a variety of books, magazines, newsletters, other literature, and television and radio programs.

Among the people interviewed were men and women working in all aspects of radio, television, film, video, theater, fashion, advertising, newspapers, magazines, book publishing, sports, and entertainment. Information was also gathered from academies, colleges, trade schools, vocational-technical schools, trade associations, and human resources departments.

100 Best Careers for Writers and Artists is divided into the following thirteen general employment sections. Within each section are descriptions of many individual careers.

- Careers for Writers in Radio, Television, and Film
- Careers for Writers in the Entertainment and Sports Industries
- Careers for Writers in Newspapers and Magazines
- Careers for Writers in Book Publishing
- Careers for Writers in Advertising, Public Relations, Marketing, and Communications
- Miscellaneous Careers for Writers
- Careers for Artists in Theater
- Careers for Artists in Design
- Careers for Artists in Television, Film, and Video
- Careers for Artists in Advertising and Graphic Design
- Careers for Artists in Fine Arts and Crafts
- Careers for Artists in Teaching
- Miscellaneous Careers for Artists

There are two parts to each job entry. The first part offers job facts in an overview chart. The second part presents descriptive information in a narrative text.

The text details the job description and responsibilities, employment opportunities, earnings, advancement opportunities, education and training, experience and qualifications, additional sources of information, and tips for obtaining the job.

Names, addresses, and phone numbers of trade associations, organizations, and unions are listed in the Appendix to provide resources for further information.

By reading this book, you are taking the first step not only toward finding a career that is in demand but also toward preparing for it. Job opportunities exist throughout the country and the world. No matter which facet of the job market you choose to enter, you can find a career that is rewarding and enjoyable. The jobs are out there waiting for you. You just have to go after them.

Shelly Field

ACKNOWLEDGMENTS

I thank every individual, company, corporation, agency, association, and union that provided information, assistance, and encouragement for this book.

First and foremost, I acknowledge with appreciation my editor, Linda Bernbach, for providing the original impetus for this book. I also thank Eve Steinberg for her editing expertise. I gratefully acknowledge the assistance of Ed and Selma Field for their ongoing support and encouragement in this project.

Others whose help was invaluable include: Academy of Hospital Public Relations; Advertising Club of New York; Advertising Council; Advertising Research Foundation; Advertising Women of New York, Inc.; Harrison Allen; American Advertising Federation; American Association of Advertising Agencies; American Federation of Musicians (AFM); American Hospital Association; American Society for Hospital Marketing and Public Relations; American Society of Composers and Publishers; Joanne Anderson; Art Directors Club, Inc.; Barbara Ashworth, Beauty School of Middletown; Association of National Advertisers; Association of Theatrical Press Agents and Managers; Dan Barrett; Allan Barrish; Jan Behr, associate business agent, Local 162 IATSE; Warren Bergstrom; Eugene Blabey, WVOS Radio; Steve Blackman; Joyce Blackman; Fredda Briant, business representative, Theatrical Wardrobe Union; Broadcast Music, Inc.; Theresa Bull; Katrina Bull; Business/Professional Advertising Association; Liane Carpenter; Earl "Speedo" Carroll; Mary Cawley; Anthony Cellini; Karen Cobham, Broadway unit coordinator of Makeup Artists and Hairstylists; Andy Cohen; Bernard Cohen, Horizon Advertising; Dr. Jessica L. Cohen; Lorraine Cohen; Norman Cohen; Gina Colozzi; Community General Hospital, Harris, N.Y.; Kathleen Conry, director/actress; Jan Cornelius; Crawford Memorial Library Staff; Meike Cryan; Daniel Dayton; W. Lynne Dayton; Direct Mail/Marketing Association, Inc.; Direct Marketing Educational Foundation, Inc.; Jane Donohue; The Dramatists Guild; Michelle Edwards; Scott Edwards; Ernest Evans; Valerie Esper; John Fasciano; Sara Feldberg; Field Associates, Ltd.; Danny Field; Deborah K. Field, Esq.; Gregg Field; Lillian (Cookie) Field; Mike Field; Robert Field; Finkelstein Memorial Library Staff; Rob Fior, Slot Manager, California Hotel and Casino; Anna Gatto; Cara Gatto; John Gatto; Sheila Gatto; Gina Giambiattista, administrator, University/Resident Theatre Association, Inc.; Sally Gifft, assistant business representative, United Scenic Artists; Tina Gilbert; George Glantzis; Kaytee Glantzis; Sam Goldych; Gail Haberle; Joyce Harrington; Hermann Memorial Library Staff; Terry Hooks; Joan Howard; Jo Hunt, DeLyon-Hunt & Associates; International Alliance of Theatrical Stage Employees (IATSE); International Brotherhood of Electrical Workers; Jimmy "Handyman" Jones; Margo Jones;

K-LITE Radio; Howard Kaiser, Raleigh Hotel; Dave Kleinman; Janice Kleinman; Dr. John C. Koch, Sullivan County Performing Arts Council; Tom Lagrutta; Bob Leone, Songwriters Guild; Liberty Public Library Staff; Lipman Advertising; Michael Madzy; Ginger Maher; Dorothy Marcus; Ernie Martinelli; Robert Masters, Esq.; Richard Mayfield, District Assistant for U.S. House of Representatives; McCann-Erikson; Lois McCluskey; Judy McCoy; Werner Mendel, New Age Health Spa; Phillip Mestman; Rima Mestman; Metropolitan Opera; Beverly Michaels, Esq.; Martin Michaels, Esq.; Mitchel Miller; Shelly Miller; Jason Milligan; Monticello Central High School Guidance Department; Monticello Central School High School Library Staff; Monticello Central School Middle School Library Staff; Sharron Morris; Music Business Institute; Music Educators Conference; Florence Naistadt; National Association of Broadcast Employees and Technicians; National Association of Broadcasters; National Music Publishers Associations; Chris Nelson; Earl Nesmith; New Dramatists; Marvin Newman; Jim Newton; New York State Employment Service; New York State Nurses Association; Peter Notarstefano; The One Club; Ed Pearson, Nikkodo, USA; Karen Pizzuto, Communications Director, IATSE; Debra Pless; Robert Pless; Anita Portas, IATSE; Public Relations Society of America; Harvey Rachlin; Ramapo Catskill Library System; Doug Richards; Martin Richman, Executive Director, Community General Hospital, Sullivan County, N.Y.; John Riegler; David Rosenberg, Human Resources Manager, Grey Advertising; Gary Roth, BMI; Genice Ruiz; Jim Ryan, business representative, United Scenic Artists; Saatchi and Saatchi Advertising; Richard Sandquist, Producer, Forestburg Playhouse; Richard Schaefer, lighting designer; Nelson Sheeley, freelance director; Matt Sjoquist; M.D. Smith, slot office secretary, California Hotel and Casino; Society of Illustrators; Laura Solomon; The Songwriter Guild; Debbie Springfield; Matthew E. Strong; Sullivan County Community College; Sullivan County Performing Arts Council; Tom Sutton; The Teenagers; Jordan Thomas; Thrall Library Staff; Marie Tremper; Turning Stone Casino; Leo S. Ullman, Esq.; United States Department of Labor; Brenda Walker; Carol Williams; John Williams; John Wolfe; Johnny World; WSUL Radio; George Wurzbach; and WVOS Radio.

My thanks also to the many associations, companies, organizations, and people who provided material for this book but who wish to remain anonymous.

INTRODUCTION

The history of mankind has been recorded over the years by the creative artists and writers of their times. Every society has had its bards and poets, its record keepers, and its storytellers. Each successive generation has been enriched by the culture of the past. Indeed, we learn a great deal about a culture from its artistic endeavors, visual arts, fabric and costume design, prose and poetry, scrolls, scripts, and stories.

Almost every industry in the world depends to some extent on the creativity of its personnel. There are literally thousands of people working in jobs revolving directly around the written word or artistic creativity, and there is room for thousands more. One of them could be you.

Creative careers fall into two overall categories: those using words and those using art. At least one of these, and often both, finds a place in every inudstry.

Our lives are affected every day by writers. Without writers, we could not have books, magazines, or newspapers to read. There would be no television shows, no movies, and no songs on the radio without writers. We would not even have the directions for popping a frozen dinner into the microwave without the skills of writers.

Our lives are similarly affected by artists and those using artistic skills. Every time we see a painting, mural, photograph, cartoon, sculpture, or piece of jewelry, we are enjoying the fruits of artists. However, artistic creativity is not limited to fine arts. Artists and designers work in many industries, among them theater, fashion, television, and film.

Creative artists design and lay out ads, book and record jackets, and packaging for the food that we eat. They design the interiors of our houses and the clothes we wear.

Within each section of this book, you will find information to acquaint you with job possibilities for artists and writers in a specific industry. A key to the organization of each entry follows.

JOB DESCRIPTION AND RESPONSIBILITIES

Every effort has been made to give well-rounded job descriptions. Because no two companies are identically structured, no two positions with the same job title or function will be identical.

Keep in mind that job titles may vary from company to company. In some instances, the duties of two jobs are the same; only the names differ. At other times, different duties apply to the same job titles.

EMPLOYMENT OPPORTUNITIES

This section discusses various employment opportunities and/or settings for jobs in each area.

EARNINGS

Salary ranges for the job titles in this book are as accurate as possible. Exact earnings depend on the size and location of a company as well as on the experience, education, training, and responsibilities of the individual in the position. In many instances, earnings are influenced by the talent and professional reputation of the specific individual.

ADVANCEMENT OPPORTUNITIES

A variety of options for career advancement has been included. However, there are no hard-and-fast rules for climbing to the top in your career. While work performance is important, advancement in many jobs is based on experience, education, talent, and attitude.

EDUCATION AND TRAINING

Because the best-qualified people are the most likely to be hired, this section presents the minimum educational and training requirements for each job area. These requirements may include technical and vocational schools, colleges and universities, and on-the-job training.

EXPERIENCE AND QUALIFICATIONS

This section discusses required or helpful experience, qualifications, and skills.

FOR ADDITIONAL INFORMATION: This section lists trade associations, organizations, and unions that offer career assistance, advice, or information. Many also provide scholarships, fellowships, seminars, or other beneficial programs. Addresses and phone numbers are located in the Appendix at the end of the book.

TIPS

This section contains ideas on how to get a job, how to gain entry into your area of interest, or how to become more successful in a current position.

This book will help you prepare for a career you will enjoy and find rewarding for years to come. Don't get discouraged. Keep knocking on doors, sending out resumes, and applying for jobs until you get the job you want. Then use your talent, drive, and determination to become the best you can be.

Good luck!

CHAPTER 1

Careers for Writers in Radio, Television & Film

Today's society is greatly influenced by radio, television, and film. Radio came on the scene in 1920, and people still tune in often to their favorite radio station to hear music, news, or an interesting talk show, especially while driving in their cars and early and late in the day. Television entered our living rooms almost half a century ago, and the first sound movie was released almost seven decades ago. Expansion of audiences in both size and variety of interests and the growth of competition among the media have sparked many career possibilities in the world of radio, television, and film.

Careers for writers in radio, television, and film cover a broad spectrum. Space alone limits the list. This chapter covers the following careers:

Advertising Copywriter—Radio/Television
News Writer—Radio
News Reporter—Radio
News Reporter—Television
News Writer—Television
Desk Assistant—Television
Community Affairs Director—Television Station
Public Relations and Promotions Director—Television Station
Screenwriter
Soap Opera Writer
Sitcom Writer

ADVERTISING COPYWRITER—RADIO/TELEVISION

JOB DESCRIPTION: *Write copy for advertisements to be aired on radio or television.*

EARNINGS: *$18,000 to $75,000+ per year.*

RECOMMENDED EDUCATION AND TRAINING: *A bachelor's degree in advertising, communications, journalism, marketing, English, public relations, or liberal arts.*

SKILLS AND PERSONALITY TRAITS: *Excellent writing skills; good command of the English language; creativity.*

EXPERIENCE AND QUALIFICATIONS: *Experience requirements vary.*

JOB DESCRIPTION AND RESPONSIBILITIES

To sell effectively, every advertisement to be heard on radio or seen on television must be well planned and carefully written. Advertising copywriters handle this job.

The copy developed for radio and television ads differs from that written for print advertising. Radio and television ads are delivered under time limitations. The words that the announcers or actors speak must be clear, concise, and easy to understand. The words must get the message across and make it memorable. Because radio provides no pictures or graphics, the words used in radio ads must create an image in the listener's mind. Copy used in television ads must relate to and coordinate with the pictures or video. Copywriters working in advertising departments of radio and television stations usually prepare ads for local, cable, and syndicated programs. Copywriters in advertising agencies usually prepare advertisements that air nationally.

Duties and responsibilities of advertising copywriters vary, depending on the size and structure of the television or radio station and its advertising department. Copywriters working at larger stations usually have more specific duties and responsibilities than those working at smaller stations. The major responsibility of all advertising copywriters is developing copy for ads. Other duties include conceiving the concepts for advertisements as well as producing them and getting them on air. At some smaller stations, advertising copywriters might also be expected to sell the ads themselves. Advertising copywriters might be responsible for writing copy for just one ad for a client or for developing an entire broadcast campaign. Often the copywriter develops several different drafts of copy for advertisements. He or she then asks the advertiser to choose and approve one. If the advertiser likes the copy, the ad can move ahead and be produced. If not, the copywriter must rewrite and change the copy until the advertiser approves.

Copywriters must be able to write in a variety of styles. They might write straight textual copy or perhaps prepare dialogue. Writing dialogue often requires the copywriter to prepare stage directions and instructions for necessary sound effects, voice-overs, and so on. The copywriter can do so with the help of a storyboard to make it easier to see the words that go with specific graphics. Copywriters must be able to write crisp, clear, and credible language. They also must be able to write condensed copy that fits into the ad's required time frame.

Other responsibilities of advertising copywriters for radio and television might include the following:

- Developing copy to be used for both television and radio commercials
- Working with directors, producers, senior copywriters, graphic designers, art directors, models, actors, actresses, announcers, and camera people

EMPLOYMENT OPPORTUNITIES

Many employment opportunities are open for copywriters who can write clear, concise, and imaginative copy. Copywriters can locate jobs throughout the country. Those without much experience often find positions at smaller stations where turnover is high. Those with experience can often find work in larger stations or in major-market television or radio. Employment possibilities include the following:

- Radio stations
- Local cable stations
- Network-affiliated television stations
- Independent television stations
- National cable stations
- Networks

EARNINGS

Earnings for advertising copywriters in radio and television range from $18,000 to $75,000 or more annually depending on the specific station's size and location as well as the copywriter's experience, expertise, responsibilities, and professional reputation.

ADVANCEMENT OPPORTUNITIES

Advertising copywriters might advance their careers by locating similar positions in larger or more prestigious stations. Some copywriters climb the career ladder by becoming senior copywriters or by obtaining copywriting jobs in advertising agencies.

EDUCATION AND TRAINING

Most radio and television stations prefer their copywriters to hold a college degree. Good majors include advertising, journalism, communications, marketing, English, public relations, and liberal arts. Many aspiring copywriters find seminars, workshops, and classes on copywriting, scriptwriting, advertising, and the broadcasting industry helpful for securing positions.

EXPERIENCE AND QUALIFICATIONS

Experience requirements for advertising copywriters working in broadcasting vary from station to station. Smaller stations often hire copywriters directly out of college. Larger stations usually require some sort of experience. You can obtain such experience through jobs at smaller stations or through internships.

Copywriters must be creative and imaginative and have excellent writing skills. The ability to write clear, concise, and condensed copy is essential.

FOR ADDITIONAL INFORMATION: Aspiring copywriters can learn more about this career by contacting the National Cable Television Association, Inc. (NCTA), the National Association of Broadcasters (NAB), the American Advertising Federation (AAF), the Radio Advertising Bureau (RAB), American Women in Radio and Television (AWRT), and the Writers Guild of America (WGA).

TIPS

- Look in the newspaper classified section for jobs advertised under such headings as "Copywriter," "Advertising," "Radio," "Television," or "Broadcasting."
- Look for internships at television and radio stations. You might also find internships through college intern programs.
- Write as much as you can. The more practice you have, the more polished your writing skills and techniques will become.
- Send your resume with a short cover letter to radio and television stations to inquire about openings.
- Take seminars, workshops, and classes in copywriting, advertising, and the broadcast industry. These are useful for honing skills and making important contacts.
- Attend seminars and conferences offered by trade associations.
- Get a job at a smaller station, gain experience, and then move on to a better job.

NEWS WRITER—RADIO

JOB DESCRIPTION: *Develop and write copy for radio newscasts; gather information; check facts.*

EARNINGS: *$16,000 to $45,000+ per year.*

RECOMMENDED EDUCATION AND TRAINING: *A bachelor's degree preferred or required.*

SKILLS AND PERSONALITY TRAITS: *Excellent writing skills; good command of the English language; research skills; interview skills.*

EXPERIENCE AND QUALIFICATIONS: *Experience writing news for radio, television, or print media is helpful.*

JOB DESCRIPTION AND RESPONSIBILITIES

Radio news writers are responsible for developing and writing the stories or scripts read by radio news anchors and in-studio reporters. The responsibilities of individual news writers vary depending on the size and structure of the station and the newsroom.

Radio news writers are expected to gather information from a variety of sources. These include reporters, wire services, press releases, and research. News writers must check their information for accuracy. Some radio news writers have additional responsibilities. They might be required to write news briefs, special reports, and short "teases" that are aired to pique interest in the news. Radio news writers might be responsible for writing and broadcasting sports reports, weathercasts, traffic conditions, features, or other types of stories as well as news.

Finished radio news reports must be interesting, understandable, accurate, and credible. The writer must tailor each story to fit into its allotted time period. Depending on the specific station, news writers might be news generalists or be responsible for specialized areas of news. These areas might include entertainment, politics, health, business, consumer information, sports, and so on. Radio news writers might work various shifts—daytime, evening, or overnight.

Other responsibilities of radio news writers might include the following:

- Rewriting wire stories from news services or other sources for use on the air
- Developing scripts for news specials and public affairs programs
- Acting as reporters or anchors themselves

EMPLOYMENT OPPORTUNITIES

News writers can find employment opportunities throughout the country. At many smaller stations, the news writers are also the reporters. Employment settings include the following:

- Network radio
- Public radio stations
- Independent radio stations

EARNINGS

Radio news writers can earn between $16,000 and $45,000 or more depending on the station's size, location, and prestige as well as the news writer's experience, responsibilities, and professional reputation. Writers starting out at smaller stations will have lower salaries. As writers obtain experience and locate jobs at larger stations and in more metropolitan areas, their salaries increase.

ADVANCEMENT OPPORTUNITIES

Radio news writers usually start their careers at small stations. At this stage of their careers, news writers usually are news reporters as well. Radio news writers climb the career ladder by locating positions at larger or more prestigious stations or networks. Some news writers advance their careers by becoming news directors, editors, producers, or reporters. Others move into television news writing.

EDUCATION AND TRAINING

As a rule, radio stations prefer or require their news writers to hold a minimum of a bachelor's degree. Good majors include journalism, communications, English, political science, broadcasting, mass communications, journalism, or a related field. Some smaller stations might waive the educational requirement. However, career advancement will be difficult without the degree. Seminars, workshops, and courses in all facets of writing and broadcasting are helpful in honing skills and making important contacts.

EXPERIENCE AND QUALIFICATIONS

Those seeking jobs in small stations might find jobs right out of college. Any type of experience writing news for radio, television, or print media is useful. Writers can gain experience through summer or part-time jobs at local or school radio stations or with print media. Internships are also helpful.

Radio news writers must have excellent writing skills and a good command of the English language. They must also be able to write simple, clear, crisp copy.

FOR ADDITIONAL INFORMATION: If you are interested in a career in this field, you can get additional information from the National Association of Broadcast Employees and Technicians (NABET), the Writers Guild of America (WGA), American Women in Radio and Television (AWRT), and the Radio-Television News Directors Association (RTNDA).

TIPS

- Look in the newspaper classified section for jobs advertised under such headings as "News," "News Writer," "Radio News," or "Broadcasting."
- Get some experience in a smaller market, then move up the career ladder.
- Keep up with current affairs and news items. Interviewers often ask questions before they hire you.
- Write as much as you can. The more practice you have, the more polished your writing skills and techniques will become.
- Send your resume with a short cover letter to radio stations to inquire about openings. Ask that they keep your resume on file if they have no current openings.
- Obtain experience working part time or summers at local newspapers and radio and television stations.
- Put together a portfolio of scripts and other news stories that you have written. Make sure that you bring these to job interviews.

NEWS REPORTER—RADIO

JOB DESCRIPTION: *Write copy for radio news stories; develop and report news stories; check facts.*

EARNINGS: *$15,000 to $50,000+ per year.*

RECOMMENDED EDUCATION AND TRAINING: *A bachelor's degree is preferred.*

SKILLS AND PERSONALITY TRAITS: *Excellent writing skills; good command of the English language; pleasant speaking voice; articulateness.*

EXPERIENCE AND QUALIFICATIONS: *Experience working in radio or writing news stories for print media is helpful.*

JOB DESCRIPTION AND RESPONSIBILITIES

Radio news reporters announce the news on the air. Reporters might be responsible for reporting local, regional, state, national, or international news, or any combination of these. Some radio news reporters are responsible for writing and broadcasting sports reports, weathercasts, traffic conditions, or other types of stories and activities.

Specific responsibilities for radio news reporters vary with the size of the station. A reporter working at a smaller station at which he or she is the only news reporter might also act as the news director. News reporters working at larger stations often work with an entire news staff. At some stations, radio news reporters are expected to look for news stories. At other stations, news directors or editors assign specific stories for each news reporter to cover. Whatever the method of obtaining the story, news reporters must find ways of developing interesting broadcasts. Radio news reporters must interview people to secure their comments. Sometimes radio news reporters bring their material to news editors who coordinate the information with other reporters' stories.

Radio news reporters must write their stories clearly and concisely. Stories must be interesting and easy for listeners to understand. Radio news reporters might work from the station or live, on location. They might be expected to tape-record interviews and statements in person or by a telephone hookup. The reporter must then decide how to edit interviews and what he or she will say during the broadcast.

Radio news reporters work various shifts—daytime, evening, or overnight.

Other responsibilities of radio news reporters might include the following:

- Compiling and rewriting wire stories from news services or other sources
- Attending meetings or events to gather news

EMPLOYMENT OPPORTUNITIES

Employment opportunities can be located throughout the country at large, medium, and small stations. Every radio station needs at least one news reporter; most have more. Stations in major markets often have large news staffs. Major markets for radio include metropolitan cities such as New York City, Los Angeles, Chicago, Boston, and Atlanta.

EARNINGS

Radio news reporters can earn between $15,000 and $50,000 or more depending on the station's size, location, and prestige as well as the reporter's experience, responsibilities, and professional reputation. Reporters starting out in smaller stations earn the least. As a reporter gains experience and locates jobs in larger stations in larger cities, his or her salary will increase.

ADVANCEMENT OPPORTUNITIES

Advancement opportunities are good for those seeking to work in radio news. Reporters can advance their careers in several ways. The most common is for radio news reporters to gain experience and find jobs in larger, more prestigious stations. Other radio news reporters climb the career ladder by becoming news directors or editors. Some reporters seek advancement opportunities in other media such as newspapers, magazines, or television.

EDUCATION AND TRAINING

Most radio stations prefer at least a bachelor's degree when filling this position. Majors such as communications, journalism, broadcasting, broadcast journalism, and liberal arts are good choices for aspiring radio news reporters. Seminars, workshops, and courses in all facets of writing are also useful.

EXPERIENCE AND QUALIFICATIONS

Usually all but the smallest stations require experience working in journalism or broadcasting. Reporters can gain such experience through summer or part-time jobs at local stations, through internships, or by working at school radio stations.

Radio news reporters must have good writing skills. A pleasant speaking voice is also necessary.

FOR ADDITIONAL INFORMATION: Aspiring reporters can get additional information from the National Association of Broadcasters (NAB), the Radio Television News Directors Association (RTNDA), the National Association of Broadcast Employees and Technicians (NABET), and American Women in Radio and Television (AWRT).

TIPS

- Look in the newspaper classified section for jobs advertised under such headings as "News," "Broadcast Journalism," "Radio News," "Radio," "News Reporter," or "Broadcasting."
- Check radio and other entertainment trade publications such as *Radio and Records*, *Broadcasting*, and *Billboard* for advertised positions.
- Write as much as you can. The more practice you have, the more polished your writing skills and techniques will become.
- Send your resume with a short cover letter to radio stations to inquire about openings.
- Get experience at your high school or college radio station.

- Obtain additional experience working part time or summers at local newspapers.
- Try getting a job at a smaller station, gaining experience, then moving on to a better job.

NEWS REPORTER—TELEVISION

JOB DESCRIPTION: *Develop and report news stories; gather information; check facts; write copy for television news stories.*

EARNINGS: *$22,000 to $200,000+ per year.*

RECOMMENDED EDUCATION AND TRAINING: *A bachelor's degree is required.*

SKILLS AND PERSONALITY TRAITS: *Excellent writing skills; good command of the English language; a pleasant speaking voice and appearance; articulateness.*

EXPERIENCE AND QUALIFICATIONS: *Experience writing news for radio, television, or print media is preferred.*

JOB DESCRIPTION AND RESPONSIBILITIES

News reporters working in television report news stories and features on the air. Reporters might be responsible for reporting local, regional, state, national, and international news or might specialize in only some of these. Television news reporters might be responsible for writing and broadcasting sports reports, weathercasts, traffic conditions, features, or other types of stories.

Specific responsibilities for television news reporters vary depending on the station's size. Reporters working at smaller stations have more diverse duties. News reporters working at larger stations usually have more specific responsibilities. Some stations expect their television news reporters to look for news stories. At others, news directors or editors assign specific stories for each reporter to cover. Whatever the method of obtaining the story, news reporters must devise ways of developing interesting broadcasts. Television news reporters must interview people to secure comments from them. The reporters might do investigations, search out leads, check facts for accuracy, and organize reports. Finished television news reports must be interesting, easy to understand, accurate, and credible. Television news reporters often must write their own copy for what they will say on air. Talented television reporters can make even run-of-the mill stories seem interesting.

Depending on the specific station, news reporters might be responsible for handling either general or specialized areas of news. Specialized areas include entertainment, politics, health, business, consumer information, sports, and so on. Some news reporters cover local events and functions. Others might report only national events. Television news reporters might work various shifts—daytime, evening, or overnight.

Other responsibilities of television news reporters might include the following:

- Compiling and rewriting wire stories from news services or other sources
- Attending meetings or events to gather news
- Traveling to regions of breaking stories throughout the country or the world
- Developing stories and features

EMPLOYMENT OPPORTUNITIES

Television reporters can find employment opportunities throughout the country in any area hosting television or cable stations. The most marketable reporters have knowledge about special subjects such as health, business, entertainment, and consumer issues. Television news reporters might work in a variety of settings, including major, midsize, and small markets. Opportunities exist in the following:

- Network television
- National cable stations
- Public television stations
- Local cable stations
- Independent television stations
- Affiliated television stations

EARNINGS

Television news reporters can earn between $22,000 and $200,000 or more depending on the station's size, location, and prestige as well as the reporter's experience, responsibilities, and professional reputation. Reporters starting out at smaller stations have lower salaries. As reporters gain experience and locate jobs in larger stations and more metropolitan areas, their salaries increase.

ADVANCEMENT OPPORTUNITIES

Television news reporters usually start out at small stations. They advance their careers by locating positions at larger or more prestigious television stations or with networks. Some news reporters climb the career ladder by becoming news directors or editors.

EDUCATION AND TRAINING

Usually, television stations require their news reporters to hold a minimum of a bachelor's degree for this position. It is wise to major in broadcasting, mass communications, journalism, political science, liberal arts, or a related field. Seminars, workshops, and courses in all facets of writing, broadcasting, and television are helpful in learning new skills and making important contacts.

EXPERIENCE AND QUALIFICATIONS

Reporters can find jobs at small stations right out of college. However, employers usually prefer experience writing news for radio, television, or print media. Reporters can gain other experience through summer or part-time jobs at local stations, through internships, or by working at school radio or television stations or on local newspapers.

Television news reporters must have good writing skills. A pleasant speaking voice and appearance are also necessary.

FOR ADDITIONAL INFORMATION: If you are interested in seeking a career in this field, you can get additional information from the National Association of Broadcasters (NAB), the Radio Television News Directors Association (RTNDA), the National Association of Broadcast Employees and Technicians (NABET), the Writers Guild of America (WGA), and American Women in Radio and Television (AWRT).

TIPS

- Look in the newspaper classified section for jobs advertised under such headings as "News," "Broadcast Journalism," "Television News," "Television," "News Reporter," "Correspondent," "Cable Television," or "Broadcasting."

- Write as much as you can. The more practice you have, the more polished your writing skills and techniques will become.

- Send your resume with a short cover letter to television and cable stations to inquire about openings.

- Get a job in a small market, gain experience, then move up the career ladder.

- If you have experience, look for an agent to help you locate a better job and negotiate your earnings package.

- Obtain experience working part time or summers at local newspapers or radio or television stations.

NEWS WRITER—TELEVISION

JOB DESCRIPTION: *Develop and write copy for newscasts; gather information; check facts.*

EARNINGS: *$18,000 to $55,000+ per year.*

RECOMMENDED EDUCATION AND TRAINING: *A bachelor's degree is required.*

SKILLS AND PERSONALITY TRAITS: *Excellent writing skills; good command of the English language; research skills; interview skills.*

EXPERIENCE AND QUALIFICATIONS: *Experience writing news for radio, television, or print media is helpful.*

JOB DESCRIPTION AND RESPONSIBILITIES

Television news writers are responsible for developing and writing the stories or scripts read by news anchors and in-studio reporters. A television news writer's responsibilities vary depending on the size and structure of the station and the newsroom. Television news writers might gather information from reporters, wire services, press releases, or research. They must check the information for accuracy. After gathering and checking information, television news writers must develop the scripts and stories. In addition to writing news stories, writers might also be responsible for writing introductions for stories, commentaries, and the transitional phrases that lead the anchor from one story to the next.

Some news writers have additional responsibilities. They might be required to write news briefs, special reports, and short "teases" that air to pique interest before the news is shown. Television news writers might be responsible for writing and broadcasting sports reports, weathercasts, traffic conditions, features, or other types of stories as well as strict news. Finished television news reports must be interesting, easy to understand, accurate, and credible. Creative, talented television writers can make even run-of-the mill stories seem exciting and interesting. Writing for the television medium must be clear and concise. Writers must tailor stories for the time period allotted for each. In addition, the story must integrate with the visuals on screen. Depending on the specific station, news writers might be responsible for general news or for specialized news areas. These areas might include entertainment, politics, health, business, consumer information, sports, and so on. Television news writers might work various shifts—daytime, evening, or overnight.

Other responsibilities of television news writers might include the following:

- Rewriting wire stories from news services or other sources for use on the air
- Developing scripts for news documentaries, specials, and public affairs programs
- Acting as reporters or anchors themselves

EMPLOYMENT OPPORTUNITIES

Television news writers can find employment opportunities throughout the country in any area hosting television or cable stations. The more knowledgeable writers are about special subjects such as health, business, entertainment, and sports, the more marketable they are. Television news writers might work in a variety of settings, including major, midsize, and small markets. Opportunities might exist at the following:

- Network television
- National cable stations
- Public television stations
- Local cable stations
- Independent television stations
- Affiliated television stations

EARNINGS

Television news writers can earn between $18,000 and $55,000 or more depending on the station's size, location, and prestige as well as the writer's experience, responsibilities, and professional reputation. News writers starting out at smaller stations have lower salaries. As writers obtain experience and find jobs at larger stations and in more metropolitan areas, their salaries increase.

ADVANCEMENT OPPORTUNITIES

Television news writers usually start their careers at small stations. They climb the career ladder by locating positions at larger or more prestigious television stations or with networks. Some news writers advance their careers by becoming news directors, editors, producers, or reporters.

EDUCATION AND TRAINING

Usually, television stations require their news writers to hold at least a bachelor's degree. Good majors include journalism, communications, English, political science, broadcasting, mass communications, journalism, or a related field. Seminars, workshops, and courses in all facets of writing, broadcasting, and television are helpful in honing skills and making important contacts.

EXPERIENCE AND QUALIFICATIONS

News writers seeking jobs at small stations can find jobs right out of college. Any type of experience writing news for radio, television, or print media is useful. Writers can gain experience through summer or part-time jobs at local or school television or radio stations or with print media. Internships are also helpful. Some news writers start as desk assistants before landing their jobs as news writers at television stations.

Television news writers must have excellent writing skills and a good command of the English language. They must also be able to write simple, clear, crisp copy.

FOR ADDITIONAL INFORMATION: If you are interested in a career in this field, you can get additional information from the National Association of Broadcast Employees and Technicians (NABET), the Writers Guild of America (WGA), American Women in Radio and Television (AWRT), and the Radio-Television News Directors Association (RTNDA).

TIPS

- Get some experience and then move up the career ladder. It is usually easier to break into this field in a smaller market.
- Look in the newspaper classified section for jobs advertised under such headings as "News," "News Writer," "Broadcast Journalism," "Television News," "Television," "Cable Television," or "Broadcasting."
- Write as much as you can. The more practice you have, the more polished your writing skills and techniques become.
- Send your resume with a short cover letter to television and cable stations to inquire about openings.
- Obtain experience working part time or summers at local newspapers or radio or television stations.
- Put together a portfolio of scripts and other news stories that you have written. Make sure that you bring these to job interviews.
- Keep up with current affairs and news items. Interviewers often ask questions before they hire you.

DESK ASSISTANT—TELEVISION

JOB DESCRIPTION: *Handle clerical tasks in the newsroom; provide assistance to newsroom staff.*

EARNINGS: *$16,000 to $25,000+ per year.*

RECOMMENDED EDUCATION AND TRAINING: *A bachelor's degree is preferred.*

SKILLS AND PERSONALITY TRAITS: *Writing skills; good command of the English language; motivation; ability to work under tight deadlines.*

EXPERIENCE AND QUALIFICATIONS: *Prior journalism experience is helpful.*

JOB DESCRIPTION AND RESPONSIBILTIES

To break into television news, as is the case with entering most other forms of media, you often must "pay your dues." Working as a desk assistant—that is, working in the newsroom assisting personnel to do their jobs—is a common way to break in.

Specific responsibilities of the desk assistant depend on the job. However, employers usually expect desk assistants to handle many of the clerical tasks in the newsroom. Desk assistants sometimes type letters and reports. They make calls for those in the newsroom and, when necessary, take messages as well. Desk assistants might be required to screen telephone calls for producers and reporters. In addition to handling clerical and office duties, desk assistants do get to work in the news operation in a limited manner. They might be responsible for monitoring wire service terminals and giving these stories to the correct reporters. An important task of desk assistants is to help get scripts ready for the newscast. Desk assistants might type scripts as well as update them, making changes when necessary. They must make sure that scripts are delivered to the appropriate people in the newsroom.

Other responsibilities of desk assistants might include the following:

- Obtaining video from the station's tape library
- Accompanying reporters on assignment in the field
- Collecting background information and checking facts for reporters

EMPLOYMENT OPPORTUNITIES

Desk assistants can find jobs throughout the country in any area hosting television stations, including major, midsize, and small markets. Opportunities exist in the following:

- Network television
- National cable stations
- Public television stations
- Local cable stations
- Independent television stations
- Affiliated television stations

EARNINGS

Desk assistants working in television news earn between $16,000 and $25,000 or more depending on their experience, responsibilities, and education as well as the station's size, prestige, and geographic location.

ADVANCEMENT OPPORTUNITIES

Desk assistant is often an entry-level job working in the newsroom. Desk assistants can climb the career ladder by locating positions within the newsroom as reporters or producers, depending on their career aspirations.

EDUCATION AND TRAINING

Although not all desk assistants have four-year degrees, higher education is necessary for the climb up the career ladder. Good majors for this work include communications, liberal arts, English, journalism, mass media, or a related field.

EXPERIENCE AND QUALIFICATIONS

Experience working in any form of journalism is helpful in obtaining this type of job. Such experience might include work on school or local newspapers or with radio or television stations.

Excellent writing skills are mandatory for this position. Desk assistants must be organized, detail-oriented, and able to work under tight deadlines.

FOR ADDITIONAL INFORMATION: To learn more about careers in this field, contact the National Association of Broadcast Employees and Technicians (NABET), the American Federation of Television and Radio Artists (AFTRA), and the Writers Guild of America (WGA).

TIPS

- Learn as much as you can and do more than your employers expect of you. Then, when a position opens up, you will have a better chance at being recommended. Desk assistant is an entry-level job that can lead to a career in television news.
- Look in newspaper classified sections for jobs advertised under such headings as "Desk Assistant," "News," and "Television."
- Contact television stations to see whether they offer internship programs in the news department.
- Send your resume and a short cover letter to television stations. Ask them to keep your resume on file if no jobs are currently available.

- Check *Broadcasting Yearbook and Television Factbook* for names and addresses of television stations throughout the country.
- Break into television news by working in a small station in a small market. After gaining some experience, move up the career ladder.
- Ask the networks whether they have vacation relief programs in which they hire temporary help during the times when regular employees are on vacation.

COMMUNITY AFFAIRS DIRECTOR—TELEVISION STATION

JOB DESCRIPTION: *Develop and write community affairs programming and public service announcements for television stations.*

EARNINGS: *$20,000 to $55,000+ per year.*

RECOMMENDED EDUCATION AND TRAINING: *A bachelor's degree.*

SKILLS AND PERSONALITY TRAITS: *Writing skills; communications skills; articulateness; ability to work well with others.*

EXPERIENCE AND QUALIFICATIONS: *Experience working with community or not-for-profit groups is helpful.*

JOB DESCRIPTION AND RESPONSIBILTIES

Every licensed television station must give a certain amount of time to public service and community affairs. All public service and community affairs activities are logged for documentation for the Federal Communications Commission (FCC). Both commercial and public television stations hire community affairs directors to develop public service programming.

Community affairs directors have several responsibilities depending on the specific size and structure of the station for which they work. The station might expect them to develop, write, and produce public affairs programs. These programs might include local news, coverage of community groups, or discussion of important issues. Shows can be presented in a variety of formats. Some programming might be presented as talk shows with a panel of guests. Others might be presented as documentaries.

Community affairs directors are also responsible for putting together public service announcements (PSAs) for the station to air. These might include announcements for meetings for not-for-profit groups, warnings about not drinking and driving, or the importance of prenatal care for teen mothers. Community affairs directors must determine what the PSAs should focus on as well as how they are presented. Community affairs directors might write the announcements along with supervising their production for airing.

Other responsibilities of community affairs directors might include the following:

- Meeting with local not-for-profit groups and with civic and service groups to obtain their ideas for air time
- Representing the station at meetings of the organizations
- Planning public service and community affairs events sponsored or cosponsored by the station

EMPLOYMENT OPPORTUNITIES

Community affairs directors can find jobs throughout the country in any area hosting television stations, including major, midsize, and small markets. Opportunities might exist in the following:

- Network television
- National cable stations
- Public television stations
- Local cable stations
- Independent television stations
- Affiliated television stations

EARNINGS

Community affairs directors working in television earn between $20,000 and $55,000 or more annually depending on the station's size, location, and prestige as well as the director's experience, responsibilities, and professional reputation. Community affairs directors starting in smaller stations earn smaller salaries; as they gain experience and find jobs in larger stations and more metropolitan areas, their salaries increase.

ADVANCEMENT OPPORTUNITIES

Community affairs directors can advance their careers by locating similar positions in larger or more prestigious stations. Some move into similar positions in community affairs in other fields.

EDUCATION AND TRAINING

Employers usually require a bachelor's degree for this position. Good majors for this work include communications, liberal arts, English, journalism, mass media, social sciences, public relations, or a related field.

EXPERIENCE AND QUALIFICATIONS

Employers require or prefer candidates to have had prior experience working in community affairs or community relations or with not-for-profit organizations. Experience working in any form of journalism is helpful.

Excellent writing skills are mandatory for this position. Candidates must also have good verbal communications skills and the ability to work well with others. Community affairs directors should be organized and detail-oriented. A familiarity with the community's needs is necessary.

FOR ADDITIONAL INFORMATION: If you are interested in pursuing a career in this area, you should contact the Public Relations Society of America (PRSA) and the Writers Guild of America (WGA).

TIPS

- Get experience by volunteering with local not-for profit organizations.
- Look in newspaper classified sections for jobs advertised under such headings as "Television," "Broadcasting," "Community Affairs," "Community Affairs Director," "Community Relations Director," or "Public Service Director."
- Contact television stations to see whether they offer internship programs.
- Send your resume and a short cover letter to television stations. Ask that they keep your resume on file if no jobs are currently available.
- Look up names and addresses of television stations throughout the country in the *Broadcasting Yearbook and Television Factbook.*
- Try breaking into television at a small station in a small market. Get some experience; then move up the career ladder.

PUBLIC RELATIONS AND PROMOTIONS DIRECTOR— TELEVISION STATION

JOB DESCRIPTION: *Handle public relations, publicity, and promotions for a television station; supervise the department; develop and write press releases, publicity, and copy for promotions.*

EARNINGS: *$20,000 to $85,000+ per year.*

RECOMMENDED EDUCATION AND TRAINING: *A bachelor's degree in public relations, communications, journalism, advertising, English, liberal arts, or a related field.*

SKILLS AND PERSONALITY TRAITS: *Excellent writing skills; good command of the English language; verbal communications skills; creativity; detail orientation; organizational skills.*

EXPERIENCE AND QUALIFICATIONS: *Public relations, publicity, promotion, or journalistic experience is necessary.*

JOB DESCRIPTION AND RESPONSIBILITIES

The public relations and promotions director of a television station is an important part of the development and implementation of public relations campaigns. He or she also is ultimately responsible for handling the publicity and promotion of the station itself, its personalities, and its programs. Specific responsibilities vary depending on the station's size and structure.

The public relations and promotions director is responsible for developing special promotions that will attract media and public attention. These often include contests as well as events cosponsored by community organizations, other businesses in the community, or affiliates of the station. The director might also schedule station personalities for interviews or appearances at public functions or other events to help promote the station. He or she must make the station as visible in the community as possible while improving its pubic image. These tasks are important because they help attract both viewers and advertisers.

A major responsibility of the job is developing and writing press releases, feature stories, fact sheets, and other copy for media distribution. The director also develops press kits, flyers, and other written material about the station, its programs, and its personalities. In some cases, assistants handle some of these responsibilities. As part of the job, the director must do a great deal of research to try to determine the nature of the audience that the station is trying to reach and find ways to attract that audience's attention. The public relations and promotions director is expected to work with other station departments to attract new viewers and advertisers. These other departments might include traffic and continuity, community relations, advertising, and programming.

Other responsibilities of a television station public relations and promotions director might include the following:

- Acting as spokesperson for the station
- Attending industry or community events on behalf of the station
- Supervising assistants and others in the department

EMPLOYMENT OPPORTUNITIES

Public relations and promotions directors can find employment opportunities throughout the country. Most opportunities are located in larger metropolitan areas that have more than one station. The following settings might offer employment opportunities:

- Networks
- National cable stations
- Public television stations
- Local cable stations
- Independent television stations
- Affiliated television stations

EARNINGS

Pubic relations and promotions directors working at television stations earn between $20,000 and $85,000 or more annually depending on the station's size, location, and prestige as well as the director's experience, responsibilities, and professional reputation. Those starting at smaller stations have lower salaries; as they obtain experience and locate jobs in larger stations and more metropolitan areas, their salaries increase.

ADVANCEMENT OPPORTUNITIES

The most common way for public relations and promotions directors at television stations to advance their careers is to find similar positions at larger or more prestigious stations. Others climb the career ladder by finding similar positions in radio, film, or unrelated fields. Some public relations directors begin their own public relations or publicity agencies.

EDUCATION AND TRAINING

Usually, television stations require their public relations and promotions directors to hold at least a bachelor's degree. Good majors include public relations, journalism, communications, English, broadcasting, mass communications, liberal arts, or a related field. Seminars, workshops, and courses in all facets of writing, broadcasting, public relations, promotion, and publicity are helpful for honing skills and for making important contacts.

EXPERIENCE AND QUALIFICATIONS

The amount of experience required for this job varies from station to station. As a rule, the larger the station, the more experience is required. Candidates seeking jobs at small stations might find jobs right out of college. Any type of journalism, publicity, public relations, or promotion experience is helpful. Some gain experience through internships or become promotion assistants at television or radio stations. Others gain experience in journalism, publicity, and promotion in unrelated fields.

Public relations and promotion directors must meet a multitude of qualifications. Mastery of public relations, publicity, and promotional skills is a must. Excellent writing and verbal skills are also essential. Creativity is necessary. The candidate also needs an understanding of the television industry.

FOR ADDITIONAL INFORMATION: If you are seeking a career in this field, you can get additional information from Broadcast Promotion and Marketing Executives (BPME) or the Public Relations Society of America (PRSA).

TIPS

- Send your resume with a short cover letter to television and cable stations to inquire about openings. Ask them to keep your resume on file if there are no current openings.
- Look in the newspaper classified section for jobs advertised under such headings as "Television," "Cable Television," "Broadcasting," "Public Relations," "Promotions," "Publicity," or "Promotion Director."
- Check industry trade publications for advertised openings.
- Write as much as you can. The more practice you have, the more polished your writing skills and techniques will become.
- Try breaking into this field in a smaller market. Get some experience; then move up the career ladder.
- Obtain experience working part time or summers at local television or cable television stations.
- Gain other experience by contacting television or radio stations to see whether they have openings for assistants in the public relations or promotion departments.
- Contact trade associations to see what seminars and workshops they offer. These are useful for developing skills and making contacts.

SCREENWRITER

JOB DESCRIPTION: *Develop and write scripts for motion pictures, films, and television programs.*

EARNINGS: *Impossible to determine due to the nature of the job.*

RECOMMENDED EDUCATION AND TRAINING: *No educational requirement.*

SKILLS AND PERSONALITY TRAITS: *Excellent writing skills; good command of the English language; ability to write dialogue; creativity; imagination.*

EXPERIENCE AND QUALIFICATIONS: *Knowledge of scriptwriting techniques; writing experience is helpful.*

JOB DESCRIPTION AND RESPONSIBILITIES

Movies, films, and television shows all begin with scripts. Screenwriters write these scripts. These writers might be responsible for developing an entire script or might work from ideas that others have developed. Some screenwriters work on their own while others collaborate with other writers. Daytime soap operas, for example, usually have a head writer and several other writers who work under his or her direction. The head writer develops the main story line, and the other writers handle day-to-day writing activities such as dialogue.

Screenwriters developing screenplays for motion pictures might pen scripts for a variety of different types of films including comedies, dramas, thrillers, and musicals. Screenwriters writing for television might prepare scripts for dramas, made-for-television movies, soaps, comedies, and so on. Those who write scripts for nonfiction television such as documentaries or news, talk, and variety shows are usually called *scriptwriters*. These scripts require different types of research and style.

Screenwriters must determine the most effective way to tell a story. Some scripts are written with the characters looking back. Others start the story at the beginning and move forward. To write a script, the screenwriter must choose a subject and style. Before writing a full script, the screenwriter usually develops a plot outline and a treatment. This plan must describe the story's events as they occur in the script and define the characters. The screenwriter can then write a script. The script contains *dialogue*—the lines that each character speaks. Scripts also include the settings of scenes, descriptions of the sets, and suggestions for movements that each character should make. Screenwriters might create original scripts or adapt themes from other sources, such as real-life dramas. Screenwriters must create and develop characters and settings for the story and introduce conflicts and resolutions.

Other responsibilities of screenwriters might include the following:

- Meetings with producers and directors to make changes in the script
- Finding literary agents to sell scripts

EMPLOYMENT OPPORTUNITIES

Most opportunities for screenwriters are in Los Angeles and New York City. These cities are where most motion pictures and television shows are produced. The producers or directors of these projects hire or retain screenwriters. Most screenwriters freelance. Staff positions for screenwriters may be available with the following:

- Studios
- Networks
- Independent production companies

EARNINGS

Determining the earnings for screenwriters is difficult. Like other creative freelancers, screenwriters might write scripts that never sell and may never earn a penny. Others, however, can earn millions over the years. Factors affecting earnings for screenwriters include the specific films or television shows for which they write scripts as well as the writers' experience, responsibilities, and reputation. The Writers Guild of America (WGA) often sets minimum earnings for screenwriters who write scripts for television shows. In addition to other factors, the length and type of program for which the script is being written determine minimum earnings. Minimum earnings for thirty-minute sitcoms are approximately $15,000. For hour-long dramas, minimum earnings are greater. Writers who have developed other successful scripts and those working on scripts for well-known shows usually negotiate higher fees. The WGA might also negotiate minimum earnings for film screenwriters. In these cases, compensation might be based on such factors as the film's budget. Screenwriters who develop scripts for high-budget feature films might receive $1 million or more plus royalties.

ADVANCEMENT OPPORTUNITIES

One of the great features of being a screenwriter is that success can come at any time. Advancement opportunities include writing screenplays for popular television shows or feature films that turn into box office hits. Some screenwriters climb the career ladder by becoming television or film directors as well as writers.

EDUCATION AND TRAINING

No formal education is necessary to become a screenwriter. However, many feel that a college background is useful in this field because of the education and experience that it provides. Good majors include communications, English, liberal arts, theater arts, radio, television, or film. Seminars, workshops, and classes in a variety of aspects of playwriting, scriptwriting, and screenwriting are helpful for learning basic techniques.

EXPERIENCE AND QUALIFICATIONS

Screenwriters must have experience writing and rewriting. That is how they hone their skills. Screenwriters should be creative, talented, and imaginative with a good command of the English language. The ability to bring stories to life in an exciting and believable fashion is imperative. The ability to write dialogue is also necessary.

FOR ADDITIONAL INFORMATION: Aspiring screenwriters can learn more about this career by contacting the Writers Guild of America (WGA) and the American Film Institute (AFI).

TIPS

- Join writers' groups and attend their meetings. These are useful for having other writers critique your work, making contacts, and honing skills.
- Write as much as you can. The more practice you have, the more polished your writing skills and techniques will become.
- Join the WGA as soon as you can. This union provides professional guidance and support.
- Try to find a reputable literary agent to represent you. Contact the WGA to get a list of agents.
- Read books on screenwriting and scriptwriting to learn basic techniques.
- Look for workshops, seminars, classes, and lectures about screenwriting as well as other aspects of the television and film industry.

SOAP OPERA WRITER

JOB DESCRIPTION: *Develop and write scripts for soap operas.*

EARNINGS: *Impossible to determine due to the nature of the job.*

RECOMMENDED EDUCATION AND TRAINING: *No educational requirement.*

SKILLS AND PERSONALITY TRAITS: *Excellent writing skills; good command of the English language; ability to write dialogue; creativity; imagination.*

EXPERIENCE AND QUALIFICATIONS: *Knowledge of scriptwriting techniques is needed; writing experience is helpful.*

JOB DESCRIPTION AND RESPONSIBILITIES

Daytime television has grown over the years. Today, serials (more commonly called "soap operas" or simply "soaps") are attracting larger audiences than ever. Soap operas are a type of television that people either love and never miss, or hate and can't understand why anyone else watches. Soaps usually have several story lines occurring within the show. Usually, at least three different story lines run simultaneously. Soaps are open-ended series. Soap opera writers must develop interesting openings every day. They then must build tension during each show, introduce one or more conflicts, and end the day's show with viewers waiting for tomorrow's episode.

Soap operas have a head writer plus a staff of other writers who work under his or her direction. The head writer develops the main story line, and the other writers handle day-to-day writing activities such as dialogue. A truly talented team of soap opera writers can keep people watching the show for years. Soap writers, like all other screenwriters, must develop plot outlines and treatments. These plans describe the events of the story lines as they occur in the script and define the characters. Then the writers can begin writing the scripts. The script contains dialogue and indicates the lines that each character will speak. Scripts also include the settings of scenes and explain how each character should behave. Soap opera writers must create and develop characters and settings for the story while they introduce conflicts and resolutions. Soap operas do not take a summer hiatus like other shows. Writers must develop scripts for five shows a week, fifty-two weeks a year.

Other responsibilities of soap opera writers might include the following:

- Attending meetings with the writing team to discuss long-range plans for story development
- Meetings with producers and directors to make changes in the script
- Performing research so that they can write an accurate script on the subject at hand

EMPLOYMENT OPPORTUNITIES

Those interested in becoming soap opera writers must live in either New York City or Los Angeles where the shows are produced. Popular soap operas include the following:

- *One Life to Live* (ABC)
- *General Hospital* (ABC)
- *Sunset Beach* (NBC)
- *Another World* (NBC)
- *As the World Turns* (CBS)
- *All My Children* (ABC)
- *Port Charles* (ABC)
- *Days of Our Lives* (NBC)
- *The Young and the Restless* (CBS)
- *The Bold and the Beautiful* (CBS)

EARNINGS

The Writers Guild of America (WGA) sets minimum earnings for soap opera writers. The length of the program, as well as other factors, determine minimum earnings. Minimum earnings for writers of thirty-minute soaps are approximately $1,284 per week. Minimum earnings for writers on an hour-long soap are $2,372 per week. Head writers and writers who have developed other successful scripts usually negotiate for higher fees.

ADVANCEMENT OPPORTUNITIES

Soap opera writers advance their careers by becoming head writers. This promotion results in increased responsibilities and earnings.

EDUCATION AND TRAINING

No formal education is necessary to become a soap opera writer. However, many feel that a college background is useful in this field for the experience and training. Good majors include communications, English, liberal arts, theater arts, radio, television, or film. Seminars, workshops, and classes in a variety of aspects of playwriting, scriptwriting, and screenwriting are helpful in learning basic techniques.

EXPERIENCE AND QUALIFICATIONS

Soap opera writers need prior writing experience. The ability to write imaginative, believable, and moving dialogue is essential in this field. Soap writers must be able to bring stories to life in an exciting and believable manner. Writers should be creative, talented, and imaginative and have a good command of the English language.

FOR ADDITIONAL INFORMATION: Aspiring soap opera writers can learn more about this career by contacting the Writers Guild of America (WGA).

TIPS

- Be prepared to move to New York City or Los Angeles. These are the cities in which most soap operas are taped. To write for soaps, you must live near one of these areas.
- Watch soaps to understand how they are put together and written.
- Join writers' groups and attend their meetings. These are useful for having your work critiqued, for making contacts, and for honing skills.
- Develop a story line on "spec" or speculation (that is, write a story line and then try to sell it) for a soap. Producers and head writers might be interested if you demonstrate talent and creativity, write moving dialogue, and create exciting situations.
- Write as much as you can. The more practice you have, the more polished your writing skills and techniques will become.

- Join the WGA as soon as you can. This union provides professional guidance and support.
- Try to find a reputable literary agent to represent you. Contact the WGA to get a list of agents.
- Read books on screenwriting and scriptwriting to learn basic techniques.

SITCOM WRITER

JOB DESCRIPTION: *Develop and write scripts for situation comedy television shows.*

EARNINGS: *Impossible to determine due to the nature of the job.*

RECOMMENDED EDUCATION AND TRAINING: *No educational requirement.*

SKILLS AND PERSONALITY TRAITS: *Excellent writing skills; good command of the English language; a humorous way of looking at things; the ability to write dialogue; creativity; imagination.*

EXPERIENCE AND QUALIFICATIONS: *Knowledge of scriptwriting techniques is needed; writing experience is helpful.*

JOB DESCRIPTION AND RESPONSIBILITIES

At one time or another, almost everyone watches situation comedies (*sitcoms*) on television. Many of us laugh at the situations that characters get themselves into. Perhaps this is because we can often relate to similar situations.

Sitcom writers are screenwriters who specialize in writing situation comedies for television. A sitcom writer might develop an entire script or work from ideas that others have developed. Some sitcom writers work on their own while others collaborate with different writers. To write the script, a sitcom writer must choose a subject and style. Before writing a full script, the sitcom writer must develop a plot outline and a treatment. This plan defines the characters and describes the story's events as they will occur in the script. The writer can then write a full script. The script contains dialogue indicating which lines each character will speak. Scripts also include the settings of scenes and descriptions of the sets and prescribe the movements that each character should make. Sitcom writers must create and develop characters and settings for the story and also introduce conflicts and resolutions. When developing scripts for sitcoms, writers must find ways to make the words and actions funny. To do so, writers might include humorous dialogue, involve characters in embarrassing activities, or create a situation or setting that others will find humorous. Sitcom writers, like all freelance screenwriters, often write scripts on "spec" or speculation—that is, they write a script and then try to sell it. Sometimes a producer will read a script that he or she does not want or even like, but will recognize from the script that the writer has potential. The producer might then retain the sitcom writer to rewrite that script or to write a different one.

Other responsibilities of screenwriters might include the following:

- Finding literary agents to sell scripts
- Meeting with producers and directors to make changes in the script

EMPLOYMENT OPPORTUNITIES

Although writers can write their scripts anywhere, the greatest number of opportunities for sitcom writers are in Los Angeles where most sitcoms are produced. Most screenwriters freelance. Staff positions for screenwriters are available at the following:

- Studios
- Networks
- Independent production companies

EARNINGS

Determining the earnings for sitcom writers is difficult. Like other freelance writers, sitcom writers might write scripts that never sell and might never earn a penny. Others, however, can earn millions over the years. Factors affecting earnings include the specific films or television shows for which the writer writes scripts as well as the writer's experience, responsibilities, and reputation. The Writers Guild of America (WGA) sets minimum earnings for television screenwriters. The length and type of program for which the script is being written, as well as other factors, determine minimum earnings. Minimum earnings for thirty-minute sitcoms are approximately $15,000. Writers who have developed other successful scripts or who are working on scripts for well-known shows usually command higher fees.

ADVANCEMENT OPPORTUNITIES

An appealing aspect of writing sitcoms is that success can come at any time. Advancement opportunities include developing a script for a show that becomes a major comedy hit.

EDUCATION AND TRAINING

No formal education is necessary to become a sitcom writer. However, many feel that a college background is useful in this field because of the experience and training that it offers. Good majors include communications, English, liberal arts, theater arts, radio, television, or film. Seminars, workshops, and classes in a variety of aspects of playwriting, scriptwriting, and screenwriting are helpful for learning basic techniques. Courses in comedy writing are also useful.

EXPERIENCE AND QUALIFICATIONS

Sitcom writers, like all screenwriters, must get experience writing and rewriting to hone their skills. They should be creative, talented, and imaginative and have a good command of the English language. The ability to see life and daily occurrences in a humorous manner is imperative. Sitcom writers also must be able to bring stories to life in an exciting and believable manner. The ability to write dialogue is essential.

FOR ADDITIONAL INFORMATION: Aspiring sitcom screenwriters can learn more about this career by contacting the Writers Guild of America (WGA).

TIPS

- Join writers' groups and attend their meetings. These are useful for having your work critiqued, making contacts, and honing skills.
- Watch a variety of sitcoms to see how they set up situations and resolve conflicts in a humorous manner.
- You don't always have to come up with a new show idea. Many producers of established sitcoms buy scripts for the shows from freelance sitcom writers. Producers might also decide that they like your ability to write dialogue and situations and hire you to work on purchased scripts.
- Write as much as you can. The more practice you have, the more polished your writing skills and techniques will become.
- Join the WGA as soon as you can. This union provides professional guidance and support.
- Try to find a reputable literary agent to represent you. Contact the WGA to get a list of agents.
- Read books on screenwriting and scriptwriting to learn basic techniques.

CHAPTER 2

Careers for Writers in the Entertainment and Sports Industries

The entertainment and sports industries encompass a great many jobs and careers, some highly visible and others behind the scenes. Both industries offer vast opportunities for a wide range of people with a variety of skills. Most visible to the public are entertainers, singers, dancers, actors, musicians, and sports figures. These celebrities all require the services of support people who have a tremendous impact even though they are not usually in the spotlight or on center stage.

From publicizing a tour to penning a sports column or writing the words to a song or libretto, opportunities in the entertainment and sports industries are plentiful for those with writing skills.

Careers for writers in entertainment and sports cover a broad spectrum. Space restrictions make it impossible for this chapter to include all possible opportunities. This chapter discusses the following careers:

Press Agent   Sports Writer
Tour Publicist   Sports Columnist
Theatrical Press Agent   Playwright
Unit Publicist   Librettist
Entertainment Journalist—Print   Songwriter/Lyricist
Critic/Reviewer—Print Media   Comedy Writer
Critic/Reviewer—Broadcasting

PRESS AGENT

JOB DESCRIPTION: *Develop publicity campaigns for those in the entertainment, sports, and music industries; implement campaigns.*

EARNINGS: *$20,000 to $150,000+ per year.*

RECOMMENDED EDUCATION AND TRAINING: *A bachelor's degree in journalism, public relations, marketing, English, advertising, or communications.*

SKILLS AND PERSONALITY TRAITS: *Excellent writing skills; telephone skills; communications skills; aggressiveness; persuasiveness; creativity.*

EXPERIENCE AND QUALIFICATIONS: *Experience working in journalism, public relations, publicity, or entertainment is helpful.*

JOB DESCRIPTION AND RESPONSIBILITIES

Press agents in the entertainment, sports, and music industries work with a variety of entertainers and entertainment events—performing artists, television and movie stars, actors and actresses, disc jockeys, radio personalities, models, singers, recording groups, comedians, sports figures, theatrical productions and revues, television shows, sporting events, musical concerts, festivals, and more. The main function of press agents is getting their clients' names in front of the public as frequently as possible. They must make the public and media aware of the client as well as of any projects or events in which the client is taking part.

Press agents develop and implement publicity campaigns for their clients. These campaigns are often written proposals outlining specific ideas to generate and garner publicity and media attention. Entertainers and entertainment events need to be in the spotlight. Press agents must constantly work to gain exposure for their clients. The methods used and type of exposure depend on the degree of popularity and fame that a client already enjoys. Clients who are already well known are sought out for interviews by many editors, journalists, talent coordinators, reporters, and so on. Press agents for these clients must be selective and must choose the best opportunities to obtain the most effective exposure for the clients. Press agents working with lesser known clients face a different type of challenge in seeking exposure for clients. To pique the interest of the media, press agents must develop, write, prepare, and distribute a variety of press releases, media kits, and such. Press agents in these situations must find ways to draw attention to their clients to compete with others who might be better known.

Press agents spend a great deal of time on the telephone. They attempt to persuade reporters and other media people to arrange feature stores on their clients. They also must constantly talk about their clients to people who are in positions to help promote them. These people might include reporters, photographers, journalists, television and radio producers, and talent coordinators. This is not a nine-to-five job. The business and social lives of press agents often intermingle among attending events, press parties, dinners, luncheons, and other functions to promote their clients as well as to attract new clients. Press agents have an interesting life. Many who are really good at what they do consider it a lifestyle rather than a job.

Other responsibilities of press agents might include the following:

- Developing media events and promotions with interesting and unique hooks and angles
- Arranging interviews between entertainers and the media
- Arranging and coordinating press conferences on behalf of clients
- Writing biographies, press releases, articles, media kits, and so on

EMPLOYMENT OPPORTUNITIES

Press agents might be employed on staff or freelance as independents. Those who freelance must find their own roster of clients. Although employment can be located throughout the country, most opportunities exist in large, culturally active cities with a great many entertainers and entertainment events. Among others, press agents might represent the following:

- Recording artists
- Magicians
- Radio personalities
- Sports figures
- Record companies
- Entertainment complexes
- Singers, musicians, or musical groups
- Comedians
- Television or film stars
- Theatrical companies
- Sports arenas

EARNINGS

The range of earnings for press agents is tremendous—anywhere from $20,000 annually to $150,000 or more. Factors affecting earnings include whether an agent is freelancing or on staff at a company, as well as the agent's experience, responsibilities, qualifications, and professional reputation. Another important factor is the client list's popularity and prestige.

ADVANCEMENT OPPORTUNITIES

Advancement opportunities for press agents depend largely on the path that an agent wants to take. Some press agents climb the career ladder by becoming freelance press agents and starting their own companies. Others advance their careers by finding or being assigned more prestigious clients.

EDUCATION AND TRAINING

The recommended education for a job in this field is a bachelor's degree with a major in journalism, public relations, communications, marketing, English, advertising, or a related field. There are also many seminars, courses, and workshops in publicity, promotion, writing, business, marketing, and the entertainment industry. These are helpful for honing skills and for making contacts.

EXPERIENCE AND QUALIFICATIONS

Many press agents start out as journalists, reporters, or public relations people. Experience requirements vary. Often, aspiring press agents can find jobs as assistants or interns to other press agents.

Press agents must have excellent written and verbal communications skills. To come up with unique ideas, they must be very creative. An understanding of the entertainment industry is imperative.

FOR ADDITIONAL INFORMATION: If you are interested in learning more about a career as a press agent, you can obtain additional information by contacting the National Entertainment Journalists Association (NEJA), the Publicists Guild (PG), the Public Relations Society of America (PRSA), and the Association of Theatrical Press Agents and Managers (ATPAM).

TIPS

- Look for apprenticeships and internships. These are often available through large entertainment-oriented public relations and publicity firms, record companies, and television and radio stations.
- Look in the classified section of newspapers for jobs advertised under such headings as "Press Agent," "Entertainment," or "Publicist."
- Also look in trade publications such as *Variety* and *Billboard* for other jobs that might be advertised.
- Get experience writing for a local newspaper.
- Make professional contacts by joining trade associations and attending their meetings and conferences.

TOUR PUBLICIST

JOB DESCRIPTION: *Go on the road with entertainers, music groups, and similar groups to publicize the artist, tour, and recordings.*

EARNINGS: *$25,000 to $100,000+ per year.*

RECOMMENDED EDUCATION AND TRAINING: *A bachelor's degree in music business, public relations, communications, journalism, music merchandising, or a related field.*

SKILLS AND PERSONALITY TRAITS: *Excellent written and verbal communications skills; enjoy traveling; creativity; aggressiveness.*

EXPERIENCE AND QUALIFICATIONS: *Prior experience working in publicity, public relations, or the entertainment industry.*

JOB DESCRIPTION AND RESPONSIBILITIES

Tour publicists go on tour with entertainers and handle their publicity requirements from the road. Many people envy tour publicists their exciting jobs. The major responsibilities of tour publicists begin as soon as the artist leaves on tour. The tour publicist is part of the tour's entourage. He or she is responsible for every aspect of publicity that involves the act.

Depending on the specific situation, either the tour publicist or another staff publicist will be responsible for handling several publicity requirements before a tour begins. A publicist arranges media interviews with television, radio, newspapers, and magazines in cities where appearances are scheduled to take place. The tour publicist also compiles press kits and develops news releases. The publicist must also arrange press conferences and parties and work out other promotional details. On the road, the tour publicist arranges for interviews, photography sessions, press conferences, and television, radio, and other personal appearances that were not scheduled prior to the tour. The tour publicist accompanies the artist to all appearances, concerts, and interviews. In many cases, the publicist meets with the show producers or talent coordinators prior to interviews to discuss the interview's possible direction. The tour publicist must take advantage of every opportunity to provide positive media exposure for the act. Unexpected events that might generate positive publicity often occur on the road. By the same token, difficulties, dilemmas, and problems that might cause negative publicity can also occur while an act is on tour. The tour publicist must attempt to block negative publicity and give it a positive spin. The tour publicist keeps in constant contact with the artist's management. This contact is important to keep management aware of everything happening on the road.

Other responsibilities of tour publicists might include the following:

- Determining who should get press and backstage passes and issuing them
- Preparing press releases and statements for the media
- Scheduling and approving interviews and photo shoots before and after appearances
- Presenting merchandising gifts to the media

EMPLOYMENT OPPORTUNITIES

Tour publicists might be on staff with a variety of entertainers, groups, or organizations. They might also freelance as independents. Employers or clients might include the following:

- Recording artists
- Entertainment managers
- Comedians
- Entertainment-oriented public relations companies
- Entertainment-oriented publicity firms
- Record companies
- Entertainment management firms
- Magicians

EARNINGS

Tour publicists may earn between $25,000 and $100,000 or more annually. Variables affecting earnings include the type of employer and the specific act that must be publicized. Other factors affecting earnings include the publicist's experience, professional reputation, and responsibilities. Tour publicists usually are paid more than home-based publicists because they travel for extended periods of time with their client on tour. Publicists working with top-name acts earn the highest salaries. Tour publicists on staff with a record company or management firm are usually paid a weekly salary plus a stipend to cover personal expenses on the road. Either the act or its management firm covers all travel expenses. Tour publicists who work as independents receive a weekly or monthly fee plus expenses.

ADVANCEMENT OPPORTUNITIES

Tour publicists can climb the career ladder in several different ways. As they obtain experience and prove themselves, they might be assigned more prestigious tours with better known acts. This results in increased earnings. Tour publicists can also advance their careers by becoming tour managers or tour coordinators. Some publicists strike out on their own and become independent tour publicists.

EDUCATION AND TRAINING

Aspiring tour publicists should have at least a bachelor's degree. Majors might include public relations, communications, music business, music merchandising, journalism, liberal arts, or a related field.

EXPERIENCE AND QUALIFICATIONS

Tour publicists are usually required to have had prior experience in publicity, public relations, or some aspect of the entertainment or music industry.

Publicists must be creative and have excellent writing and verbal communications skills. Tour publicists should be able to work under a great deal of pressure. This job can be quite stressful.

FOR ADDITIONAL INFORMATION: If you are interested in obtaining additional information regarding careers in this field, contact the Touring Entertainment Industry Association (TEIA) and the Public Relations Society of America (PRSA).

TIPS

- Look for an an internship in the publicity department of a record company or entertainment-oriented public relations or publicity firm. You won't go on the road at this point, but you will get valuable experience and make important contacts.

- Consider sending your resume and a short cover letter inquiring about tour publicist positions to record companies, management companies, and music- and entertainment-oriented publicity and public relations firms.

- If you can't find a job as a tour publicist, look for a home-based publicist position at an entertainment-oriented public relations firm or record company. Get your foot in the door and discuss your aspirations with supervisors.

- Take seminars and workshops in publicity, the entertainment business, the music industry, writing, and so on. The more qualified you are, the more marketable you will be.

THEATRICAL PRESS AGENT

JOB DESCRIPTION: *Publicize and promote theatrical productions; develop publicity campaigns; write press releases; compile press kits.*

EARNINGS: *$600 to $1,600+ per week.*

RECOMMENDED EDUCATION AND TRAINING: *A three-year apprenticeship is required.*

SKILLS AND PERSONALITY TRAITS: *Excellent written and verbal communications skills; creativity; detail orientation; aggressiveness.*

EXPERIENCE AND QUALIFICATIONS: *Prior experience in publicity, public relations, or the entertainment industry.*

JOB DESCRIPTION AND RESPONSIBILITIES

If no one knows about a Broadway show, no one will come to see it. Publicity is critical to the success of theatrical productions; it must generate ticket sales. Theatrical press agents are responsible for handling the publicity for Broadway shows, off-Broadway shows, and regional theater group productions.

Theatrical press agents have a multitude of responsibilities. They handle some of these responsibilities before the show opens; they take care of others after opening night. Theatrical press agents must develop publicity campaigns designed to attract audiences. They must create and implement ideas that attract the attention of the media, which, in turn, makes people aware of the production. The theatrical press agent must handle routine publicity requirements such as compiling press kits, preparing biographies of the stars and the cast, writing press releases, and dealing with the media. The theatrical press agent also arranges interviews and personal appearances for stars of the show. The more attention the stars and the show receive, the more tickets will be sold. Theatrical press agents plan special media events to generate more publicity and interest in the production. Many people compete fiercely for media attention. Therefore, these media events must be creative. Press agents must develop interesting ideas and angles for feature, entertainment, and assignment editors as well as for reporters and columnists. On opening night, the theatrical press agent calls critics and reviewers to ensure that they are attending the show. That night, the press agent must be at the opening answering media questions and passing out press kits and other pertinent information. The press agent also schedules and implements opening night parties and other media events.

Other responsibilities of theatrical press agents might include the following:

- Determining who should get press passes and issuing backstage passes
- Keeping media attention focused on the show throughout its run

- Compiling media lists
- Supervising theatrical press agent apprentices

EMPLOYMENT OPPORTUNITIES

Most employment opportunities are in large, culturally active cities like New York City, Los Angeles, Washington D.C., Seattle, Chicago, Philadelphia, and Atlanta.

EARNINGS

The Association of Theatrical Press Agents and Managers (ATPAM), an AFL-CIO union, negotiates minimum weekly salaries for theatrical press agents. Negotiated earnings include a minimum salary plus a percentage for vacation pay, pension, and a specific amount for a welfare fund. Determining the annual earnings for theatrical press agents is difficult because agents are usually paid for specific productions. Factors affecting earnings include the number of projects for which the agent is hired each year as well as the length of each project. Other variables include the type and size of theater that the production is in. The theater's seating capacity determines the minimum salary for those working on off-Broadway productions. Those handling the job in small theaters earn a minimum of $600 per week. The minimum weekly salary for theatrical press agents working on Broadway shows is $1,600. Agents who have built up their professional reputations can receive much higher weekly salaries.

ADVANCEMENT OPPORTUNITIES

Theatrical press agents can advance their careers by building up their professional reputations and commanding high weekly earnings. Some agents advance by being hired to work on more prestigious shows. The top rung on the career ladder for theatrical press agents is handling the publicity for a Broadway show.

EDUCATION AND TRAINING

Theatrical press agents must go through a three-year apprenticeship with a member of ATPAM. Although a college degree is not required, it is recommended. Good majors include public relations, communications, English, journalism, advertising, business, or theater arts.

EXPERIENCE AND QUALIFICATIONS

Theatrical press agents obtain their needed experience through the required three-year apprenticeship. Experience in publicity, theater, or the entertainment industry is also useful.

Agents should have excellent written and verbal communication skills. They must also be creative and aggressive.

FOR ADDITIONAL INFORMATION: Obtain additional information regarding careers in this field by contacting ATPAM and the Public Relations Society of America (PRSA).

TIPS

- Call or write ATPAM to find a branch office near you to get specifics on the apprenticeship program. (The address and phone number are in the back of this book.)
- Find a sponsor to take part in the apprenticeship program. If you do not know anyone in the ATPAM union, the union will help you find a sponsor with whom to work.
- Learn as much as you can from your apprenticeship sponsor. Do not take the easy way out.
- Get experience by volunteering to handle the publicity requirements for a school, college, or community theater production.
- Get additional experience by taking a summer job with a local theatrical company.
- Take seminars and workshops in publicity, theater, and various aspects of writing. The more qualified you are, the more marketable you will be.

UNIT PUBLICIST

JOB DESCRIPTION: *Handle publicity and promotion for television shows and movies.*

EARNINGS: *$25,000 to $100,000+ per year.*

RECOMMENDED EDUCATION AND TRAINING: *A bachelor's degree in public relations, communications, journalism, English, or liberal arts.*

SKILLS AND PERSONALITY TRAITS: *Excellent writing skills; verbal communications skills; publicity, promotion, and public relations skills; creativity; persuasiveness; a pleasing personality; telephone skills.*

EXPERIENCE AND QUALIFICATIONS: *Experience in publicity, journalism, public relations, entertainment, or related fields.*

JOB DESCRIPTION AND RESPONSIBILITIES

Every season, new television shows come out and new movies are released. Television and movie studios and production companies must find ways to make their shows or films stand out, get attention, and attract viewers. Unit publicists are hired to handle the promotion and publicity for television shows, films, and movies.

Unit publicists work with the studio, network, or production company responsible for the show or film. Their job often starts before the release of the new film or television show. Unit publicists must develop a plan for creating interest and excitement in the show or film to attract a larger audience. The publicist must also find ways to garner media attention. The unit publicist arranges media interviews with the stars of the film or television show. These often include interviews with editors, reporters, and columnists from the print as well as broadcast media. The unit publicist might set up interviews with networks, cable, or syndicated media. Depending on the specific project, he or she might arrange interviews with local, national, or international media.

In many cases, the unit publicist travels with the project's star. In other situations, he or she might assign an assistant or escort to travel with the star promoting the project. Whoever is responsible for this task must ensure that the celebrity arrives on time and must provide clips, press releases, bios, photographs, and press kits to the editor, producer, or reporter.

The unit publicist is responsible for developing press kits and for writing press releases and fact sheets about the film or show along with providing relevant information about the stars. The publicist also arranges for still shots as well as video clips. He or she must make sure that press information is distributed to the proper media.

Unit publicists are usually assigned or retained for a specific film or television show. After a film has been out for a period of time, the project no longer needs exposure. The unit publicist might then be assigned to another project. Unit publicists for television shows are usually retained for longer periods of time.

Other responsibilities of the unit publicist include the following:

- Scheduling press conferences and press parties
- Arranging screenings for critics or reviewers
- Generating tremendous amounts of publicity for the project

EMPLOYMENT OPPORTUNITIES

Most opportunities for unit publicists are in Los Angeles and New York City. Unit publicists might work in the the following capacities:

- Public relations agencies
- Independent publicists
- Networks
- Independent television production companies
- Freelancing
- Publicity agencies
- Independent press agents
- Independent film production companies
- Television studios
- Motion picture studios

EARNINGS

Unit publicists earn between $25,000 and $100,000 or more annually. Factors affecting earnings include the specific project and work situation as well as its prestige. Other factors include the publicist's experience, professional reputation, and responsibilities. Unit publicists might belong to the Publicists Guild (PG), which negotiates and sets minimum earnings for members working in studios, television stations, production companies, and agencies that have agreements with the guild. Unit publicists who freelance or work independently might not have as steady an income as those on staff with a public relations or publicity firm, studio, or production company.

ADVANCEMENT OPPORTUNITIES

Unit publicists can advance their careers by locating similar positions with more prestigious projects. Some publicists climb the career ladder by becoming independent or freelance unit publicists. Advancement opportunities in this field are based on the publicist's talent, drive, and determination as well as being in the right place at the right time.

EDUCATION AND TRAINING

Aspiring unit publicists should have at least a bachelor's degree. Helpful majors include public relations, communications, English, journalism, and liberal arts. Any courses or seminars about the entertainment industry, film, public relations, writing, or publicity are also useful.

EXPERIENCE AND QUALIFICATIONS

Experience in publicity, public relations, and writing in some aspect or form of the entertainment industry is necessary for this position. You can gain such experience through prior positions as an entertainment journalist, as assistant to other unit publicists or to a press agent, or through an internship.

The ability to work under pressure is essential. Unit publicists must also be able to develop creative and unique ideas geared toward attracting both media attention and viewers.

FOR ADDITIONAL INFORMATION: Aspiring unit publicists can learn more about careers in this field by contacting the Public Relations Society of America (PRSA), the Publicists Guild (PG), and the National Entertainment Journalist Association (NEJA).

TIPS

- Look for internships in larger public relations agencies, television and film production companies, and television stations. Such internships are a great way to make contacts, break into the field, and learn skills. Write to the personnel director inquiring about internship possibilities. Include a resume. If you don't receive a response in a week or two, call and ask whether you can talk to someone about an internship.

- Get experience by volunteering to handle publicity for community theater productions or other entertainment events put on by not-for-profit organizations.

- Contact your school or local newspaper to see whether you can become its entertainment critic, reviewer, or reporter. You can then talk to managers, agents, and entertainers who come to your town. This is another great way to make contacts in the entertainment world.

- Join trade associations. Attend their conferences and meetings. Don't turn down the opportunity to make any contacts. All will be helpful.

- Read the trade papers. Get familiar with the entertainment industry.

- As you read the trades, notice the low-budget films being produced. Contact the production company for a possible assignment.

- Remember to print business cards and give them to everyone that you encounter in the entertainment industry. Don't forget entertainment journalists and critics.

- Place a small advertisement of your availability as a unit publicist in one of the trade publications.

ENTERTAINMENT JOURNALIST—PRINT

JOB DESCRIPTION: *Write articles, columns, and feature stories about entertainers, entertainment events, and news.*

EARNINGS: *$15,000 to $100,000+ per year.*

RECOMMENDED EDUCATION AND TRAINING: *A bachelor's degree in journalism, communications, English, or liberal arts.*

SKILLS AND PERSONALITY TRAITS: *Excellent writing skills; creativity; objectivity; good command of the English language.*

EXPERIENCE AND QUALIFICATIONS: *Journalism and other writing experience are helpful.*

JOB DESCRIPTION AND RESPONSIBILITIES

Entertainers and celebrities make news. Entertainment journalists write about that news and about the entertainers and celebrities who make the news. They also write about entertainment events, happenings, performances, and so on.

Entertainment journalists might write about all facets of entertainment or might specialize in a specific area such as music, theater, television, or film. Journalists working at smaller publications usually have more varied responsibilities and report on a variety of entertainment events. In some instances, entertainment journalists develop story ideas on their own. In others, they are assigned stories. Entertainment journalists must write interesting factual and creative articles with unique angles. Entertainment journalists gather information through interviews, tips, leads, and research. Press agents and publicists often send entertainment journalists press kits, bios, news releases, and photographs for their use. Entertainment journalists might be responsible for writing stories about international, national, or local entertainment news. They might also write about entertainment events or celebrities who are coming to town. Whatever they write, entertainment journalists must be sure that they check all information for accuracy. Errors, especially in the entertainment world, are usually not tolerated and can lead to lawsuits.

Entertainment journalists might attend press conferences, opening parties, and other entertainment media events to gather news. They also must often attend plays, ballets, operas, movies, and concerts.

Other responsibilities of entertainment journalists might include the following:

- Reviewing or critiquing concerts, plays, movies, television shows, or recordings
- Taking photographs to go with print stories

EMPLOYMENT OPPORTUNITIES

Although major entertainment news is usually centered in cities such as New York City, Hollywood, or Los Angeles, entertainment journalists can find employment opportunities throughout the country. Often print journalists relate national news to the local scene. Entertainment journalists can locate full- or part-time positions. Opportunities in this field include the following:

- Daily newspapers
- Trade papers, magazines, and journals
- General-interest magazines
- Weekly newspapers
- Entertainment-oriented magazines and newspapers

EARNING

Entertainment journalists working in print earn between $15,000 and $100,000 or more annually depending on the publication's size, type, and geographic location. Other factors include the journalist's experience, responsibilities, and professional reputation. Those working on small-town weeklies usually have the lowest earnings. Salaries rise in relation to the publication's size and circulation. Some journalists working for nationally known publications can earn million-dollar salaries. Such salaries, however, are rare.

ADVANCEMENT OPPORTUNITIES

Entertainment journalists advance their careers by locating similar positions at larger or more prestigious publications. Some journalists climb the career ladder by specializing in a specific type of entertainment, such as music, television, or films. Others might advance their careers by becoming broadcast entertainment journalists.

EDUCATION AND TRAINING

Smaller publications might not have educational requirements. However, journalists usually need education for career advancement. Usually, employers require or prefer a bachelor's degree in journalism, communications, English, liberal arts, or a related field. Any courses or workshops in writing and journalism are helpful in honing skills.

EXPERIENCE AND QUALIFICATIONS

To land a job as an entertainment journalist, you usually need writing experience. Small weeklies might require only a minimum of experience; larger publications usually require more. You can gain experience by working on school or college newspapers. You might also gain such experience through summer or part-time jobs with newspapers or magazines. Internships are also valuable for learning skills and making contacts.

FOR ADDITIONAL INFORMATION: Aspiring entertainment journalists can learn more about this career by contacting the National Critics Institute (NCI), the American Newspaper Publishers Association Foundation (ANPAF), the Community College Journalism Association (CCJA), the National Newspaper Association (NNA), or the Newspaper Guild (NG).

TIPS

- Look for internships at newspapers and magazines to get hands-on experience and on-the-job training. Although it is helpful for an internship to be in the entertainment field, it is not necessary.
- Consider contacting your local newspaper to see whether it might be interested in a weekly column on some facet of entertainment. Although the pay will probably be low or nonexistent, the experience will be well worthwhile.
- If you are still in school, get involved with your school's newspaper or literary magazine.
- Look in the newspaper classified section for jobs advertised under such headings as "Entertainment Journalist," "Entertainment," "Writer," "Journalist," "Music," "Theater," and "Dance."
- Put together a portfolio of your best writing samples. Bring it to interviews with you.

CRITIC/REVIEWER—PRINT MEDIA

JOB DESCRIPTION: *Write reviews for plays, theatrical productions, concerts, movies, and television shows for print media.*

EARNINGS: *$15,000 to $100,000+ per year.*

RECOMMENDED EDUCATION AND TRAINING: *A bachelor's degree is required or preferred.*

SKILLS AND PERSONALITY TRAITS: *Excellent writing skills; objectivity; interest in entertainment; ability to work under tight deadlines.*

EXPERIENCE AND QUALIFICATIONS: *Prior writing experience is helpful.*

JOB DESCRIPTION AND RESPONSIBILITIES

Critics working in print media review a variety of entertainment productions or events. These include plays, theatrical productions, movies, television shows, concerts, records, and more. Critics might work for newspapers or magazines. They might review works for small weekly papers or for large, prestigious dailies. Some critics work for entertainment publications; others work for local, regional, or national magazines.

Critics attend openings of plays, concerts, and other performing art productions and screenings of new movies. They then must write objective reviews of the performances. Reviews discuss how well a production was performed and address the performance of the main actors and actresses or other principals. For smaller publications, critics might review all the performing arts. For larger publications, some critics specialize in a specific area such as theater, opera, movies, music, or television. The more specialized a critic, the more he or she must know about that specific medium.

Other responsibilities of critics working in print media might include the following:

- Writing and reporting on non-entertainment subjects
- Writing entertainment columns
- Attending opening parties and galas to meet the stars

EMPLOYMENT OPPORTUNITIES

Critics working in the print media can find jobs throughout the country. Most newspapers and many magazines have entertainment sections that employ critics. Depending on the publication's size, the entertainment reporter might double as the critic. Critics might work in the following settings:

- Weeklies
- Midsize and larger dailies
- Entertainment magazines
- Small dailies
- Entertainment newspapers
- Regional publications

EARNINGS

Earnings for most critics working in print media range from $15,000 to $65,000 or more annually depending on the specific publication that the critic works for as well as his or her experience, responsibilities, and professional reputation. Nationally known critics might earn $100,000 or more annually. However, such critics are few and far between. Some critics work on a per-review basis. Such reviews are usually done for smaller publications. Earnings can range from a few cents a word to a flat fee up to $150 or more.

ADVANCEMENT OPPORTUNITIES

Critics working in print media can take several paths toward career advancement. They might climb the career ladder by locating similar jobs with larger or more prestigious publications. They might also become specialists in one type of entertainment, such as theater, movies, or television. Some critics working in print advance by locating reviewing positions in television.

EDUCATION AND TRAINING

Most publications prefer or require their employees to hold a bachelor's degree. Good majors include journalism, public relations, theater arts, communications, English, liberal arts, or a related field. Workshops and seminars in all aspects of writing are useful.

EXPERIENCE AND QUALIFICATIONS

Employers usually require prior experience working for a print publication. You can gain such experience by working on a college newspaper or magazine. Critics must have excellent writing skills and objectivity. Interest and knowledge in entertainment, theater, movies, television, and the performing arts are vital. The ability to write interesting, clear, concise, and unbiased reviews is necessary.

FOR ADDITIONAL INFORMATION: If you are interested in a career as a critic in the print media, you can learn more about this field by contacting the New York Drama Critics Circle (NYDCC), the Outer Critics Circle (OCC), and the Music Critics Association (MCA).

TIPS

- Look for an internship in the entertainment department of a newspaper or magazine.
- Get experience by reviewing movies, plays, concerts, records, television shows, and theatrical performances for your school newspaper.
- Consider contacting editors to see whether they have any openings for a freelance critic.
- Send your resume and a short cover letter to newspapers and magazines inquiring about openings. You can find names and addresses of daily newspapers in the *Editor and Publisher International Yearbook* available in many libraries throughout the country.

CRITIC/REVIEWER—BROADCASTING

JOB DESCRIPTION: *Attend plays, theatrical productions, concerts, movies, and other performances; view television shows; listen to music; write and broadcast reviews over television or radio.*

EARNINGS: *$18,000 to $100,000+ per year.*

RECOMMENDED EDUCATION AND TRAINING: *A bachelor's degree is required or preferred.*

SKILLS AND PERSONALITY TRAITS: *Excellent writing skills; objectivity; interest in entertainment; ability to work under tight deadlines; pleasant appearance and speaking voice.*

EXPERIENCE AND QUALIFICATIONS: *Prior experience in journalism or broadcasting is required.*

Job Description and Responsibilities

Critics working in broadcasting review performing arts and theatrical productions as well as television shows, movies, or music. They attend plays, theatrical productions, operas, and concerts. Critics might also attend screenings of movies or television shows or might view them in theaters or at home. Critics working in broadcasting might work in television, radio, or both. Some might also write reviews for newspapers or magazines.

Specific responsibilities of critics in broadcasting depend on the station's size and its geographic location. Critics working in major television markets such as New York, Los Angeles, and other large cities are usually responsible for reviewing plays, operas, symphonies, movies, and often new television shows. Critics working in smaller markets might also be responsible for reviewing local theatrical productions, summer stock, community and school theater, concerts by local musicians and singers, and more. Some critics specialize in a specific medium. For example, well-known broadcast critics Gene Siskel and Roger Ebert review movies.

After watching a performance, the critic must write a review. The critic must review performances with objectivity, honesty, and fairness. Reviews might include critiques of the production as well as of the performance of the main actors, actresses, or other principals. They might also include the dates, times, and locations of future performances. Critics often award ratings or stars to a production to indicate how good they think it is. Writing the review is only one part of the critic's job. The critic must then read on the air (either live or on tape) the review that he or she has written. The critic might obtain and show during the review a clip or short piece of film of the production. Sometimes, the critic might attend a performance, quickly write a review, and present the review on the air that very night. Critics working in broadcasting might do reviews every night for the entertainment segment on the news or might be assigned several shows each week to review. The larger the market, the more specialized critics' jobs become. In larger markets, critics might specialize in a specific area such as theater, opera, movies, music, or television. The more specialized a critic, the more he or she must know about that specific medium.

Other responsibilities of critics working in broadcasting might include the following:

- Writing and reporting on other entertainment subjects
- Writing and reporting on non-entertainment subjects
- Attending opening parties and galas to meet the stars

EMPLOYMENT OPPORTUNITIES

Critics can find jobs throughout the country. However, they might find it more difficult to find jobs as critics in broadcasting than do their counterparts in print media. Those without much experience often find positions at smaller stations where turnover is high. Those with experience can often find work in larger stations or in major-market television or radio. Employment possibilities include the following:

- Radio stations
- Local cable stations
- Networks
- Independent television stations
- National cable stations
- Network-affiliated television stations

EARNINGS

Earnings for critics working in broadcasting range from $18,000 to $100,000 or more annually depending on the specific station and market in which the critic works as well as the station's size, location, and prestige. Other factors affecting earnings include the critic's experience, responsibilities, and professional reputation. A few nationally known critics earn $100,000 or more annually; however, these critics are few and far between.

ADVANCEMENT OPPORTUNITIES

Critics working in broadcasting can advance their careers by locating similar jobs in larger and more prestigious stations and markets.

EDUCATION AND TRAINING

Most broadcasting stations require at least a bachelor's degree for on-air personalities such as critics. Good majors include broadcasting, journalism, mass media, theater arts, performing arts, communications, English, liberal arts, or a related field. Workshops and seminars in all aspects of writing and broadcasting are also helpful.

EXPERIENCE AND QUALIFICATIONS

Employers usually require prior experience working in journalism or broadcasting. Critics can gain such experience by working on a college newspaper or magazine or on a television or radio station. You can also obtain this experience as an intern or reporter in non-entertainment subjects.

Critics in broadcasting need to have excellent writing skills and objectivity. Interest in and knowledge of entertainment, theater, movies, television, and the performing arts are imperative. The ability to write interesting, clear, concise, and unbiased reviews is necessary. Broadcast critics and reviewers should be well groomed and have pleasant appearance. They must also be articulate and have clear and pleasant speaking voices.

FOR ADDITIONAL INFORMATION: Aspiring broadcast critics can learn more about this field by contacting the American Theatre Critics Association (ATCA), the Writers Guild of America (WGA), the American Federation of Television and Radio Artists (AFTRA), and the National Critics Institute (NCI).

TIPS

- Look for an internship at a television or radio station. Any experience is helpful. The experience doesn't necessarily have to be in the entertainment department.

- Get experience by reviewing movies, plays, concerts, records, television shows, and theatrical performances for your school radio station.

- Contact a small local radio station to see whether it is interested in reviews of entertainment events. You might not make any money, but you will get great experience and something to put on your resume.

- If you are still in school, work at the school's radio or television station. This is yet another way to get important experience.

SPORTS WRITER

JOB DESCRIPTION: *Write news reports and feature stories on sports news, events, and people.*

EARNINGS: *$16,000 to $100,000+ per year.*

RECOMMENDED EDUCATION AND TRAINING: *Educational requirements vary.*

SKILLS AND PERSONALITY TRAITS: *Excellent writing skills; good command of the English language; research skills; interview skills; basic knowledge of sports.*

EXPERIENCE AND QUALIFICATIONS: *Writing experience is necessary.*

JOB DESCRIPTION AND RESPONSIBILITIES

For someone who can write and who loves to be around sports, a career in sports writing and reporting is ideal. Sports writers are responsible for writing routine stories and feature articles about news in the sports world.

Responsibilities of sports writers vary depending on the specific type and size of the publication for which they work. Some writers specialize in just one or two sports. Other sports writers are responsible for covering a variety of sporting events, including baseball, basketball, hockey, and football games, horse races, boxing matches, golf tournaments, and skating competitions. A good portion of the job of sports writers might be devoted to attending games and other sporting events.

Sports writers gather information from a variety of sources. These include talking to the athletes, team players, coaches, club managers, team owners, public relations directors, and publicists. They also obtain information from wire service reports, press releases, press kits, and biographies. Sports writers must check the accuracy of their information.

Sports writers are usually assigned specific games or sporting events to cover. They might develop articles to report the actual game or match, events leading up to the game or match, and reactions after the event. Newspapers and other print publications have tight deadlines. Sports writers might outline a story from the venue where the game or match is taking place and either phone or fax the article to editor. Sometimes the sports writer is responsible for developing sports-related feature articles. In these cases, the writer might be expected to come up with subject matter or to give a unique angle to the assigned subject.

Sports writers who cover the day-to-day activities of specific teams are often known as *beat writers*. These sports writers, usually working for larger newspapers in areas hosting professional teams, report the news of every game that the specific team plays. Such sports writers must consistently turn in a standard amount of copy about their assigned team, even when nothing much is actually happening. These writers must build a good working relationship with the team players, coaches, and managers for the team that they are covering.

Sports writers working for smaller newspapers might be responsible for writing about news of school, college, and amateur sports in addition to professional sports.

Other responsibilities of sports writers might include the following:

- Rewriting wire stories from news services or other sources
- Reporting scores of local or national teams
- Taking photographs to accompany stories
- Attending press conferences scheduled by sports teams and sport-related groups

EMPLOYMENT OPPORTUNITIES

Sports writers can find employment opportunities throughout the country. At smaller papers, sports writers sometimes handle other writing responsibilities. Larger newspapers often have entire sports departments on staff. Employment settings exist in the following:

- Daily newspapers
- Local and regional magazines
- Weekly newspapers
- National magazines and periodicals

EARNINGS

There is a tremendous range of earnings for sports writers. They earn between $16,000 and $100,000 or more depending on the publication's size, location, and prestige as well as the writer's experience, responsibilities, and professional reputation. Writers starting out in smaller publications have earnings at the lower end of the salary scale. As writers obtain experience and locate jobs in larger, more prestigious publications, their salaries increase. A few writers have built such a reputation in sports writing that they command and receive $100,000 or more per year.

ADVANCEMENT OPPORTUNITIES

Sports writers usually start their careers at small newspapers. At this point in their careers, they might have additional writing and reporting responsibilities outside the realm of sports. Sports writers advance by locating similar positions in larger and more prestigious publications. Those writing for small weeklies might climb the career ladder when hired by dailies. Writers working for dailies might advance their careers by finding jobs at larger publications or national magazines.

EDUCATION AND TRAINING

Although small weeklies might only require sports writers to hold a two-year degree, dailies and larger magazines usually require a bachelor's degree. Therefore, those seeking a career in this field should obtain a four-year degree. Good majors include journalism, English, communications, or a related field. Seminars, workshops, and courses in all facets of writing and sports studies are helpful.

EXPERIENCE AND QUALIFICATIONS

Writers seeking jobs in small weeklies might find jobs right out of college. Any type of experience writing is useful. Writers can gain such experience by writing for school or college newspapers or by taking part in internship programs.

Sports writers must have excellent writing skills and a good command of the English language. They must also be able to write simple, clear, crisp, and interesting copy. Sports writers must have a basic knowledge of sports and must enjoy attending sporting events.

FOR ADDITIONAL INFORMATION: If you are interested in seeking a career in this field, you can obtain additional information from the National Sportscasters and Sportswriters Association (NSSA).

TIPS

- Look in the newspaper classified section for jobs advertised under such headings as "News," "Sports News," "Sports Writer," or "Sports Reporter."
- Try breaking into this field in a smaller market. Get some experience with a small weekly and then move up the career ladder.
- Write as much as you can. The more practice you have, the more polished your writing skills and techniques will become.
- Send your resume with a short cover letter to newspapers inquiring about openings. Ask that they keep your resume on file if no current openings are available.
- Obtain experience working part time or summers at local newspapers.
- Put together a portfolio of sports articles and other stories that you have written. Make sure that you bring your portfolio to job interviews.
- Look for freelance assignments. You can often find these by coming up with interesting stories and angles. Call your local newspaper's sports editor and ask whether he or she might be interested.

- Consider writing on "spec" (or speculation)—that is, come up with an idea, write the story, submit it, and see whether the newspaper's sports editor wants to use it. If he or she does, fine; if not, you have gained some experience.
- Look for internships with the sports departments of newspapers or local radio stations.

SPORTS COLUMNIST

JOB DESCRIPTION: *Writing a regular sports column for a publication.*

EARNINGS: *$18,000 to $100,000+ per year.*

RECOMMENDED EDUCATION AND TRAINING: *Educational requirements vary.*

SKILLS AND PERSONALITY TRAITS: *Excellent writing skills; good command of the English language; research skills; interview skills; basic knowledge of sports; creativity; ability to work under pressure.*

EXPERIENCE AND QUALIFICATIONS: *Writing experience is necessary.*

Job Description and Responsibilities

A sports columnist writes a regular column on some facet of the sports industry for a newspaper, magazine, or other periodical. In some cases, the column is *syndicated*—that is, the column is purchased and published in several newspapers or magazines.

Sports columns usually have a name or title. The sports columnist has a byline. A photograph of the columnist often appears with the column. The frequency of sports columns can vary. Some columnists are responsible for daily columns. Others write them weekly, biweekly, or monthly. This depends on the specific publication.

Sports columnists differ from sports writers. Sports writers must report the sports news as it occurs. Sports columnists, on the other hand, usually offer their opinions of a sports event or provide in-depth feelings on a specific sports subject. Sports columnists also are not usually assigned stories. Instead, they must develop unique ideas for columns with interesting angles. Sports columnists might write about athletes, events, specific sports, and so on. To write their columns, sports columnists spend a great deal of time talking to people involved in the sports industry. They talk on the phone and attend press conferences, press parties, dinners, games, tournaments, and so on to obtain information. Sometimes sports columnists do not have to attend a sports event; instead, they watch it live or taped on television.

Other responsibilities of sports columnists might include the following:

- Socializing with athletes, managers, and others in the sports industry
- Writing general sports news in addition to the column

EMPLOYMENT OPPORTUNITIES

Sports columnists can find employment opportunities throughout the country. For many smaller papers, sports columnists also handle other writing responsibilities. Larger newspapers often have entire sports departments on staff. Employment settings might exist in the following:

- Daily newspapers
- Local and regional magazines
- Weekly newspapers
- National magazines and periodicals

EARNINGS

There is a tremendous range of earnings for sports columnists. A columnist can earn between $18,000 and $100,000 or more depending on the publication's size, location, and prestige as well as his or her personal experience, responsibilities, and professional reputation. Those starting out with columns in smaller publications have lower salaries. As columnists obtain experience, become better known, and write for more prestigious publications, their salaries increase. Syndicated columnists in major publications might have earnings near $100,000 or more.

ADVANCEMENT OPPORTUNITIES

Sports columnists advance their careers by being hired to write sports columns in larger or more prestigious publications. They usually advance their careers by building a following. Obtaining a syndicated column in prestigious publications is the top rung of the career ladder in this profession.

EDUCATION AND TRAINING

Educational requirements for sports columnists vary. Although small weeklies might require sports columnists to hold only a two-year degree, dailies and larger magazines usually require at least a bachelor's degree. Good majors include journalism, English, communications, or a related field. Educational requirements are often waived for sports columnists who are retired athletes, sportscasters, commentators, and so on. Seminars, workshops, and courses in all facets of writing and sports studies are helpful.

EXPERIENCE AND QUALIFICATIONS

Sports columnists usually have had experience in some facet of writing. Any type of writing experience is useful. You can gain such experience by writing for school or college newspapers or by taking part in internship programs. Many sports columnists start out as sports writers and then move up the career ladder.

Sports columnists are usually totally sports-oriented; they would eat and sleep sports even if they didn't work in the industry. They must have excellent writing skills and a good command of the English language. They must also be able to write clear, crisp, interesting copy.

FOR ADDITIONAL INFORMATION: If you are interested in seeking a career in this field, you can get additional information from the National Sportscasters and Sportswriters Association (NSSA).

TIPS

- Consider writing a sports column on "spec" for your school or local newspaper. Write an interesting column, vent your opinion, and then call or visit the sports editor to see whether he or she might be interested.

- Look for part-time or freelance positions as a sports columnist in weeklies or small dailies.

- Look in the newspaper classified section for jobs advertised under such headings as "Sports Columnist," "Columnist," or "Sports Writer."

- Try breaking into this field in a smaller market. Get some experience in a small weekly; then move up the career ladder.

- Write as much as you can. The more practice you have, the more polished your writing skills and techniques will become.

- Send your resume and a short cover letter to newspapers inquiring about openings. Ask that they keep your resume on file if no openings are currently available.

- Put together a portfolio of sports columns and articles that you have written. Make sure that you bring your portfolio to job interviews.

- Look for internships in the sports departments of newspapers.

PLAYWRIGHT

JOB DESCRIPTION: *Develop and write scripts for plays and other theatrical productions.*

EARNINGS: *Impossible to determine due to the nature of the job.*

RECOMMENDED EDUCATION AND TRAINING: *No educational requirement.*

SKILLS AND PERSONALITY TRAITS: *Excellent writing skills; good command of the English language; ability to write dialogue; creativity; originality.*

EXPERIENCE AND QUALIFICATIONS: *Knowledge of scriptwriting techniques.*

Job Description and Responsibilities

Someone is responsible for developing and writing the script for every play and for every theatrical production of any kind. This person is the playwright. He or she is responsible for developing a story and then writing it in a specific form called a "script for the theater." The script contains dialogue indicating the lines that each character will speak. Scripts also include the settings of scenes and prescribe the movements that each character should make. Playwrights might create original productions or adapt themes from other sources. In some situations, the playwright might write a play and then try to find a producer to finance the production. Producers also might retain playwrights to develop scripts. Before writing a play, the playwright must develop an idea for the story. He or she must then determine how to tell the story. The playwright might create the work as a comedy, mystery, thriller, or musical. He or she must create and develop characters and settings for the story and introduce conflicts and resolutions.

Other responsibilities of playwrights might include the following:

- Making changes in the script at the producer's request
- Locating producers to finance shows and put them into production

Employment Opportunities

Anyone can write a play. However, not everyone can become a successful playwright. Some people write scripts on "spec" or speculation and then try to find a producer to finance the show. The better (but more difficult) way for playwrights to work is to have producers contact them to develop and write scripts. Most opportunities in this field are in culturally active cities. Aspiring playwrights can seek positions as playwrights in residence at repertory, community, or school theaters.

Playwrights might also submit scripts to aspiring producers who are also trying to break into the business. Playwrights might submit scripts to the following:

- Experimental theaters
- College theaters
- Community theaters

EARNINGS

Some playwrights never earn a penny from this profession; others have made millions of dollars in this field. Several factors determine earnings for playwrights. Playwrights can write scripts and sell them outright for an agreed-on amount of money. They might also write a script and accept an option payment from a producer. This gives the producer the rights to the script for a certain amount of time. During this period, the producer looks for financing for the project. If the producer finds financing, he or she negotiates for the rights to use the script. With this method, the playwright is paid a royalty every time that the script is performed.

ADVANCEMENT OPPORTUNITIES

Advancement for playwrights occurs on several levels. Those who have never had a play produced climb the career ladder when they sell the rights to their first script. Others advance by selling more scripts or by seeing several of their scripts turned into productions. The highest level of success that a playwright can attain is to pen a script that is turned into a major production on Broadway.

EDUCATION AND TRAINING

No formal education is necessary to become a playwright. However, many feel that college is useful. Schools with majors in theater, theater arts, or scriptwriting often offer opportunities not available to other aspiring playwrights. These might include programs in which the school can develop, work on, and produce plays. Seminars, workshops, and classes in a variety of aspects of writing, stage, or theater are also useful for honing skills and developing contacts.

EXPERIENCE AND QUALIFICATIONS

Playwrights should have had a tremendous amount of writing experience in a variety of areas. Many playwrights have written other types of works including short stories, novels, or articles for various media.

Playwrights must also be very creative and have an excellent command of the English language. The ability to bring stories to life on stage in an exciting and creative manner is essential. The ability to write dialogue is also necessary.

FOR ADDITIONAL INFORMATION: Aspiring playwrights can learn more about this career by contacting both the New Dramatist and the Dramatist Guild (DG).

TIPS

- Write as much as you can. The more practice you have, the more polished your writing skills and techniques will become.
- Look for playwriting contests and competitions to enter. Organizations, local and national theater groups, play publishers, or colleges and universities often sponsor such competitions.
- Go to as many theater productions as possible, including those put on by local, community, and school theater groups, regional and experimental theaters, and Broadway productions. These will help give you ideas and the opportunity to see how other writers' ideas have been developed.
- Most important, do not take the rejection of any of your scripts personally. Believe in yourself and keep writing.
- Start making contacts in the theatrical world. Begin with local theater groups as well as with summer stock and regional theater groups.
- Take seminars, workshops, and courses to help hone skills, make contacts, and learn new techniques.

LIBRETTIST

JOB DESCRIPTION: *Write the libretto; develop the story of any opera.*

EARNINGS: *$12,000 to $65,000+ per opera.*

RECOMMENDED EDUCATION AND TRAINING: *No educational requirement.*

SKILLS AND PERSONALITY TRAITS: *Understanding of opera; writing skills; ability to develop a story line; creativity.*

EXPERIENCE AND QUALIFICATIONS: *Prior experience writing scripts is helpful.*

JOB DESCRIPTION AND RESPONSIBILITIES

An opera is a theatrical production set to music. The difference between an opera and a play is that most, if not all, of the dialogue in an opera is sung instead of spoken.

Every opera must have a story. The libretto is the book that tells the story of the opera. The libretto is really a musical script. The person who writes the libretto is called the librettist. A libretto is approximately one-third the length of a theatrical play, but still the librettist can be compared to a playwright.

The major responsibility of the librettist is to write the actual words that a composer then sets to music. Before the librettist can write an opera, someone must come up with the idea. Sometimes, the librettist is responsible for developing the story; other times, someone else develops the story and gives it to the librettist. He or she then writes the words or dialogue that opera singers later sing. The librettist must write dialogue for all the singers—the principals (or *leads*), the support singers, and the members of the chorus. Librettists might write original works or adapt themes from other sources. They often work with others, including composers or producers. There is no set time for a librettist to write a libretto. Sometimes it takes weeks; other times, it might take years. As a rule, librettists do not work normal business hours.

Other responsibilities of librettists might include acting as the composer for the libretto.

EMPLOYMENT OPPORTUNITIES

Either a composer or a producer hires or commissions librettists. Opportunities are limited because people tend to want to work with those who have a track record, but they might exist in areas hosting regional opera companies. Opera companies, some with very fine reputations, are springing up in small cities throughout the United States, and opportunities might be available in areas that support these companies. Still, the opera capital of the United States is New York City.

EARNINGS

Earnings for librettists range from $12,000 to $65,000 per opera. Factors affecting earnings include the librettist's experience, responsibilities, and professional reputation as well as the nature of the specific piece being commissioned.

ADVANCEMENT OPPORTUNITIES

Librettists advance their careers by being commissioned to write librettos for more prestigious productions.

EDUCATION AND TRAINING

Although no formal education is required to become a librettist, a college background can be helpful because of the opportunities and experience that it affords.

Good majors include theater arts or music. Classes, workshops, and seminars in the performing arts, theater, opera, scriptwriting, English, music, and literature are also helpful.

EXPERIENCE AND QUALIFICATIONS

Prior experience writing any type of scripts is useful. A librettist can gain other good experience through internships in college or with trade associations or opera companies. Librettists should be creative and have good writing and language skills. They must understand and have a full knowledge of opera. They also need a sense of staging and drama.

FOR ADDITIONAL INFORMATION: If you are interested in learning more about careers in this field, you can contact Opera America (OA) for additional information.

TIPS

- Seek internships. They offer one of the best ways to get involved in this field. They can help you to hone skills as well as to make important contacts.
- Contact Opera America. This organization often offers a variety of seminars and workshops helpful to aspiring librettists.
- Learn as much as you can about operas. Visit the library to review librettos from operas; attend live operas and watch them on television.

SONGWRITER/LYRICIST

JOB DESCRIPTION: *Compose music and/or lyrics for songs; develop ideas for words and/or music.*

EARNINGS: *Impossible to determine due to the nature of the job.*

RECOMMENDED EDUCATION AND TRAINING: *No formal educational requirements.*

SKILLS AND PERSONALITY TRAITS: *Creativity; understanding of music theory; musical talent.*

EXPERIENCE AND QUALIFICATIONS: *Experience composing music or writing lyrics or poetry is helpful.*

JOB DESCRIPTION AND RESPONSIBILITIES

Songwriters write the lyrics and/or the music of songs. They are also known as composers, writers, or lyricists. Some songwriters work alone; others collaborate. Sometimes one person writes the words while another composes the music. Songwriting is an attractive vocation for many because a tune can turn into a hit at any time. Some songwriters have written tunes and made deals with music publishers; then, several years later, major recording artists have recorded their tunes and turned them into big hits.

Songwriters develop ideas for songs. A person might attempt to write a song when he or she is inspired by a feeling, situation, or idea or might be responsible for writing tunes on a regular basis. Songwriters must protect their tunes after they write them so that others cannot steal the words or music. The most common way to protect tunes is by applying for and obtaining a copyright from the federal government.

Actually writing a song is not always the most difficult aspect of the job for songwriters attempting to make a living at this craft. Selling the tune or rights to it can often prove to be more difficult. After copyrighting a tune, a professional songwriter must find a way to exploit the song. The songwriter must find someone who is interested in recording or using the song. He or she might handle this task personally or might have a representative handle these details. After finding a publisher or recording artist who is interested in the song, the songwriter might sell the tune outright or just sell the rights to use it. The songwriter should be offered a contract spelling out the terms of the agreement.

Other duties of songwriters might include the following:

- Performing or recording their own tunes
- Making demos to showcase new tunes

EMPLOYMENT OPPORTUNITIES

Although almost anyone can write a song and become a songwriter, not everyone can become a commercially successful songwriter. The problem with this career is that no matter how good a song is, the songwriter must still find someone to publish and record it to make it a commercial success. Some songwriters write hundreds of songs and never sell one. Others are lucky enough to produce hit after hit. Songwriters can work either full or part time. They can write tunes for themselves or for others to record or perform, write tunes for radio or television jingles, or write music for plays, films, or television shows. Songwriters might work on staff in several employment settings, including the following:

- Record companies
- Record producers
- Recording artists

EARNINGS

Determining the earnings of songwriters is impossible due to the nature of the job. One songwriter can write hundreds of songs and never make a dime from any, whereas another can write a song that turns into a major commercial success. After publishing a song, the songwriter can receive royalties for the rest of his or her life. Songwriters might receive a percentage of monies every time that a tune is played, performed, recorded, or used. They, therefore, can earn a great deal of money and achieve financial success at almost any time. Some successful songwriters earn over $1 million annually. Earnings can continue indefinitely, especially when tunes turn into standards or classics or when new artists record remakes of old hits.

Variables affecting the earnings of songwriters include the number of songs that the songwriter has had published or sold, the number of times that each tune is played, performed or used, and the popularity of each song. Earnings also depend on the specific type of agreement made for tunes. These agreements might include the rights to use the songs or might entail selling the tunes outright. Songwriters can receive writer's royalties as well as publisher's royalties. The number of collaborators and the method used for splitting monies received must also be taken into account.

ADVANCEMENT OPPORTUNITIES

Songwriters advance their careers by writing songs that turn into major hits and then become standards or classics, which can result in financial and artistic success.

EDUCATION AND TRAINING

No formal education or training is necessary to become a songwriter. Some songwriters go through formal training at music conservatories, colleges, and universities. Others attend workshops, seminars, and classes in songwriting. Some very successful songwriters have had no training at all.

EXPERIENCE AND QUALIFICATIONS

In some cases, a songwriter's first song turns into a hit. However, experience writing lyrics, music, and poetry is helpful in honing skills in this field.

To succeed, songwriters should have a combination of talent, luck, and perseverance. A complete knowledge and understanding of the music industry is also useful.

FOR ADDITIONAL INFORMATION: Aspiring songwriters can obtain additional career information from the American Society of Composers, Authors, and Publishers (ASCAP), Broadcast Music, Inc. (BMI), SESAC, Inc. (Society of European Songwriters, Authors and Composers), the Songwriters Guild (SG), and the National Academy of Recording Arts and Sciences (NARAS).

TIPS

- Protect your songs. Copyrighting is your best protection.
- Locate songwriting workshops and seminars to obtain inspiration, advice, and tips.
- Do not get involved with people who ask you to pay to publish your songs. Publishers are the ones who pay writers for their work, not the other way around.
- Look for staff positions in songwriting in the recording capitals such as New York City, Nashville, and Los Angeles.

COMEDY WRITER

JOB DESCRIPTION: *Write humorous material for comedians or publication.*

EARNINGS: *$20,000 to $100,000+ per year.*

RECOMMENDED EDUCATION AND TRAINING: *No formal education or training requirements.*

SKILLS AND PERSONALITY TRAITS: *Excellent writing skills; good command of the English language; a sense of humor; ability to see things humorously.*

EXPERIENCE AND QUALIFICATIONS: *Writing experience is helpful.*

JOB DESCRIPTION AND RESPONSIBILITIES

Comedians amuse their audiences by performing funny material. Comedy writers often develop this material. In some cases, the comedy writers are the comedians themselves. In others, comedy writers develop the material and then sell it to comedians for use in their performances. Comedy writers might develop humorous monologues, funny skits, jokes, or songs with a twist.

Comedy writers often must rewrite monologues or jokes several times. Sometimes the comedian cannot put over a specific line, even if the monologue is funny, and the writer simply must revise it. In addition to writing for comedians, comedy writers also develop skits, jokes, and gags for other entertainers to use in their acts. They might also write humorous speeches for people in business or industry.

Other responsibilities of comedy writers might include the following:

- Writing humorous material for books, magazines, or newspapers
- Writing situation comedies
- Developing humorous segments of television variety shows

EMPLOYMENT OPPORTUNITIES

Comedy writers might work full or part time. Employment opportunities include:

- Freelance
- Newspapers
- Staff writer at radio or television show
- Magazines

EARNINGS

Annual earnings of comedy writers range from $20,000 to $150,000 or more. Factors affecting earnings include the type of comedy that the comedy writer writes as well as his or her professional reputation. Those who write for comedians might receive between $100 and $2,500 or more per minute. A five-minute monologue might start at $100 and fetch up to $5,000 or more if the writer has a track record.

ADVANCEMENT OPPORTUNITIES

Comedy writers advance their careers by selling a consistent supply of material to prestigious entertainers. Some comedy writers become comedians in their own right; others go on to develop and write successful sitcoms.

EDUCATION AND TRAINING

There are no formal education or training requirements for comedy writers. Some people just pick up the skill on their own. Others attend comedy-writing classes.

EXPERIENCE AND QUALIFICATIONS

Some comedy writers have had prior experience as comedians writing material for themselves. Comedy writers have a unique way of looking at events and usually see them in a humorous way. Excellent writing skills are mandatory to this job.

FOR ADDITIONAL INFORMATION: If you are interested in learning more about a career in this field, you can contact the Hollywood Comedy Club (HCC) or the Association of Entertainers (AE).

TIPS

- Look for seminars and workshops in comedy writing. These can help you hone skills.
- Look for up-and-coming comedians who might need material. You won't make a lot of money, but you will get experience.
- Visit comedy clubs and showcases to get inspiration.

CHAPTER 3

Careers for Writers in Newspapers and Magazines

Newspapers and magazines play a key role in our society. Newspapers let us know about the day's happenings and inform us about local, state, national, and international events. Some present points of view on current issues or report on the actions of various groups. In addition to news and views, periodicals offer facts, fiction, and features as well as criticism and commentary.

Periodical publications cover myriad subjects and interests. From news to entertainment to cooking to collecting to contesting, there is virtually no subject that doesn't have its own publication. Opportunities for writers in these publications exist in small communities as well as in large cities.

Careers for writers in newspapers and magazines are nearly unlimited. Space restrictions, however, make it impossible for this chapter to discuss all possible opportunities. This chapter discusses the following careers:

Editor—Newspaper	Newspaper Reporter
Editorial Writer	Wire Service Correspondent
Columnist—Newspaper/Magazine	Magazine Staff Writer
Copy Editor—Newspaper/Magazine	Magazine Researcher

EDITOR—NEWSPAPER

JOB DESCRIPTION: *Handle day-to-day decisions of the paper; oversee reporters; decide the general content of the paper.*

EARNINGS: *$23,000 to $100,000+ per year.*

RECOMMENDED EDUCATION AND TRAINING: *A bachelor's degree.*

SKILLS AND PERSONALITY TRAITS: *Supervisory skills; editing skills; communications skills; interpersonal skills; organizational skills; detail orientation.*

EXPERIENCE AND QUALIFICATIONS: *Prior editing experience is required.*

JOB DESCRIPTION AND RESPONSIBILITIES

Editors working on newspapers handle the day-to-day activities and operations of the newspaper's newsroom. At various levels, editors might carry such titles as executive editors, news editors, or city editors. Newspaper editors are responsible for deciding which stories the newspaper should cover and which reporters should cover them. Newspaper editors must determine the stories that are most important and those that should be given the most coverage. Editors might cut articles that they feel are too long and rewrite stories as they feel necessary. Editors decide what the lead story should be and choose front-page photos. They might write the headlines or work with others who handle the task. The lead headline is important because it helps attract readers.

Depending on the newspaper's size and structure, editors might have one or two assistant editors or section editors working with them. In small newspapers, the editor might have sole responsibility for the entire newsroom.

Other responsibilities of newspaper editors might include the following:

- Acting as liaisons between the paper and the community
- Attending events on behalf of the newspaper
- Attending regular editorial meetings
- Representing the publisher at industry conventions

EMPLOYMENT OPPORTUNITIES

Newspaper editors can find employment opportunities throughout the country. Employment settings might exist with the following:

- Daily newspapers
- Tabloids
- Weekly newspapers

EARNINGS

There is a tremendous range of earnings for newspaper editors. An editor can earn $23,000 to $100,000 or more annually depending on the newspaper's size, location, and prestige as well as on his or her experience, responsibilities, and professional reputation. Those starting with smaller publications have lower salaries. As editors gain experience and become editors of more prestigious publications, their salaries increase.

ADVANCEMENT OPPORTUNITIES

Newspaper editors can advance their careers by finding similar positions at larger or more prestigious newspapers. Others climb the career ladder by moving into upper management.

EDUCATION AND TRAINING

Employers usually require newspaper editors to hold a bachelor's degree. Good majors for this field include journalism, communications, liberal arts, English, mass media, or a related field. Courses or workshops in editing, publishing, and production are useful.

EXPERIENCE AND QUALIFICATIONS

Newspaper editors must have had prior experience either in editing or journalism. They can acquire such experience through such jobs as editorial assistant, assistant editor, and section editor.

Editors should be organized and detail-oriented so that they can work on several projects at one time. They must have editing and writing skills. Supervisory skills are also necessary. The ability to work well with others is essential.

FOR ADDITIONAL INFORMATION: To learn more about careers in this field, contact the Society of Professional Journalists (SPJ), International Society of Weekly Newspaper Editors (ISWNE), and Investigative Reporters and Editors (IRE).

TIPS

- Try breaking into this field in a smaller market. Get some experience with a small weekly; then move up the career ladder.
- Send your resume and a short cover letter to newspapers to see whether they have any openings. Ask that they keep your resume on file if no current jobs are available.

- Look in the classified section of newspapers for jobs advertised under such headings as "Editor," "City Editor," "Executive Editor," or "Newspapers."

EDITORIAL WRITER

JOB DESCRIPTION: *Write regular editorials for a newspaper; screen letters to the editor.*

EARNINGS: *$18,000 to $60,000+ per year.*

RECOMMENDED EDUCATION AND TRAINING: *A bachelor's degree.*

SKILLS AND PERSONALITY TRAITS: *Excellent writing skills; good command of the English language; research skills; objectivity; persuasiveness.*

EXPERIENCE AND QUALIFICATIONS: *Journalism experience is necessary.*

JOB DESCRIPTION AND RESPONSIBILITIES

Editorial writers are responsible for the editorial page in the newspaper. They have many responsibilities depending on the specific newspaper's size and structure. Editorial writers develop and write editorials on a multitude of issues. They must thoroughly research these issues. Every editorial is written from a point of view. Before writing an editorial, the writer must determine his or her position on the issue. Editorial writers must keep abreast of news, current events, and issues on a local, regional, national, and international level. They do this by reading a variety of newspapers, magazines, and other publications, by listening to radio or television broadcasts, and by talking to people involved in the news. Editorial writers might write editorials on issues facing the local circulation area or on national issues. Some react to late-breaking news events, others to news that is not as timely but important just the same.

Other responsibilities of editorial writers might include the following:

- Screening and choosing which of the public's letters to the editor to print on the editorial page
- Determining which other editorial articles to print in the newspaper

EMPLOYMENT OPPORTUNITIES

Editorial writers can find employment opportunities throughout the country. Employment settings might exist with the following:

- Daily newspapers
- Weekly newspapers

EARNINGS

Editorial writers earn between $18,000 and $60,000 or more depending on the publication's size, location, and prestige as well as on the writer's experience, responsibilities, and professional reputation. Those starting with smaller publications have lower salaries. As writers are hired for larger or more prestigious publications, their salaries increase.

ADVANCEMENT OPPORTUNITIES

Editorial writers can advance their careers by finding similar positions at larger or more prestigious publications. Some climb the career ladder by becoming senior editors.

EDUCATION AND TRAINING

Employers usually require editorial writers to hold at least a bachelor's degree. Good majors include journalism, English, communications, liberal arts, or a related field. Some editorial writers have minors in business or economics as well.

EXPERIENCE AND QUALIFICATIONS

Editorial writers need a fair amount of journalism experience. Experience working as a newsroom editor might be required as well.

Editorial writers must have excellent writing skills and a good command of the English language. They must also be able to write objective, clear, crisp, and interesting copy. An editorial writer should have a logical mind and be able to see both sides of a story.

FOR ADDITIONAL INFORMATION: For more information about careers in this field, contact the National Council of Editorial Writers (NCEW), the Society of Professional Journalists (SPJ), and the International Society of Weekly Newspaper Editors (ISWNE).

TIPS

- While in school, make sure that you are involved with your college newspaper.
- Try entering the profession by getting a job at weeklies or small dailies.

- Write as much as you can. The more practice you have, the more polished your writing skills and techniques will become.
- If you have journalism and newsroom editing experience, send your resume with a short cover letter to newspapers inquiring about openings.

COLUMNIST—NEWSPAPER/MAGAZINE

JOB DESCRIPTION: *Write a regular column for a newspaper or magazine.*

EARNINGS: *$18,000 to $100,000+ per year.*

RECOMMENDED EDUCATION AND TRAINING: *Educational requirements vary.*

SKILLS AND PERSONALITY TRAITS: *Excellent writing skills; good command of the English language; research skills; interview skills; creativity; the ability to work under pressure.*

EXPERIENCE AND QUALIFICATIONS: *Writing experience is necessary.*

JOB DESCRIPTION AND RESPONSIBILITIES

A columnist writes a regular column for a newspaper, magazine, or other periodical. In some cases, the column is syndicated. Syndicated columns are bought by and published in several newspapers or magazines. Columns usually have a title or a name. The columnist also has a *byline*—that is, he or she is given credit for writing the piece. Often a photograph of the columnist accompanies each column. Many columnists become personalities in their own right. The frequency with which columns appear can vary. Some columnists are responsible for daily columns; others might be expected to write them weekly, biweekly, or monthly. This depends on the specific publication.

Columnists write on a variety of subjects, depending on their specialties. They might write about entertainment, sports, health, pets, medicine, gardening, careers, education, finance, business, or politics. Columnists might write columns that are humorous or serious; some might be analytical; others might comment on various subjects. Columnists are not usually assigned stories. They must instead develop their own unique ideas for columns with interesting angles.

Other responsibilities of columnists might include the following:

- Writing and reporting general news
- Representing the publication at social or press functions

EMPLOYMENT OPPORTUNITIES

Columnists can find employment opportunities throughout the country. Many smaller papers expect columnists to handle other writing responsibilities. Employment settings might exist in the following:

- Daily newspapers
- Local and regional magazines
- Weekly newspapers
- National magazines and periodicals

EARNINGS

There is a tremendous range of earnings for columnists. Columnists may earn $18,000 to $100,000 or even more depending on where they are published and how well they are known. Those starting with columns in smaller publications have lower salaries. As writers gain experience, become better known, and write for more prestigious publications, their salaries increase. Syndicated columnists in major publications might have earnings near $100,000 or more.

ADVANCEMENT OPPORTUNITIES

Columnists advance in their careers by being hired to write a column in larger or more prestigious publications. The top rung of the career ladder in this profession is writing a nationally syndicated column.

EDUCATION AND TRAINING

Educational requirements for columnists vary. Although small weeklies might require columnists to hold only a two-year degree, dailies and larger magazines usually require a minimum of a bachelor's degree. Good majors include journalism, English, communications, or a related field. Employers often waive educational requirements for columnists who are experts in the field in which they write.

EXPERIENCE AND QUALIFICATIONS

Columnists usually have had experience in some facet of writing. Any type of writing experience is useful. Columnists can gain such experience by writing for school or college newspapers or by taking part in internship programs. Many columnists start as reporters or other types of journalists, then move up the career ladder.

Columnists must have excellent writing skills and a good command of the English language. They must also be able to write clear, crisp, and interesting copy with unique hooks and angles.

FOR ADDITIONAL INFORMATION: If you are interested in a career in this field, you can get additional information from the Newspaper Guild (NG) or the Society of Professional Journalists (SPJ).

TIPS

- Consider writing a column "on spec" for your school or local newspaper. Write an interesting column, vent your opinion, and then call or visit the editor to see whether he or she is interested.

- Try to find part-time or freelance positions as a columnist for weeklies or small dailies.

- Look in the newspaper classified section for jobs advertised under such headings as "Columnist," "Magazine Columnist," or "Newspaper Columnist."

- Try breaking into this field in a smaller market. Get some experience with a small weekly; then move up the career ladder.

- Write as much as you can. The more practice you have, the more polished your writing skills and techniques will become.

- Send your resume with a short cover letter to newspapers to see whether they have openings. Ask that they keep your resume on file if there are no current openings.

- Put together a portfolio of columns and articles that you have written. Make sure that you bring your portfolio to job interviews.

- Look for internships with newspapers and magazines.

COPY EDITOR—NEWSPAPER/MAGAZINE

JOB DESCRIPTION: *Review articles, captions, and columns for errors in grammar, punctuation, and spelling; check articles for readability, style, and agreement with editorial policy.*

EARNINGS: *$18,000 to $60,000+ per year.*

RECOMMENDED EDUCATION AND TRAINING: *A bachelor's degree is required or preferred for most jobs.*

SKILLS AND PERSONALITY TRAITS: *Excellent written communication skills; good command of the English language; knowledge of grammar, punctuation, and spelling.*

EXPERIENCE AND QUALIFICATIONS: *Prior writing or reporting experience is necessary.*

JOB DESCRIPTION AND RESPONSIBILITIES

Copy editors working at newspapers and magazines are responsible for reviewing articles, photo captions, columns, and other copy and for making necessary changes. Responsibilities vary depending on the size of the newspaper or magazine.

Copy editors must check articles for mistakes in grammar, spelling, and punctuation. They also must read the articles for word usage, content, and sentence structure. When going over articles, copy editors make necessary changes so that the copy is easy to read and grammatically correct. When making changes, copy editors usually use proofreaders' marks. These are special symbols that are universally used by those in the publishing industry to correct errors and make changes. Copy editors are expected to check copy for accuracy. The accuracy check might include factual information, dates, and the spelling of names, cities, and countries. They might check the accuracy of information by asking the reporter who wrote the story or by checking the newspaper's or magazine's morgue, public records, and so on. Copy editors might decide to move a certain sentence or paragraph to a different location in an article. They might choose to delete words, sentences, or portions of articles. Copy editors rewrite parts of articles to make them more interesting, accurate, or readable. At some publications, especially smaller ones, copy editors might also be responsible for handling other writing or reporting duties.

Other responsibilities of copy editors might include the following:

- Writing headlines for stories and articles
- Determining the newsworthiness of articles, stories, and features

EMPLOYMENT OPPORTUNITIES

Copy editors can find employment throughout the country. They might work in the following settings:

- Weekly newspapers
- Larger daily newspapers
- National magazines
- Small daily newspapers
- Local or regional magazines

EARNINGS

Annual earnings for copy editors working in newspapers and magazines can range from $18,000 to $60,000 or more depending on the publication's size, location, and prestige as well as the copy editor's experience and responsibilities. Usually, copy editors working at larger dailies and national magazines earn higher salaries than their counterparts in weekly newspapers and local or regional magazines.

ADVANCEMENT OPPORTUNITIES

Copy editors can advance their careers by obtaining experience and then locating similar positions with larger or more prestigious publications. A copy editor might also climb the career ladder by becoming an editorial supervisor, assistant editor, editor of a specific department, or even editor of the publication itself.

EDUCATION AND TRAINING

Although educational requirements vary, the recommended training for copy editors is a bachelor's degree. Good choices for majors include journalism, English, social sciences, liberal arts, or a related field.

EXPERIENCE AND QUALIFICATIONS

Experience requirements vary from job to job. Employers usually prefer experience writing for or editing newspapers or magazines. Copy editors can acquire experience by working on college newspapers or magazines.

Copy editors should be good writers and have a command of the English language. They must have a full knowledge of grammar, spelling, punctuation, word usage, and sentence structure. The ability to use proofreading symbols is also necessary.

FOR ADDITIONAL INFORMATION: You can get additional information regarding careers in copy editing by contacting the Newspaper Guild (NG), the Newspaper Association of America Foundation (NAAF), the National Newspaper Foundation (NNF), and the Dow Jones Newspaper Fund.

TIPS

- Look for an internship in newspapers or magazines.
- Send your resume and a short cover letter to dailies, weeklies, and magazines to see whether they have openings. Request that they keep your resume on file if there are no current openings.
- Take seminars and workshops in writing and editing.
- Look in the classified section of newspapers for jobs advertised under such headings as "Copy Editor," "Editor," "Newspaper," "Magazine," or "Publishing."
- Look for other openings advertised in magazines and similar publications.
- Be sure to contact your college's placement office.

NEWSPAPER REPORTER

JOB DESCRIPTION: *Write articles and news stories for a newspaper; gather and check facts.*

EARNINGS: *$18,000 to $75,000+ per year.*

RECOMMENDED EDUCATION AND TRAINING: *A bachelor's degree is preferred.*

SKILLS AND PERSONALITY TRAITS: *Excellent writing skills; good command of the English language; research skills; interviewing skills.*

EXPERIENCE AND QUALIFICATIONS: *Experience requirements vary.*

JOB DESCRIPTION AND RESPONSIBILITIES

Newspaper reporters are responsible for writing news stories and feature articles. They might be responsible for reporting local, regional, state, national, or international news or a combination of these.

Specific responsibilities for reporters vary depending on the newspaper's size. Reporters working for smaller papers that employ only a few news reporters might be responsible for writing articles on almost any subject. Larger publications might assign reporters to more specialized stories. Reporters might be assigned subjects to cover, such as education, entertainment, politics, or government. At some newspapers, reporters look for news stories. At others, news directors or editors assign specific stories to each news reporter to cover. Whatever the method of obtaining the basic information, news reporters must find ways to develop interesting stories. Reporters must interview people to secure comments from them. Sometimes reporters bring their material to editors who combine it with the material of other reporters. Reporters must write their stories clearly and concisely. Stories must be interesting to readers and easy to understand. Reporters might work from the newsroom, making phone calls to gather information, or might go out in the field to speak to people and obtain information for stories. The reporter must decide how to edit interviews and what he or she will use in an article. Reporters might work various shifts—daytime, evening, or overnight.

Other responsibilities of newspaper reporters include the following:

- Compiling and rewriting wire stories from news services or other sources
- Attending meetings or events to gather news
- Generating feature stories
- Taking photographs to go with stories

EMPLOYMENT OPPORTUNITIES

Newspaper reporters can find employment opportunities throughout the country. Employment settings might exist at the following:

- Daily newspapers
- Tabloids
- Weekly newspapers

EARNINGS

Newspaper reporters earn between $18,000 and $75,000 or more depending on the publication's size, location, and prestige as well as the reporter's experience, responsibilities, and professional reputation. Reporters starting at smaller publications have lower salaries. As reporters gain experience and find jobs at larger papers or in more metropolitan areas, their salaries increase.

ADVANCEMENT OPPORTUNITIES

Advancement opportunities for newspaper reporters are good. Reporters might choose from several paths to career advancement. The most common is for reporters to gain experience and find jobs in larger, more prestigious publications. Other reporters climb the career ladder by becoming assistant or section editors. Some reporters move into the public relations field or find jobs in corporate communications.

EDUCATION AND TRAINING

Most newspapers require at least a bachelor's degree for this position. Good majors include communications, journalism, English, liberal arts, or a related field. Seminars, workshops, and courses in all facets of writing are also useful.

EXPERIENCE AND QUALIFICATIONS

Experience requirements vary from job to job. Smaller papers often take reporters right out of college. Larger papers might require internships or work experience.

Newspaper reporters must have excellent writing skills with a good command of the English language. The ability to conduct research and to interview people is necessary. Reporters should be inquisitive, self-motivated, and very organized. They also need to be able to work under tight deadlines.

FOR ADDITIONAL INFORMATION: If you are seeking a career in this field, you can get additional information from the Newspaper Guild (NG), the American Society of Journalists and Authors (ASJA), or the National Federation of Press Women (NFPW).

TIPS

- Look in the newspaper classified section for positions advertised under such headings as "News," "Journalism," "Journalist," "Reporter," or "News Reporter."
- Write as much as you can. The more practice you have, the more polished your writing skills and techniques will become.
- Send your resume with a short cover letter to newspapers to inquire about openings.
- Get experience at your high school or college newspaper.
- Obtain additional experience working part time or summers at local newspapers.
- Try to get a job at a smaller newspaper, gain experience, and then move on to a better job.

WIRE SERVICE CORRESPONDENT

JOB DESCRIPTION: *Write stories about local news and events for wire services.*

EARNINGS: *$23,000 to $85,000+ per year.*

RECOMMENDED EDUCATION AND TRAINING: *A bachelor's degree.*

SKILLS AND PERSONALITY TRAITS: *Writing skills; good command of the English language; reporting skills; the ability to work on tight deadlines.*

EXPERIENCE AND QUALIFICATIONS: *Prior journalism experience is required.*

JOB DESCRIPTION AND RESPONSIBILITIES

Newspapers cannot afford to pay reporters to go to every area of the world to cover every story. Therefore, they subscribe to wire services. Wire services employ reporters and correspondents to gather and report news in their areas. The correspondents then transmit the news by electronic "wire" machines.

Just as newspapers have specialized reporters to write on various subjects, so do the wires. Wire service correspondents might report on general news, political news, entertainment news, health news, sports, and so on, depending on their specialties. A wire service might assign its correspondents a specific locality or "beat" to cover. They must regularly check in with people at that location to see what is happening and report any significant events. Wire service correspondents must be able to write accurate stories quickly because wire services work on a deadline. As soon as the news happens, the correspondent must file a report. The report is then put on the wire, and the story goes out to all the newspapers and radio and television stations that subscribe to the service. Those sources then either use the story as is or rewrite it to fit their needs.

Other responsibilities of wire service correspondents might include the following:

- Traveling to cover an event
- Attending press conferences to gather news
- Cultivating sources for in-depth reporting

EMPLOYMENT OPPORTUNITIES

Wire service reporters can find employment in many of the major cities throughout the world. The most well-known wire services are Associated Press (AP) and Reuters.

EARNINGS

Earnings for wire service correspondents range from $23,000 to $85,000 or more depending on the correspondent's experience, responsibilities, and professional reputation as well as the geographic location at which he or she is based.

ADVANCEMENT OPPORTUNITIES

Wire service correspondents can advance their careers by obtaining better assignments from the wire service or by becoming senior correspondents or wire service bureau managers.

EDUCATION AND TRAINING

Wire service correspondents must have at least a bachelor's degree. Good majors for this field include communications, liberal arts, English, journalism, mass media, or a related field. Some wire service correspondents find that minors in subjects such as economics and history have proved useful in their jobs.

EXPERIENCE AND QUALIFICATIONS

Correspondents usually must have had prior journalism experience. You can gain experience by writing for daily newspapers.

Excellent writing skills are mandatory for this type of position, as are good reporting skills. A command of the English language is also essential. The ability to write clear, concise, and accurate stories with unique angles is also necessary.

FOR ADDITIONAL INFORMATION: To learn more about careers in this field, contact the Associated Press (AP) or Reuters.

TIPS

- Get as much writing experience as you can.
- Work for your college newspaper or magazine in various positions to obtain experience in all phases of writing.
- Consider a summer or part-time job for a local weekly.
- Contact wire services to see whether they offer internship programs.
- Send your resume and a short cover letter to the wire services to learn whether they have any openings. Ask that they keep your resume on file if no current jobs are available.

MAGAZINE STAFF WRITER

JOB DESCRIPTION: *Write articles for magazines; gather and check facts.*

EARNINGS: *$18,000 to $65,000+ per year.*

RECOMMENDED EDUCATION AND TRAINING: *A bachelor's degree is required.*

SKILLS AND PERSONALITY TRAITS: *Excellent writing skills; good command of the English language; research skills; interviewing skills.*

EXPERIENCE AND QUALIFICATIONS: *Experience requirements vary.*

JOB DESCRIPTION AND RESPONSIBILITIES

Magazine staff writers are responsible for writing stories, feature articles, and columns. Specific responsibilities for magazine staff writers vary depending on the publication's size and type. Writers working at smaller periodicals might be responsible for writing articles on almost any subject that the magazine covers. Larger publications might assign more specialized stories. Depending on the type of publication, staff writers may cover such subjects as education, entertainment, travel, beauty, politics, government, and health.

Editors might assign specific stories to staff writers to cover or they might expect the writers to develop their own articles in their assigned subject areas. Writers must find ways to develop interesting, accurate, and understandable articles that are informative to readers. Staff writers might work from the magazine editorial office, making phone calls to gather information, or might work in the field, traveling to speak to people to obtain information for stories. The staff writer must decide how to edit interviews and what he or she will use in an article.

Other responsibilities of magazine staff writers might include the following:

- Checking facts for accuracy
- Making editorial changes in articles
- Generating features and story ideas

EMPLOYMENT OPPORTUNITIES

Magazine staff writers can find employment opportunities throughout the country. Most opportunities are in large cities, such as New York City, where many magazine publishers are located. Employment settings exist at the following:

- Consumer magazines
- Technical magazines
- Sunday newspaper magazine supplements
- Trade journals
- Regional magazines
- Company-sponsored magazines

EARNINGS

Magazine staff writers earn from $18,000 to $65,000 or more depending on the publication's size, type, prestige, and location and the writer's experience, responsibilities, and professional reputation. Writers starting with smaller publications have lower salaries. As writers gain experience and find jobs at larger publications, their salaries increase.

ADVANCEMENT OPPORTUNITIES

A magazine staff writer can choose several paths to career advancement. The most common is for writers to gain experience and find jobs at larger, more prestigious publications. Another path is to become an assistant and finally a full-fledged editor.

EDUCATION AND TRAINING

Most magazines require at least a bachelor's degree for this position. Good majors include communications, journalism, English, liberal arts, or a related field. Seminars, workshops, and courses in all facets of writing are also useful.

EXPERIENCE AND QUALIFICATIONS

Experience requirements vary from job to job. Smaller publications often take writers right out of college. Larger magazines might require internships or work experience.

Magazine staff writers need excellent writing skills with a good command of the English language. An understanding of the magazine's subject matter is essential. The ability to do research and to interview people is necessary. Magazine writers should be inquisitive, self-motivated, and organized.

FOR ADDITIONAL INFORMATION: If you are interested in seeking a career in this field, you can get additional information from the American Society of Magazine Editors (ASME), the American Society of Journalists and Authors (ASJA), or the National Federation of Press Women (NFPW).

TIPS

- Look in the newspaper classified section for positions advertised under such headings as "Magazines," "Journalism," "Staff Writer," "Trade Journal," or "Consumer Magazine."
- Write as much as possible. The more practice you have, the more polished your writing skills and techniques will become.
- Send your resume with a short cover letter to magazines to inquire about openings.
- You might also write to larger consumer publications to see whether they offer internships. These are valuable ways to gain on-the-job training and get your foot in the door.

MAGAZINE RESEARCHER

JOB DESCRIPTION: *Research information for magazine articles; gather and check facts, dates, and spelling.*

EARNINGS: *$18,000 to $40,000+ per year.*

RECOMMENDED EDUCATION AND TRAINING: *A bachelor's degree is required.*

SKILLS AND PERSONALITY TRAITS: *Research skills; writing skills; inquisitive mind; detail orientation.*

EXPERIENCE AND QUALIFICATIONS: *Experience requirements vary.*

Job Description and Responsibilities

Magazine stories and articles must be accurate. Researchers working at magazines are responsible for reading the articles that staff writers, columnists, and freelancers have written. They must then check and verify facts in those articles.

Researchers often speak to the authors of articles to learn where they found information for their stories. They might then check the writers' sources. For example, researchers might check with people who were quoted in an article to ensure that the quotes are accurate. Researchers might also check with experts in a given area to ensure that facts in articles are correct. In addition to checking facts, researchers must also check dates and the spelling of names, places, and so on. Magazine researchers are often expected to search for facts to make a writer's article or feature more complete. They might speak to experts, visit libraries, or go on-line to get this information.

Other responsibilities of magazine researchers might include the following:

- Informing writers and editors of necessary changes
- Proofreading articles and stories
- Writing articles

Employment Opportunities

Magazine researchers can find employment opportunities throughout the country in larger publications. Smaller magazines usually expect writers or editorial assistants to verify facts. Most opportunities are in large cities such as New York City, where there are many magazine publishers. Employment settings might exist with the following:

- Consumer magazines
- Technical magazines
- Sunday newspaper magazine supplements

- Trade journals
- Regional magazines
- Company-sponsored magazines

Earnings

Magazine researchers earn from $18,000 to $40,000 or more depending on the publication's size, type, prestige, specialty, and location and the researcher's experience and responsibilities. Researchers working on more specialized technical or scientific publications in metropolitan areas earn the highest salaries.

Advancement Opportunities

Researchers can take several paths to career advancement. Some researchers gain experience and go on to become staff writers. Others climb the career ladder by becoming assistant editors.

EDUCATION AND TRAINING

Most magazines require at least a bachelor's degree. Good majors include communications, journalism, English, liberal arts, or a related field. Courses in specialized fields are also useful.

EXPERIENCE AND QUALIFICATIONS

Experience requirements vary from job to job. At some magazines, this is an entry-level position. Other publications prefer journalistic experience.

Magazine researchers should be detail-oriented and inquisitive. They need good telephone skills for checking facts on the phone. Sound writing skills and an understanding of the magazine's subject matter are essential. The ability to research is necessary.

FOR ADDITIONAL INFORMATION: If you are interested in seeking a career in this field, you can gain additional information from the American Society of Magazine Editors (ASME), the American Society of Journalists and Authors (ASJA), or National Federation of Press Women (NFPW).

TIPS

- Look in the newspaper classified section for positions advertised under such headings as "Magazines," "Researcher," "Magazine Researcher," or "Fact Checker."
- Send your resume with a short cover letter to magazines to inquire about openings.
- Write to larger consumer publications to see whether they offer internships. These are valuable ways to gain on-the-job training and get your foot in the door.

CHAPTER 4

Careers for Writers in Book Publishing

If all the books ever printed were placed side by side, chances are they would circle the Earth many times. Book publishing is a big business. Hundreds of publishers are responsible for publishing thousands of titles each year.

Books are written for every age group, from preschoolers to seniors. Comedy, drama, poetry, and fiction books are published to appeal to a wide range of readers. Histories, biographies, how-to's, self-help, and textbooks are among the many areas of non-fiction produced to meet the needs of voracious readers, students, and researchers.

People interested in working in publishing do not necessarily have to be authors to enjoy satisfying careers. There is a broad spectrum of careers in the writing, editing, selling, marketing, and promoting of books.

Space restrictions make it impossible to discuss all possible opportunities. This chapter covers the following careers:

Senior Editor—Book Publishing
Associate Editor—Book Publishing
Copy Editor—Book Publishing
Editorial Assistant—Book Publishing
Publicity Director—Book Publishing

Literary Agent
Non-Fiction Book Author
Cookbook Author
Children's Book Author
Romance Book Author

SENIOR EDITOR—BOOK PUBLISHING

JOB DESCRIPTION: *Acquire manuscripts; develop books; oversee publications.*

EARNINGS: *$28,000 to $65,000+ per year.*

RECOMMENDED EDUCATION AND TRAINING: *Bachelor's degree.*

SKILLS AND PERSONALITY TRAITS: *Negotiation skills; decision-making skills; business skills; organizational skills.*

EXPERIENCE AND QUALIFICATIONS: *Prior experience editing.*

JOB DESCRIPTION AND RESPONSIBILITIES

Senior editors working in book publishing handle book projects from their inception through publication. Senior editors are also responsible for acquiring manuscripts.

Once a publishing house decides to publish a book, the senior editor is responsible for negotiating the contract with the author. Senior editors might negotiate with an author directly or with the author's agent. Subjects of negotiation might include advances, royalty rates, subsidiary rights, promotion of the book, and other pertinent areas. The senior editor can negotiate up to a point. However, the editor must know the limits to which he or she can go on an author's contract.

Senior editors work with the editorial director to determine publishing plans. These might include publishing schedules for new books on the list. Senior editors also are responsible for assisting with sales projections for projects on the book list. Senior editors cannot physically edit every book and still get the rest of their work done. They are, therefore, responsible for assigning books to other editors and then supervising these editors. Senior editors are also expected to oversee the production of books to make sure each adheres to deadlines.

Senior editors may be responsible for a variety of types of manuscripts depending on the publishing house. These may include:

- Fiction
- Romance
- How-to books
- Children's books
- Science fiction
- Non-fiction
- Technical books
- Cookbooks
- Textbooks

Other responsibilities of senior editors working in book publishing may include:

- Assisting in the development of publishing plans and goals
- Attending regular editorial meetings
- Representing the publisher at industry conventions

EMPLOYMENT OPPORTUNITIES

Although senior editors can find employment throughout the country, the greatest number of opportunities are located in New York City. This is where most of the large publishing houses are located. However, employment opportunities might be easier to obtain in small publishing houses scattered throughout the country.

EARNINGS

Earnings for senior editors range from $28,000 to $65,000 or more depending on the specific publishing house, its location, size, and prestige. Other factors affecting earnings include the individual's experience and responsibilities.

ADVANCEMENT OPPORTUNITIES

Senior editors can advance their careers by locating similar positions at larger or more prestigious publishing houses. Some senior editors climb the career ladder by becoming executive editors or editorial directors.

EDUCATION AND TRAINING

Senior editors must have a bachelor's degree. Good majors for this work include communications, liberal arts, English, journalism, mass media, or a related field. Courses or workshops in editing, publishing, and production will also be useful.

EXPERIENCE AND QUALIFICATIONS

Senior editors must have had prior editing experience. Most have moved up the ranks in publishing from positions as assistant and associate editors.

A senior editor must have the ability to recognize a good book idea at its initial stage. Senior editors should have negotiation and decision-making skills. Supervisory skills and business skills are also necessary. The ability to understand contracts is helpful.

FOR ADDITIONAL INFORMATION: If you are interested in learning more about a career as a senior editor, contact the Editorial Freelancers Association (EFA), Women In Communications, Inc. (WIC), the Manhattan Publishing Group (MPG), and the Women's National Book Association (WNBA).

TIPS

- Send your resume and a short cover letter to book publishers to see whether they have any openings. Ask that your resume be kept on file if no jobs are currently available.

- Look for names and addresses of book publishers in *Literary Market Place* which is available in many libraries throughout the country.

- Check the classified section of newspapers under headings such as "Publishing," "Book Publishing," "Senior Editor," "Acquisition Editor," or "Editor."

- Look for employment opportunities in smaller publishing houses— it might be easier to obtain employment there.

- Contact the several employment agencies that specialize in jobs in publishing. Remember to ask who pays the fee if you are hired— you or the employer.

ASSOCIATE EDITOR—BOOK PUBLISHING

JOB DESCRIPTION: *Edit manuscripts; screen manuscripts; recommend acquisition of books.*

EARNINGS: *$23,000 to $45,000+ per year.*

RECOMMENDED EDUCATION AND TRAINING: *Bachelor's degree.*

SKILLS AND PERSONALITY TRAITS: *Editing skills; writing skills; communication skills; interpersonal skills; organizational skills; detail orientation.*

EXPERIENCE AND QUALIFICATIONS: *Prior editing experience.*

JOB DESCRIPTION AND RESPONSIBILITIES

Associate editors working in book publishing have many responsibilities. They help determine whether an author's proposal should be recommended for a more in-depth presentation and then, eventually, for acquisition. Associate editors are expected to read manuscripts that have been directed their way. They also might be required to read manuscripts and proposals from the slush pile. The slush pile contains unsolicited manuscripts and other ideas that have been sent to the publisher. When reading through proposals, associate editors must have a full understanding of what the publisher needs and wants.

Associate editors work with others in the editorial department to determine long-range projects and deadlines for acquisitions and production. Associate editors work directly with their authors. They try to move authors along so that books are completed on schedule. After an author submits a manuscript, the associate editor is responsible for handling the editing. Depending on the publishing house, the associate editor might give the manuscript to a copy editor or an assistant editor or might choose to handle the task himself or herself. The associate editor edits for any necessary revisions, rewrites, or other changes to the manuscript.

Associate editors may be responsible for a variety of types of manuscripts depending on the publisse. These may include:

- Fiction
- Romance
- How-to books
- Children's books
- Non-fiction
- Technical books
- Cookbooks
- Textbooks

Other responsibilities of associate editors working in book publishing may include:

- Seeking authors to write specific books
- Attending regular editorial meetings
- Representing the publisher at industry conventions

EMPLOYMENT OPPORTUNITIES

Although associate editors can find employment throughout the country, the greatest number of opportunities are located in New York City. This is where most of the large publishing houses are located.

EARNINGS

Earnings for associate editors range from $23,000 to $45,000 or more depending on the specific publishing house, its location, size, and prestige. Other factors affecting earnings include the individual's responsibilities and experience.

ADVANCEMENT OPPORTUNITIES

Associate editors can advance their careers by locating similar positions at larger or more prestigious publishing houses. Some also climb the career ladder by becoming senior editors.

EDUCATION AND TRAINING

Associate editors must have a bachelor's degree. Good majors for this work include communications, liberal arts, English, journalism, mass media, or a related field. Courses or workshops in editing, publishing, and production will also be useful.

EXPERIENCE AND QUALIFICATIONS

Associate editors must have had prior editing experience. This experience is often obtained through jobs as editorial assistant and assistant editor.

By reading manuscripts and query letters, associate editors must be able to recognize whether or not an idea or author will be good for the publisher's line. Associate editors should be organized and detail oriented because they work on several projects simultaneously. They must have editing and writing skills, and supervisory skills might also be necessary. Associate editors must be able to work well with others: assistant editors, editorial assistants, people in production, and authors.

FOR ADDITIONAL INFORMATION: If you are interested in a career as an associate editor, contact the Editorial Freelancers Association (EFA), Women In Communications, Inc. (WIC), the Manhattan Publishing Group (MPG), and the Women's National Book Association (WNBA).

TIPS

- Send your resume and a short cover letter to book publishers to see whether they have any openings. Ask that your resume be kept on file if no jobs are currently available.

- Look for names and addresses of book publishers in *Literary Market Place*, which is available in many libraries throughout the country.

- Check the classified section of newspapers under headings such as "Publishing," "Book Publishing," "Associate Editor," "Project Editor," or "Editor."

- Check for job openings in *Publishers Weekly*, a publishing trade magazine.

- Look for employment opportunities in smaller publishing houses— it might be easier to obtain employment there.

- Contact the several employment agencies that specialize in jobs in publishing. Remember to ask who pays the fee if you are hired— you or the employer.

COPY EDITOR—BOOK PUBLISHING

JOB DESCRIPTION: *Read as well as correct manuscripts for consistency, style, and readability.*

EARNINGS: *$18,000 to $38,000+ per year.*

RECOMMENDED EDUCATION AND TRAINING: *Bachelor's degree.*

SKILLS AND PERSONALITY TRAITS: *Knowledge of grammar and style; patience; detail orientation.*

EXPERIENCE AND QUALIFICATIONS: *Prior production experience necessary.*

JOB DESCRIPTION AND RESPONSIBILITIES

Books do not go directly from the author's computer to the printing press. Generally, before books go into production, they must be edited. Copy editors are responsible for reading and editing a manuscript for style and consistency. Copy editors are not expected to change the substance of a manuscript. They edit for grammatical correctness, accuracy, and readability. They might add and rearrange sentences to improve clarity. Copy editors also might delete incorrect or unnecessary material.

Copy editors are charged with the important task of reading the manuscript carefully; the finished book must be as accurate as possible. Copy editors are expected to check manuscripts for all types of errors. Inaccuracies may occur in facts, dates, spelling, and punctuation. Copy editors also edit the manuscript to ensure that the grammar is correct.

Copy editors are responsible for editing the entire manuscript. This includes the table of contents, main text, bibliography, glossary, and appendices. Depending on the practice of the publishing house, the copy editor might make changes on a computer or mark changes on a hard (paper) copy of the manuscript.

Copy editors might be responsible for different types of manuscripts depending on the publisher and the projects they are assigned. These projects may include:

- Fiction
- Romance
- How-to books
- Children's books
- Non-fiction
- Technical books
- Cookbooks
- Textbooks

Other responsibilities of copy editors working in book publishing may include:

- Proofreading galleys and mechanicals for typographical errors
- Checking manuscript for agreement with editorial policy
- Verifying information with authors or through research to assure accuracy

EMPLOYMENT OPPORTUNITIES

Copy editors working in book publishing can find employment throughout the country. The greatest number of opportunities are located in New York City. This is where most of the large publishing houses are located. Opportunities also exist at the numerous small publishing houses that are scattered throughout the country. Copy editors might work full time or find freelance opportunities.

EARNINGS

Earnings for copy editors range from $18,000 to $38,000 or more depending on the specific publishing house, its location, size, and prestige. Other factors affecting earnings include the individual's experience and responsibilities.

ADVANCEMENT OPPORTUNITIES

Copy editors working in book publishing can advance their careers in many ways. Some might climb the career ladder by advancing to a production or managing editor position. Depending on training and career aspirations, a copy editor might also become an assistant editor.

EDUCATION AND TRAINING

Most publishers prefer or require copy editors to hold a bachelor's degree. Good majors for this work include communications, liberal arts, English, journalism, mass media, or a related field. Courses or workshops in editing, publishing, and production will also be useful.

EXPERIENCE AND QUALIFICATIONS

Copy editors working in book publishing usually must have had prior experience in production. Some obtain this through internships in publishing houses. Others work as production assistants. Working on college or local newspapers can also provide the necessary editing and production experience.

Copy editors must be detail oriented and have a full knowledge of grammar, style, and spelling. It is essential for copy editors to know proofreading symbols and to understand production.

FOR ADDITIONAL INFORMATION: If you are interested in a career as a copy editor, contact the Editorial Freelancers Association (EFA), Women In Communications, Inc. (WIC), the Manhattan Publishing Group (MPG), and the Women's National Book Association (WNBA).

TIPS

- Send your resume and a short cover letter to book publishers to see whether they have any openings. Ask that your resume be kept on file if no jobs are currently available.

- Look for names and addresses of book publishers in *Literary Market Place* which is available in many libraries throughout the country.

- Check the classified section of newspapers under headings such as "Publishing," "Book Publishing," "Editing," or "Copy Editing."

- Contact book publishers to inquire about freelance opportunities—they're often available.

- Contact the several employment agencies specializing in publishing jobs. Remember to ask who pays the fee if you are hired—you or the employer.

EDITORIAL ASSISTANT—BOOK PUBLISHING

JOB DESCRIPTION: *Handle minor editorial duties; perform clerical and secretarial tasks.*

EARNINGS: *$15,000 to $20,000+ per year.*

RECOMMENDED EDUCATION AND TRAINING: *Bachelor's degree required.*

SKILLS AND PERSONALITY TRAITS: *Writing skills; verbal communication skills; office skills; organizational skills; good command of the English language, grammar, and spelling.*

EXPERIENCE AND QUALIFICATIONS: *No experience necessary.*

JOB DESCRIPTION AND RESPONSIBILITIES

Although editorial assistants may seem to be the equivalents of glorified secretaries, their jobs are still coveted because editorial assistants have entree into the editorial world. Specific responsibilities of editorial assistants vary depending on the publishing house. Generally, editorial assistants are responsible for handling a great many office tasks. These include typing, filing, answering the phones, and making calls for editors.

Editorial assistants may act as liaison between an author and an editor. They may do research on simple questions such as the date a book will be released. Editorial assistants might also be expected to keep track of requisitions for advances for authors and to handle similar requests for expenses or other bills.

Editorial assistants might be assigned some general editorial duties, such as doing the initial routing of unsolicited manuscripts. Editorial assistants direct some of the manuscripts to editors who are assigned to review them. The rest of the unsolicited manuscripts are routed to what is known as the "slush pile." Editorial assistants may be expected to read the unsolicited manuscripts in the slush pile to determine if they are worthy of being passed on to an editor. The editorial assistant may be asked to prepare a short summary on promising manuscripts. He or she might also be asked to voice an opinion of the manuscript.

Individuals can be editorial assistants to editors working in various types of publishing including:

- Fiction
- Romance
- How-to books
- Non-fiction
- Technical books

Other responsibilities of editorial assistants working in book publishing may include:

- Applying for copyright applications for new books
- Keeping track of production schedules for editors

EMPLOYMENT OPPORTUNITIES

The greatest number of employment opportunities for editorial assistants in book publishing are located in New York City. However, there are small publishing houses throughout the country where such jobs can be obtained.

EARNINGS

Earnings for editorial assistants working in book publishing range from $15,000 to $20,000 or more depending on the size, prestige, and location of the publishing house as well as on the experience and responsibilities of the individual.

ADVANCEMENT OPPORTUNITIES

As this is an entry-level job, advancement prospects are good. Individuals climb the career ladder by becoming assistant editors or associate editors. People in publishing move around a lot. Editorial assistants may move up within the company or obtain a higher position in a different publishing house.

EDUCATION AND TRAINING

For editorial assistants aspiring to become editors, a minimum of a bachelor's degree is recommended. Good majors include communications, journalism, mass media, English, liberal arts, or a related field.

EXPERIENCE AND QUALIFICATIONS

This is an entry-level job useful for those interested in becoming editors. Prior experience working on a school or local newspaper or magazine is helpful but is not always required.

As a great deal of this job entails handling office tasks, office skills are necessary. The editorial assistant must be able to use office equipment, answer phones, and type letters. A good command of the English language and of grammar and spelling is essential.

FOR ADDITIONAL INFORMATION: If you are interested in a position as an editorial assistant, contact the Manhattan Publishing Group (MPG), Women's National Book Association (WNBA), and Women In Communications, Inc. (WIC).

TIPS

- Learn as much as you can in this position. Do a little extra, not just what is expected of you. Then, when a job opens up, you stand a good chance of promotion.
- If you don't live in New York City, don't despair. There are more and more independent small presses throughout the country.
- Check the classified section of newspapers under headings such as "Book Publishing," "Publishing," or "Editorial Assistant."
- Contact the several employment agencies specializing in jobs in publishing. Remember to ask who pays the fee if you are hired—you or the employer.

PUBLICITY DIRECTOR—BOOK PUBLISHING

JOB DESCRIPTION: *Obtain publicity for the company's list of books; write press releases; set up media tours.*

EARNINGS: *$20,000 to $55,000+ per year.*

RECOMMENDED EDUCATION AND TRAINING: *Bachelor's degree required.*

SKILLS AND PERSONALITY TRAITS: *Excellent writing skills; verbal communication skills; creativity; aggressiveness; organizational skills.*

EXPERIENCE AND QUALIFICATIONS: *Prior experience in publicity or public relations.*

JOB DESCRIPTION AND RESPONSIBILITIES

There are literally thousands of books published each year. The publicity director working for a book publisher is responsible for obtaining publicity for the company's list of books. A good publicity director can make the difference between a book's obtaining a great deal of media attention or none at all.

Because of the nature of certain books and authors and in consideration of financial constraints, all books and authors do not receive the same amount of publicity. Sometimes, the publicity director will just send out review copies of a new book with a press release to a few select media outlets. In other situations, the publicity director might launch a full-fledged media tour. When planning a media tour, the publicity director must determine key cities for the author to visit. The publicity director then writes letters, develops press releases, and puts together other pertinent written material to send to guest coordinators and producers of television and radio shows in the selected areas. The same information is sent to newspapers and magazines. The publicity director must then follow up with phone calls to obtain bookings on shows and to arrange print interviews. It is essential that the publicity director come up with unique press material regarding the authors and the books in order to catch the attention of the media.

The publicity director is expected to develop a library of up-to-date media lists. These lists differ depending on the type of book being publicized. A cookbook mailing would go to a different set of media than would a science fiction or technical book.

Other responsibilities of publicity directors working in book publishing may include:

- Supervising publicists and publicity trainees in the department
- Getting books reviewed in trade, specialty, and general-interest publications
- Planning publicity functions such as press parties, book signings, and so on
- Planning budgets for the publicity department

EMPLOYMENT OPPORTUNITIES

The greatest number of employment opportunities for publicity directors are located in New York City. However there are other small publishing houses located throughout the country. Individuals may become publicity directors for book publishers with various types of books or for those specializing in various areas. These include:

- Fiction and science fiction
- Non-fiction
- Romance

EARNINGS

Earnings for publicity directors working in book publishing range from $20,000 to $55,000 or more depending on the size, prestige, and location of the publishing house. Other factors affecting earnings include the experience, responsibilities, and professional reputation of the individual.

Advancement Opportunities

Publicity directors working in book publishing can advance their careers by locating similar positions in larger or more prestigious publishing houses. Some also climb the career ladder by advancing to the position of marketing director.

Education and Training

A minimum of a bachelor's degree is required by most publishers for the position of publicity director. Good majors include public relations, journalism, mass media, communications, English, liberal arts, or a related field. Workshops and seminars in all aspects of writing, publicity, promotion, and marketing are also helpful.

Experience and Qualifications

Prior experience working in publicity, public relations, or marketing is necessary for most positions. Some individuals obtain experience by holding a job as assistant publicity director for a publishing house or as publicist for other companies.

Publicity directors should have excellent writing skills and a good command of the English language. They need to be creative and aggressive. A publicity director should have a good working relationship with the media or be able to cultivate one.

FOR ADDITIONAL INFORMATION: If you are interested in a career as a publicity director in book publishing, contact the Public Relations Society of America (PRSA), the American Publicist Guild (APG), and Publishers' Publicity Association, Inc. (PPA).

Tips

- Look for employment opportunities in smaller publishing houses— it might be easier to obtain employment there. Get some experience there and then move up the career ladder.
- Seek out internships in any capacity in publicity or public relations; they will also be useful.
- If you don't live in New York City, don't despair. There are more and more independent small presses opening throughout the country.
- Check the classified section of newspapers under headings such as "Publicity," "Publicity Director," "Publishing," or "Book Publishing."

- Contact the several employment agencies specializing in publishing jobs. Remember to ask who pays the fee if you are hired—you or the employer.

LITERARY AGENT

JOB DESCRIPTION: *Market and sell authors' manuscripts to editors, publishers, and other buyers.*

EARNINGS: *$20,000 to $500,000+ per year.*

RECOMMENDED EDUCATION AND TRAINING: *Bachelor's degree required or preferred.*

SKILLS AND PERSONALITY TRAITS: *Written and verbal communications skills; ability to see raw talent; contacts in publishing industry.*

EXPERIENCE AND QUALIFICATIONS: *Prior experience working in publishing or marketing helpful.*

JOB DESCRIPTION AND RESPONSIBILITIES

An author may write a great book. However, if it does not come to the attention of the right editors and publishers, no one may ever read it. Literary agents help authors market their manuscripts to editors, publishers, and other buyers.

Literary agents have many responsibilities. They are responsible for reading, evaluating, and appraising manuscripts. They may read hundreds of manuscripts before they find one that shows promise. It is essential that the literary agent be able to see the potential a particular manuscript may hold. If the literary agent thinks an author has talent and potential, he or she is expected to try to acquire the author as a client. In some cases, the literary agent may suggest changes or revisions that might improve a manuscript that shows promise.

Agents must contact prospective publishers and editors to find one who might be interested in the manuscript. Literary agents may call these people on the phone, set up formal meetings or less formal luncheons, and so on. Agents often socialize with publishers, editors, and others in the publishing industry in order to make contacts and to market clients' manuscripts.

Other responsibilities of literary agents may include:

- Negotiating contracts on behalf of clients
- Marketing represented authors' articles to magazines

EMPLOYMENT OPPORTUNITIES

The greatest number of opportunities for literary agents is located in New York City. Other publishing-oriented cities may also have opportunities. Literary agents may handle authors in all genres of writing or may specialize in fiction, non-fiction, or children's books.

EARNINGS

Earnings for literary agents can range dramatically from $20,000 to $500,000 or more. Factors affecting earnings include the specific employment situation as well as the experience, responsibilities, and the professional reputation of the individual. Literary agents working for an agency may earn a salary plus a commission for each new client brought in. They may also receive a percentage of any deals they negotiate. Individuals freelancing on their own are usually paid a percentage of any monies earned by their clients.

ADVANCEMENT OPPORTUNITIES

Literary agents can advance their careers in a number of ways. Some individuals locate similar positions in larger or more prestigious literary agencies. Others are assigned more prestigious clients or projects. Some individuals climb the career ladder by striking out on their own.

EDUCATION AND TRAINING

Although educational requirements vary depending on the job, a college degree is usually necessary. Good majors include English, marketing, business, communications, or liberal arts.

EXPERIENCE AND QUALIFICATIONS

Aspiring literary agents may obtain experience in this field as assistants in agencies. Others gain relevant experience working in the publishing world in various capacities. Some agents were once aspiring authors themselves. Literary agents need contacts in the publishing industry in order to get manuscripts to the key people. Marketing skills are a must. Communications skills, both written and verbal, are essential.

FOR ADDITIONAL INFORMATION: If you are interested in learning more about a career as a literary agent, contact the Authors Guild (AG) or the Association of Authors' Representatives (AAR).

TIPS

- Seek out an internship with a literary agency. This is one of the best ways to get experience and get your foot in the door of this industry.
- Look for an entry-level job as an assistant—it will provide you with helpful experience.
- If you can't find a job as in a literary agency right away, consider a position working in a book publishing company. This will help you make important contacts.
- Look for openings in the classified section of newspapers under headings such as "Literary Agent," "Assistant Literary Agent," "Agent Representative," and so on.

NON-FICTION BOOK AUTHOR

JOB DESCRIPTION: *Perform research; write non-fiction books.*

EARNINGS: *Impossible to determine due to nature of work.*

RECOMMENDED EDUCATION AND TRAINING: *Educational requirements vary.*

SKILLS AND PERSONALITY TRAITS: *Writing skills; self motivation; research skills.*

EXPERIENCE AND QUALIFICATIONS: *Writing experience helpful.*

JOB DESCRIPTION AND RESPONSIBILITIES

Non-fiction books are based on factual information. The subject matter of non-fiction books is limitless. Non-fiction includes how-to books, biographies, cookbooks, reference books, and many more categories. Non-fiction book authors may select their subject matter based on their personal interests or expertise or may receive assignments from editors or publishers. Writers of non-fiction are expected to do a great deal of research to gather information. This can be done through inter views, by reading reference books, magazines, or articles, or by visiting specific locations.

Non-fiction authors may have various responsibilities depending on the specific type of books on which they are working. Cookbook authors, for example, develop recipes that must be tested and retested to assure accuracy and ease of use. Individuals who write biographies are expected to check and verify facts. Non-fiction book authors make notes when doing research. They are then responsible for developing and planning the presentation of the information and the text itself so as to write a clear, concise, and easy-to-understand book.

Non-fiction authors must develop outlines for books. After writing the manuscript, the author is responsible for reviewing the information and making any necessary corrections. The manuscript is then submitted for publication. Non-fiction book authors may write their books in different ways. Some authors dictate and have others type their work. Others write or type their manuscripts on typewriters, word processors, or computers.

Other responsibilities of non-fiction book authors may include:

- Discussing the manuscript with editors
- Going over the manuscript, galleys, and page proofs for errors
- Doing interviews and going on media tours to promote books
- Writing freelance articles for magazines or other publications

EMPLOYMENT OPPORTUNITIES

One of the great advantages to authors is that they can write in any location. Individuals may, however, seek the availability of libraries or other resources to perform research. Non-fiction authors may write for publishers or may self-publish and sell their books on their own to bookstores or through mail order.

Non-fiction authors may write a variety of types of books including:

- How-to's
- Textbooks
- History books
- Medical books
- Craft books
- Cookbooks
- Biographies
- Inspirational books
- Reference books
- Sports books

EARNINGS

Although every person can write a manuscript, not every manuscript sells. It is almost impossible to determine the earnings of non-fiction book authors. Earnings depend on the specific publisher, the contract that has been negotiated, the number and price of books sold, and the popularity of the author. Most non-fiction book authors working with major publishers receive royalties on books sold. Depending on the contract, royalties are paid on a percentage of the cover price of each book sold or are a percentage of net sums earned by the book. In most cases, non-fiction book authors negotiate advances from a few hundred dollars up to many thousands to be paid before a book is actually written and published. Royalties are then paid against advances—that is, only after the advance money has been earned.

ADVANCEMENT OPPORTUNITIES

Non-fiction book authors can advance their careers by writing and selling additional books. One of the top rungs on the career ladder for a non-fiction author is writing one or more books that become best sellers.

EDUCATION AND TRAINING

Although there may be no educational requirement for non-fiction book authors, publishers often prefer writers with a college degree. Courses in writing and research may also be helpful in honing authorial skills.

EXPERIENCE AND QUALIFICATIONS

Some type of writing experience is often required of non-fiction book authors; they must be able to demonstrate their ability to write. Authors must have excellent writing skills and a good command of the English language. The ability to research is necessary. Expertise in a specific field may be helpful.

FOR ADDITIONAL INFORMATION: If you are an aspiring non-fiction book author, you can obtain additional career information by contacting the Authors Guild or the American Society of Journalists and Authors (ASJA).

TIPS

- Get as much writing experience as possible to hone your skills and develop your craft.
- Before you send query letters to publishers, visit bookstores and libraries to see which ones handle the type of books that you write.
- Consult *Writers Digest* and *Literary Marketplace* for lists of publishers and the types of books they publish.
- Learn to write good query letters. These are needed to sell your ideas to editors.
- Be prepared to develop and write proposals for your ideas for books.
- You may need to find an agent to help you sell your work. *Literary Marketplace* offers a list of agents.
- Don't let rejections from editors and publishers get you down. Persevere. Keep sending out letters and ideas.

COOKBOOK AUTHOR

JOB DESCRIPTION: *Create recipes; collect recipes; test recipes.*

EARNINGS: *Impossible to determine due to nature of work.*

RECOMMENDED EDUCATION AND TRAINING: *Educational requirements vary.*

SKILLS AND PERSONALITY TRAITS: *Writing skills; self motivation; culinary skills.*

EXPERIENCE AND QUALIFICATIONS: *Prior culinary and writing experience helpful.*

JOB DESCRIPTION AND RESPONSIBILITIES

Thousands of cookbooks are published every year. Cookbooks may be written about cooking in general or may specialize in different areas, such as one type of food, a particular cooking method, or in regional or ethnic-based recipes. Cookbook authors might select their subject matter based on their personal interests or expertise, or they might receive assignments from editors or publishers. Some cookbook authors are professional chefs. Others have worked around food or nutrition in related areas.

Cookbook authors are responsible for creating or collecting the recipes for these books. They must make and test the recipes, assuring that the ingredients and measurements are accurate. Cookbook authors often must revise recipes many times until the perfect recipe is developed. Once a recipe has been perfected, the cookbook author must develop easy, clear, and accurate instructions so that readers will be able to duplicate it. Depending on the type of book, authors may also be required to write introductions for recipes as well as instructions, demonstrations of techniques, suggestions for serving, and other pertinent text. The author may also prepare glossaries describing cooking terms or write instructions on food safety.

Cookbook authors are responsible for arranging the presentation of recipes and instructions in the book. After a cookbook manuscript has been completed, the author is expected to review the information and make any necessary corrections. The manuscript is then submitted for publication.

Other responsibilities of cookbook authors may include:

- Preparing recipes so they can be photographed for the book
- Going over the manuscript, galleys, and page proofs for errors
- Doing interviews and going on media tours to promote books
- Writing freelance articles for magazines or other publications

EMPLOYMENT OPPORTUNITIES

Cookbook authors, like other authors, can write in any location. Cookbook authors may write for publishers or may self-publish and sell their books on their own to bookstores or through mail order. Cookbook authors also might write books on a variety of food and food-related subjects including:

- General cooking
- Baking
- Ethnic cooking
- Salads
- Crockpot cookery
- Cookie making
- Vegetarian cooking
- Candy making
- Regional cooking
- Breadmaking
- Chicken, fish, and fowl cookery

EARNINGS

It is almost impossible to determine the earnings of cookbook authors. Earnings depend on the specific publisher for which the individual writes, the contract that has been negotiated, the number and price of books sold, and the popularity of the author and his or her books. Most cookbook authors working with major publishers receive royalties on books sold. Depending on the contract, royalties are paid on a percentage of the cover price of each book sold or are based on a percentage of net earnings of the book. In most cases, cookbook authors also negotiate advances from a few hundred dollars up to many thousands. Advances are paid before a book is actually written and published. Royalties are paid only after the book has earned the advance money.

ADVANCEMENT OPPORTUNITIES

Cookbook authors can advance their careers by writing and selling more books. One of the top rungs on the career ladder for a cookbook author is writing one or more books that become best sellers in their field.

EDUCATION AND TRAINING

Although there may be no educational requirement for cookbook authors, publishers often prefer writers with a background in food and nutrition as well as a college degree. Courses in writing are often helpful in honing authorial skills.

EXPERIENCE AND QUALIFICATIONS

Prior writing experience is often required for cookbook authors in order for them to demonstrate their ability to write. Individuals must have excellent writing skills and a good command of the English language. Expertise in food, nutrition, or a related field is often required.

FOR ADDITIONAL INFORMATION: If you are an aspiring cookbook author, you can obtain additional career information by contacting the Authors Guild.

TIPS

- Learn to write good query letters. These are needed to sell your ideas to editors.
- Before you send query letters to publishers, visit bookstores and libraries to see which companies handle cookbooks.
- Consult *Writers Digest* and *Literary Marketplace* for lists of publishers and the types of books they publish.
- Get as much writing experience as possible to hone your skills and develop your craft.
- Get additional writing experience by offering to do a cooking column for your local newspaper.
- Don't let rejections from editors and publishers get you down. Persevere. Keep sending out letters and ideas.

CHILDREN'S BOOK AUTHOR

JOB DESCRIPTION: *Develop ideas for children's books; write books for youngsters.*

EARNINGS: *Impossible to determine; see text.*

RECOMMENDED EDUCATION AND TRAINING: *Educational requirements vary.*

SKILLS AND PERSONALITY TRAITS: *Writing skills; self motivation; knowledge of children's reading levels.*

EXPERIENCE AND QUALIFICATIONS: *Experience requirements vary.*

JOB DESCRIPTION AND RESPONSIBILITIES

All children love to be read to when they are very young and as they grow older, even when they are able to read to themselves. Children love repetition and want to hear old favorites over and over. They also enjoy hearing or reading something new. There is a huge market for good books for children. Authors of children's books can write on a variety of subjects for many different targeted age groups. They might write on pure inspiration and try to sell their books, or they might receive assignments from editors or publishers. Some children's authors write books for series; others produce books on a variety of unrelated subjects.

Those who write for children must understand the reading levels, abilities, and attention spans of various groups of children. Very young children, for instance, have a shorter attention span than do older youngsters. Therefore, the chapters in books for this age group must be shorter. Children's book authors must write on subjects of interest to the children to whom their stories are directed. Some appealing children's books are written in rhyme. Others, equally effective, are written in prose. Stories that lend themselves to generous illustration are important for the younger set.

Children's book authors, like other authors, must develop ideas to sell to editors and publishers. These ideas are often sent to editors in the form of query letters describing the ideas. Unproven authors may be required to write two or three chapters in addition to a query letter to demonstrate the ability to write and develop full stories.

Other responsibilities of children's book authors may include:

- Illustrating the book
- Collaborating with the illustrator
- Going over the manuscript, galleys, and page proofs for errors
- Writing freelance articles for magazines or other publications

EMPLOYMENT OPPORTUNITIES

Children's book authors can write in any location. They may write books for various age groups on a variety of subjects including fiction or non-fiction. They may write picture books, chapter books, series, or self-contained stories.

EARNINGS

It is almost impossible to determine the earnings of children's book authors. Factors affecting earnings include the specific publisher, the contract that has been negotiated, the number and price of books sold, and the popularity of the author. Those who write books that must be illustrated may also have to split earnings with illustrators or artists. The usual way in which authors are compensated is through royalties on books sold. Depending on the contract, royalties are paid on a percentage of the cover price of each book sold or as a percentage of the net revenue actually earned by the book. Children's book authors may also negotiate advances to be paid before a book is written and published.

ADVANCEMENT OPPORTUNITIES

Children's book authors can climb the career ladder in various ways. Some individuals gain professional recognition in the field of children's books. They are then sought out and commissioned by publishers. Others create a series of books and develop a following among readers. The height of success for an author of children's books is to have a book acclaimed as a "classic."

EDUCATION AND TRAINING

Although there may be no educational requirement for children's book authors, publishers often prefer writers with a college background. Some authors in this genre have education degrees. Others have degrees in just about anything—from liberal arts to business.

EXPERIENCE AND QUALIFICATIONS

Children's book authors must be able to write in an interesting style and to develop stories for a particular age group. Expertise in a specific area related to children may be helpful.

FOR ADDITIONAL INFORMATION: If you are an aspiring children's book author, you can obtain additional career information by contacting the Authors Guild.

TIPS

- Look at the children's book section of bookstores and libraries to see what types of books are currently in the marketplace.
- Learn to write good query letters. These are needed to sell your ideas to editors.
- Consult *Writers Digest* and *Literary Marketplace* for lists of publishers and the types of books they publish.
- Take a class in writing children's books. This will help hone your skills, develop your craft, and motivate you.
- Become an expert in writing for children. Offer to write a column about children's books for your local newspaper.
- Remember to mention that you are artistically talented if you can illustrate your book.

ROMANCE BOOK AUTHOR

JOB DESCRIPTION: *Develop and write romance novels.*

EARNINGS: *Impossible to determine; see text.*

RECOMMENDED EDUCATION AND TRAINING: *No formal educational requirements.*

SKILLS AND PERSONALITY TRAITS: *Excellent writing skills; good command of the English language; creativity; imagination; self motivation.*

EXPERIENCE AND QUALIFICATIONS: *Writing experience helpful.*

JOB DESCRIPTION AND RESPONSIBILITIES

The romance novel is a special type of fiction based on a stylized or simplistic love story embellished by problems, adventures, or detours. The great appeal of romance novels is that they allow their readers to escape from daily routine and reality into fantasy. Romance novels may be glitzy or glamorous or may just be centered on life in a realistic setting. However, the compelling feature of all romance novels is romantic passion. Some romance novels are based in the current time period. Others are based in historic times. Romance novelists must develop interesting plots, good story lines, and strong characters with whom readers can identify. Romance publishers may have a number of different lines appealing to different age groups or types of readers. Some romances, for example, center around first loves, whereas others focus on horror or history.

Many publishers will not read unsolicited manuscripts. They may, however, read query letters from authors regarding their ideas. In some cases, romance novelists must have a literary agent represent them in order to have publishers consider their work. Many romance novelists write under a pen name. One novelist might even use different pen names if he or she writes for more than one line of romance novels.

Other responsibilities of romance novelists may include:

- Performing research to assure accuracy of historic facts, dates, geographic locations, and so on
- Discussing manuscripts with editors and making necessary revisions
- Going over the manuscript, galleys, and page proofs for errors
- Finding agents to help sell manuscripts

EMPLOYMENT OPPORTUNITIES

Romance novelists, like other authors, can write in almost any setting. They write novels on a variety of subjects. Major publishers handling romance novels include Harlequin Romances and Silhouette Books.

EARNINGS

It is almost impossible to determine the earnings of romance novelists. Factors affecting earnings for novelists include the specific publisher and book as well as the contract that has been negotiated, the number and price of books sold, and the popularity of the author. Most romance novelists receive royalties on books sold. Depending on the contract, royalties are paid on a percentage of the cover price of each book sold or are a percentage of monies earned from the sales of each book. Authors may also negotiate advances from a few hundred dollars up to hundreds of thousands. The latter, however, are few and far between. Royalties are paid against advances.

ADVANCEMENT OPPORTUNITIES

Romance novelists advance their careers by writing books that sell more copies. Authors who write well-received romances will usually have an audience for many more of their books.

EDUCATION AND TRAINING

Reading romance novels is one of the best ways to learn the genre. There are no formal educational requirements for romance novelists. Courses in writing romance novels and in fiction writing may be helpful for learning the basic formula as well as for honing your skills.

EXPERIENCE AND QUALIFICATIONS

Those who write romance novels usually have had some sort of prior writing experience, although this is not necessarily required. Successful romance writers, however, usually have read romances and enjoy them. Individuals must have excellent writing skills and a good command of the English language. Creativity and a great imagination are essential in developing interesting story lines and plots. An understanding of personal relationships and an ability to describe feelings that readers can identify with are important.

FOR ADDITIONAL INFORMATION: If you are an aspiring romance novelist, you can obtain additional career information by contacting the Romance Writers of America (RWA).

TIPS

- Read a variety of romance novels to see how the story lines, plots, and characters are developed.
- Take courses sponsored by the Romance Writers of America (RWA). These will help you learn this craft and develop your skills as a romance novelist.
- Write to the publishing houses that publish romance novels to see what their guidelines are for submissions.
- Consult *Writers Digest* and *Literary Marketplace* for lists of publishers and the types of books they publish.
- Develop a full outline, and write a number of chapters by way of proposals to editors or agents.

CHAPTER 5

Careers for Writers in Advertising, Public Relations, Marketing & Communications

The advertising, public relations, marketing, and communications industries are multi-billion dollar businesses. Almost every type of company, not-for-profit organization, political group, and government entity uses the services of these companies in one form or another. Radio, television, print commercials, and billboards along with articles in newspapers, magazines, and other publications all influence what the public thinks and believes. Opportunities to make an impact on purchasing habits and decision making are available in agencies, corporations, trade associations, government, not-for-profit organizations, and on a freelance basis.

Careers in advertising, public relations, marketing, and communications cover a broad spectrum. Space restrictions limit inclusion of all possible opportunities here. Careers included in this section are:

Account Executive—Agency
Copywriter—Agency
Copywriter—Freelance
Direct Mail Specialist
Public Relations Specialist
Marketing Manager
Placement Specialist

Publications Coordinator—Corporate/
 Industry
Public Information Officer
Employee Relations Coordinator
Press Secretary—Government/Politics
Speechwriter—Freelance

ACCOUNT EXECUTIVE—AGENCY

JOB DESCRIPTION: *Oversee advertising and/or public relations campaigns; act as liaison between departments in advertising agency and client.*

EARNINGS: *$23,000 to $150,000+ per year.*

RECOMMENDED EDUCATION AND TRAINING: *Bachelor's degree in advertising, marketing, communications, journalism, liberal arts, business, or related field.*

SKILLS AND PERSONALITY TRAITS: *Creativity; good writing skills; organizational skills; detail orientation.*

EXPERIENCE AND QUALIFICATIONS: *Prior experience working in advertising or public relations agency preferred.*

JOB DESCRIPTION AND RESPONSIBILITIES

Account executives in advertising and public relations agencies are responsible for overseeing specific client accounts. An account executive may handle one or more accounts. He or she must keep clients satisfied with the agency's services. The account executive acts as a liaison between the various departments in the agency and the client. He or she meets with clients to determine the direction they want to take and the goals they hope to achieve. The account executive continues to meet with the client to pitch new ideas as well as to get approval or suggestions.

The account executive is responsible for planning the type of advertising to use for each client as well as the timing and placement of ads. He or she determines the use of public relations, publicity, and special promotions during the client's campaign. It takes a great deal of creativity on the part of the account executive to design unique, interesting campaigns that grab the interest and attention of the public. Once the account executive does develop the campaign, he or she is expected to meet with the creative department of the agency to explain general creative concepts needed for the campaign. The creative department then comes up with specific ideas for the approval of the account executive and client.

Account executives are expected to develop advertising budgets and then make sure they are adhered to. They must supervise media selection, including deciding whether a campaign will use broadcast or print media, or both. Account executives oversee the copywriters and graphic artists to make sure ads are effective.

Many feel that the life of an account executive is stressful. He or she must always be concerned that the client is happy and the campaign is going well. Regardless of where fault actually lies, the account executive takes responsibility for failure of any campaign.

Other responsibilities of account executives may include:

- Bringing in new clients
- Keeping time sheets to account for work accomplished on behalf of clients
- Attending functions and events on behalf of the agency

Employment Opportunities

Account executives may find employment throughout the country. Although there are many agencies located in smaller cities, the greatest number of opportunities exist in areas where there are many agencies. These areas include New York City, Chicago, Los Angeles, Atlanta, Detroit, Dallas, Cleveland, and Boston.

Earnings

There is a huge salary range for account executives in agencies. Earnings range from $23,000 to $150,000 or more annually depending on the experience and responsibilities of the individual as well as on the size, location, and prestige of the agency and its clients. Usually, account executives working in larger agencies in more metropolitan areas have the highest earnings.

Advancement Opportunities

Account executives can take a number of paths toward career advancement. Some stay at the same agency and obtain larger or more prestigious clients or become account supervisors. Others locate similar positions at larger agencies. Some account executives strike out and open up their own agencies.

Education and Training

A minimum of a bachelor's degree is generally required for this type of position. Good majors include advertising, marketing, communications, English, journalism, liberal arts, business, or a related field. Additional seminars, conferences, and workshops in advertising, marketing, and public relations are useful for their educational content as well as for networking and making contacts.

Experience and Qualifications

Prior agency experience is required for account executives. Usually, individuals move up the ranks in agencies from trainees to junior or assistant account executives.

Creativity is essential in order to develop unique ideas for campaigns. Good writing skills and verbal communication skills are also needed. Organizational skills and the ability to work under pressure are absolute necessities.

FOR ADDITIONAL INFORMATION: If you are interested in learning more about careers in this field, contact the Advertising Club of New York, the Advertising Research Foundation (ARF), the American Advertising Federation (AAF), and the Business/Professional Advertising Association (B/PAA).

TIPS

- Check for job openings in the classified section of newspapers under headings such as "Advertising," "Public Relations," "Agency," "Account Executive," or "Account Manager."
- Contact the several employment agencies specializing in advertising and public relations careers. Remember to ask who pays the fee if you are hired—you or the employer.
- Look for internships in agencies.
- Join trade associations and attend their meetings and conferences. Networking is important in this field.

COPYWRITER—AGENCY

JOB DESCRIPTION: *Develop and write copy for ads for print, broadcast, and outdoor media.*

EARNINGS: *$20,000 to $85,000+ per year.*

RECOMMENDED EDUCATION AND TRAINING: *Bachelor's degree.*

SKILLS AND PERSONALITY TRAITS: *Excellent writing skills; good command of the English language; research skills; creativity; organizational skills.*

EXPERIENCE AND QUALIFICATIONS: *Writing and agency experience useful.*

JOB DESCRIPTION AND RESPONSIBILITIES

Every advertisement we see was written by a copywriter. Copywriters working in agencies are expected to develop the copy for clients' advertisements. The copywriter may be required to write the headline, the body copy, or both. Agency copywriters are responsible for developing the ideas and concepts necessary to sell a client's product. Agency copywriters work with the client and account executive and must create a central theme for an advertising campaign so that all ads and commercials for the same product or product family will be recognizably related.

One of the differences between working as a freelancer and working in an agency is that there is often a great deal of teamwork in the agency. The copywriter may work with the client, account executive, research team, creative director, and artists in developing the best ads possible. It is essential that the agency copywriter understand the ad concepts and directions that the client is interested in taking. The copywriter might meet with the client to determine this information. He or she may also perform research on the product or have the agency research department handle this task. The purpose of research is for the copywriter to come up with themes that set the product apart from competitive products. With this information, the copywriter works to find a unique way or interesting angle for persuading people to purchase the product. Copywriters must find the most creative way to say what the client wants said. Ads, unlike books, do not necessarily need many words to be effective. An attention-grabbing headline of three or four words may be all that is necessary to sell a product.

Agency copywriters are often responsible for preparing the copy for scripts for television commercials. These are usually done with the help of a storyboard. A storyboard is a sheet of paper or cardboard with areas resembling television screens. Graphics, indicating the video of what will be seen, are placed in the storyboard areas. The dialogue is typed under each picture. In some cases, the copywriter writes the script much like a television or movie script. In these situations, the script indicates not only dialogue but scene settings and action as well.

Copywriters may be retained to handle ad copy for print ads and scripts for broadcast commercials. They must make sure the copy is as appealing as possible to attract the greatest amount of attention and interest. In addition to writing copy for ads, agency copywriters may also prepare copy for articles, brochures, sales letters, direct mail pieces, speeches, booklets, and instructional manuals. Copywriters may be expected to develop scripts for training films, press releases, product slogans, or anything else requiring words.

Other responsibilities of agency copywriters may include:

- Writing scripts for radio commercials
- Developing copy for billboards and other outdoor advertising
- Obtaining approval of rough drafts from the client
- Revising copy that the client is not happy with

EMPLOYMENT OPPORTUNITIES

Talented and creative copywriters can usually find employment throughout the country. The greatest number of opportunities is located in large cities hosting large advertising agencies. These include New York City, Washington, DC, Los Angeles, Boston, Chicago, Atlanta, Detroit, Pittsburgh, and Cleveland.

EARNINGS

Agency copywriters can earn between $20,000 and $85,000 or more annually. Factors affecting earnings include the size, location, and prestige of the specific agency and the experience, responsibilities, and professional reputation of the individual. Generally, copywriters with a great deal of experience working in large agencies in metropolitan areas earn the highest salaries.

ADVANCEMENT OPPORTUNITIES

Copywriters can advance their careers by locating similar positions in larger or more prestigious agencies or by being assigned more prestigious clients at the same agency. Copywriters can also climb the career ladder by becoming copy supervisors or senior copywriters at their agencies.

EDUCATION AND TRAINING

Most agencies require copywriters to hold a bachelor's degree. Good choices for majors include advertising, public relations, communications, liberal arts, English, or related fields. Workshops, seminars, and classes in advertising, copywriting, and other facets of writing are also useful.

EXPERIENCE AND QUALIFICATIONS

Writing experience is usually necessary. Individuals may have had prior experience as a junior copywriter or as copywriter in a non-agency setting.

An understanding of the advertising industry is needed for this type of job. Individuals must have excellent writing skills and a flair for writing attention-grabbing, creative copy. Copywriters work under deadlines. They must be able to work on many different projects at the same time without getting flustered.

FOR ADDITIONAL INFORMATION: If you are an aspiring copywriter, you can learn more about this career by contacting the American Advertising Federation (AAF), the Public Relations Society of America (PRSA), the Writers Guild of America (WGA), and the One Club.

TIPS

- Check for openings in the newspaper classified section under headings such as "Advertising," "Copywriter," or "Agency."
- Write as much as you can. The more practice you have, the more polished your writing skills and techniques will become.

- Send your resume with a short cover letter asking about openings to agencies. The *Advertising Red Book* has names, addresses, and phone numbers. Remember to ask that your resume be kept on file if there are no current openings.

- Write to agencies to see if they offer internship programs. The *Advertising Red Book* can help you with this, too.

- Put together a portfolio of copy you have prepared. Make sure you bring your portfolio to interviews.

COPYWRITER—FREELANCE

JOB DESCRIPTION: *Develop and write copy for advertisements, sales pieces, speeches, training films, press releases, articles, and so on.*

EARNINGS: *$18,000 to $85,000+ per year.*

RECOMMENDED EDUCATION AND TRAINING: *Bachelor's degree helpful.*

SKILLS AND PERSONALITY TRAITS: *Excellent writing skills; good command of the English language; research skills; creativity; organizational skills.*

EXPERIENCE AND QUALIFICATIONS: *Writing experience useful.*

JOB DESCRIPTION AND RESPONSIBILITIES

Copywriters who freelance handle a multitude of copywriting needs. Individuals might work from their homes or from their own offices. Freelance copywriters might also work in the offices of their clients. Freelance copywriters may develop and prepare copy for a variety of products, services, events, or advertisements. Freelancers may work with advertising agencies, public relations agencies, television or radio stations, magazines or newspapers, corporations, printers, publishing companies, not-for-profit organizations, trade associations, and municipalities.

One of the main responsibilities of the freelance copywriter is to find the most creative way to say what the client wants said. It is therefore essential that the copywriter understand the concepts that the client wants to convey. Copywriters who freelance are expected to attend meetings with clients and potential clients. The freelance copywriter must determine what the client wants to get across, any possible styles that need to be followed, deadlines that need to be met, and so on. The copywriter must also find out who is responsible for approval of the copy and how that party can be contacted. Because the copywriter is not on staff, he or she must discuss fees for completed work and how those fees will be paid. Sometimes, the individual is paid up front. In other cases, all work must be completed prior to payment.

Copywriters may be retained to handle ad copy for print ads and scripts for broadcast commercials. They must make sure the copy is as appealing as possible to attract the greatest amount of attention. In addition to writing copy for ads, freelance copywriters may also prepare copy for articles, brochures, sales letters, direct mail pieces, speeches, booklets, and instructional manuals. Copywriters may be expected to develop scripts for training films, press releases, product slogans, or anything else requiring words.

Other responsibilities of freelance copywriters may include:

- Obtaining approval on rough drafts from the client
- Revising copy with which the client is not happy
- Doing research to gather information for copy

EMPLOYMENT OPPORTUNITIES

Talented, creative copywriters can find clients in locations throughout the country. Many organizations that utilize the services of copywriters need them only on an irregular basis or prefer to use them on a per-project basis instead of in a staff position. Potential clients include:

- Radio stations
- Corporations
- Trade associations
- Magazines
- Politicians
- Television stations
- Industry
- Newspapers
- Not-for-profit organizations
- Small businesses

EARNINGS

Freelance copywriters can earn between $18,000 and $85,000 or more annually. They may be compensated in a number of different ways. Some are hired on a per-project basis. Others are paid on an hourly basis or are retained on a monthly basis. Annual earnings are based on various factors and are difficult to determine. These factors include the amount of work the individual does, the number and prestige of his or her clients, and how successful he or she is.

ADVANCEMENT OPPORTUNITIES

Freelance copywriters can advance their careers by finding more consistent work, a greater number of clients, or clients who are more prestigious. Some individuals become staff copywriters for large corporations or advertising agencies.

EDUCATION AND TRAINING

Generally, there are no educational requirements for copywriters who freelance. However, a college background and degree are useful. Good majors include public relations, advertising, communications, liberal arts, English, or related fields. Workshops, seminars, and classes in advertising, copywriting, and other facets of writing will also be useful.

EXPERIENCE AND QUALIFICATIONS

Writing experience is necessary. Some freelance copywriters have a flair for writing copy for ads; others for speeches, booklets, or longer pieces. The most marketable individuals are those with experience writing in a variety of areas.

Copywriters work under deadlines. They must be able to work on many different projects at the same time without getting flustered. Successful freelance copywriters need excellent writing skills, a good command of the English language, and the ability to write creative copy.

FOR ADDITIONAL INFORMATION: If you are an aspiring copywriter, you can learn more about this career by contacting the Public Relations Society of America (PRSA), the Writers Guild of America (WGA), the American Advertising Federation (AAF), and the One Club.

TIPS

- Check for freelance positions in the newspaper classified section under headings such as "Freelance," "Part Time," "Copywriter," or "Writer."

- Consider looking for opportunities in a smaller market where more people know you—it's usually easier to break into the field this way. Get some experience and then move up the career ladder.

- Write as much as you can. The more practice you have, the more polished your writing skills and techniques will become.

- Send your resume with a short cover letter asking about freelance copywriting to corporations, trade associations, radio and television stations, political candidates, not-for-profit organizations, and so on. Consult the *Advertising Red Book* for names, addresses, and phone numbers.

- Obtain experience volunteering to write copy for not-for-profit organizations.

- Join community groups, civic groups, and volunteer organizations. Membership is useful for helping people know what you do and making contacts.

- Put together a portfolio of copy you have prepared. Make sure you bring your portfolio to interviews with potential clients.
- Consider taking a small ad in your local newspaper announcing your business specialty. Make it creative. You can't expect people to hire you if your ad doesn't catch their eye.

DIRECT MAIL SPECIALIST

JOB DESCRIPTION: *Develop and write copy for direct mail advertising and sales pieces.*

EARNINGS: *$18,000 to $80,000+ per year.*

RECOMMENDED EDUCATION AND TRAINING: *Bachelor's degree required.*

SKILLS AND PERSONALITY TRAITS: *Excellent writing skills; persuasiveness; understanding of direct mail advertising.*

EXPERIENCE AND QUALIFICATIONS: *Prior writing experience necessary.*

JOB DESCRIPTION AND RESPONSIBILITIES

Today, more than ever, companies are selling products and services through direct response and mail order. Direct mail specialists develop the copy used in direct mail advertising and literature. Direct mail advertising is often referred to as direct response advertising. Direct mail specialists are responsible for preparing the copy to sell almost any product or service. These include magazines, clothing, food products, books, insurance, jewelry, and collectibles. Direct mail specialists are expected to develop copy for product ads and sales letters sent via mail or sold by phone contact. They might also prepare literature to be sent out with monthly credit card statements. Some direct mail specialists write copy for visual ads shown on television. These commercials usually sell products using a toll-free, 800, phone number. Others write copy for catalog sales.

Direct mail specialists have a challenging job. They must develop persuasive, interesting, and factual copy to sell products or services. Their words must convince people to buy, without benefit of their being able to feel or smell the products. Even if the product is shown on television or in photographs, the words themselves must paint a visual image for the potential purchaser. Direct mail specialists must write copy for a targeted market to interest them in the product. Direct mail copy is prepared to advertise a product or service that is sold mainly through mail or phone instead of at retail outlets. Direct mail specialists may write copy for print advertisements, catalog pieces, sales letters, brochures, marketing pieces, or copy for television or radio commercials. Good direct mail copy induces people to see or hear the ad and to immediately call or write in to order the item.

Other responsibilities of direct mail specialists may include:

- Developing advertising and sales concepts
- Developing ideas to use as selling points

EMPLOYMENT OPPORTUNITIES

Direct mail specialists who can develop copy that brings in a good response are always in demand. Individuals may work for direct mail marketing agencies or for advertising agencies. A variety of jobs is available for direct mail specialists throughout the country. The greatest number of opportunities for direct mail specialists is in agencies located in larger metropolitan areas such as New York City, Los Angeles, Chicago, Boston, Philadelphia, and Washington, DC.

EARNINGS

Annual earnings for direct mail specialists range from $18,000 to $80,000 or more depending on the location, size, and prestige of the specific agency as well as on the experience, responsibilities, and professional reputation of the individual. Those just entering the field may earn between $18,000 and $23,000. As individuals obtain experience, their earnings increase. Direct mail specialists with experience under their belts and working in larger agencies in more metropolitan areas earn the highest salaries.

ADVANCEMENT OPPORTUNITIES

Direct mail specialists may advance their careers by locating similar positions in larger or more prestigious agencies. Others climb the career ladder by becoming copy supervisors.

EDUCATION AND TRAINING

A minimum of a bachelor's degree is generally required for direct mail specialists. Good majors include advertising, marketing, public relations, communications, English, liberal arts, or a related field. Courses, seminars, and workshops specifically on developing and writing direct mail pieces are very helpful.

EXPERIENCE AND QUALIFICATIONS

The direct mail business offers entry-level positions as well as those requiring prior copywriting experience. Direct mail specialists must have excellent writing skills. A good command of the English language is necessary. The ability to write attention-grabbing copy with a persuasive flair is essential.

FOR ADDITIONAL INFORMATION: Individuals interested in learning more about this career may obtain additional information by contacting the Direct Marketing Association (DMA), the Direct Mail/Marketing Association (DM/MA), and the Mail Advertising Service Association (MASA).

TIPS

- Check for jobs in the classified section of newspapers under headings such as "Direct Mail Specialist," "Direct Response Specialist," "Copywriter," or "Advertising."
- Look in trade journals for advertised openings.
- You might also contact trade associations to see what internships are available.
- Develop a portfolio of your writing samples demonstrating your ability to write attention-grabbing copy for ads and other direct response materials.

PUBLIC RELATIONS SPECIALIST

JOB DESCRIPTION: *Develop public relations and publicity campaigns; create positive image for clients; write news releases, annual reports, and speeches.*

EARNINGS: *$18,000 to $150,000+ per year.*

RECOMMENDED EDUCATION AND TRAINING: *Bachelor's degree in public relations, journalism, marketing, English, advertising, or communications.*

SKILLS AND PERSONALITY TRAITS: *Excellent writing skills; communication skills; creativity.*

EXPERIENCE AND QUALIFICATIONS: *Writing, journalism, publicity, or marketing experience.*

JOB DESCRIPTION AND RESPONSIBILITIES

Every successful company and organization in some way incorporates public relations into its business. Public relations specialists are the individuals who develop public relations campaigns. Public relations specialists are expected to build a positive image for a company, organization, industry, person, or project and then keep that image in the public eye as much as possible.

Public relations specialists may have varied responsibilities depending on the specific employment situation. Much of their work involves writing. Public relations specialists may be expected to develop and write copy for brochures, leaflets, booklets, instructional manuals, and advertisements. P.R. specialists also write press releases, biographies, annual reports, and speeches. They must be adept at fielding media questions, editing copy, supervising the layout of publications, and designing brochures and sales pieces.

It is essential that P.R. specialists develop and maintain accurate media and mailing lists. These lists are used to send press releases, articles, and other written material to the media. P.R. specialists must be comfortable dealing with the media in all its aspects whether it be talking to reporters about a story, personally appearing on television or radio, or being interviewed by the print media as a spokesperson for a client. In some instances, an individual may be hired by a corporation to handle one or all of the company's public relations responsibilities. In other situations, a P.R. specialist may be retained to serve as the company spokesperson or to advise a client on how to respond to the press.

Other responsibilities of P.R. specialists may include:

- Developing media events and promotions with interesting and unique hooks and angles
- Arranging interviews between clients and the media
- Booking clients on television and radio talk shows
- Arranging and coordinating press conferences

EMPLOYMENT OPPORTUNITIES

Public relations specialists may find employment throughout the country. As more and more organizations vie for the attention of the public and attempt to develop a positive image, public relations has become a business necessity. Almost every corporation and organization has a public relations department that must be staffed. Employment settings include:

- Public relations firms
- Corporate industry
- Entertainment companies
- Trade associations
- Health care facilities
- Freelance
- Advertising agencies
- Not-for-profit organizations
- Tourism and hospitality
- Political candidates
- Retail businesses

EARNINGS

Earnings for public relations specialists can vary greatly depending on the specific job or client. Other factors affecting compensation include the individual's responsibilities, education, experience, and geographic location. Annual earnings can range from $18,000 to $150,000 or more. P.R. specialists who work on a freelance or consulting basis may be paid a set fee from a client on a per-project basis. They may also be paid a monthly retainer or may charge by the hour for their services. Retainers can range from $50 to $10,000 a month or more. Hourly rates can run between $10 and $250 or more depending on the individual's experience and reputation in the field. Keep in mind that many individuals who freelance have more than one client. Earnings for full-time, in-house P.R. specialists in corporations range from $18,000 to $150,000 or more; it depends on the experience and responsibilities of the individual and the size and location of the business, company, or organization. In general, people working in larger, more metropolitan areas earn more than their counterparts in smaller suburban locations.

ADVANCEMENT OPPORTUNITIES

Advancement opportunities for public relations specialists depend to a great extent on the path individuals wish to take. Some individuals locate similar jobs in larger or more prestigious companies. Others become the director of a public relations department. There are some public relations specialists who freelance or open their own firms.

EDUCATION AND TRAINING

A minimum of a four-year college degree is required for most jobs in public relations. A master's degree is often helpful both for both attaining a job and for advancing a career. Good choices for majors include public relations, journalism, communications, marketing, English, or liberal arts. Seminars, courses, or workshops in public relations, publicity, marketing, and all types of writing will also be helpful to those just entering the workforce as well as to career changers.

EXPERIENCE AND QUALIFICATIONS

Experience requirements vary. Though many people decide to pursue public relations while in college, others opt for this career when they realize that they have been handling public relations projects in voluntary positions throughout their lifetimes. Such activities include volunteering to work on a political campaign, acting as a publicity chairperson, or running a fund-raising event for a not-for-profit organization such as the PTA or hospital auxiliary.

Public relations specialists must have excellent writing and verbal communication skills. They must be very creative to come up with unique ideas.

FOR ADDITIONAL INFORMATION: If you are interested in learning more about a career as a public relations specialist, contact the Public Relations Society of America (PRSA).

TIPS

- Look for apprenticeships and internships. These are often available through large public relations and publicity firms as well as in the public relations departments of many corporations.
- Check for job opportunities in the classified section of newspapers under headings such as "Public Relations Specialist," "Public Relations Generalist," "Public Relations Counselor," "Public Relations," or "Corporate Public Relations."
- Look in trade journals for advertised openings.
- Contact the several employment agencies specializing in public relations jobs.
- Get experience by volunteering to do public relations for a local not-for-profit or civic group.

MARKETING MANAGER

JOB DESCRIPTION: *Develop marketing campaigns; implement campaigns; write sales material.*

EARNINGS: *$20,000 to $150,000+ per year.*

RECOMMENDED EDUCATION AND TRAINING: *Bachelor's degree in marketing, public relations, advertising, journalism, English, communications, or liberal arts.*

SKILLS AND PERSONALITY TRAITS: *Excellent writing skills; communication skills; ability to research; creativity.*

EXPERIENCE AND QUALIFICATIONS: *Experience in marketing, advertising, promotion, and public relations.*

JOB DESCRIPTION AND RESPONSIBILITIES

Marketing is a complex affair. To accomplish their jobs, marketing managers work with many other departments in a corporation; among them are sales, promotion, advertising, and public relations. The marketing manager is responsible for developing concepts and campaigns designed to introduce and promote a company's products and services. The marketing manager is responsible for determining the amount of advertising and type of media that will be used to sell a product or service. The marketing manager is also responsible for determining the types of promotions, public relations, and selling techniques that will be most effective.

This position involves a great deal of writing. The marketing manager must develop letters, press releases, reports, proposals, sales pieces, brochures, newsletters, and memos. An important responsibility of the marketing manager is determining the viability of new products. He or she may do extensive consumer research and test marketing on new products to see how well they are accepted. The marketing manager may also perform or supervise other research. This can include interviewing people, developing questionnaires, searching through libraries and databases, and using information provided by trade associations. The marketing manager must tabulate and review information gathered after research and test marketing is completed.

Other responsibilities of marketing managers may include:

- Supervising the marketing department
- Leading sales meetings
- Training sales and marketing people
- Attending trade shows, conventions, and fairs on behalf of the company

EMPLOYMENT OPPORTUNITIES

Marketing managers may locate job opportunities throughout the country in both metropolitan and suburban areas. Industries that employ marketing managers include:

- Book publishing
- Pharmaceuticals
- Service industries
- Not-for-profit organizations
- Geriatric facilities
- Insurance
- Hotels/motels
- Educational institutions
- Cosmetics
- Retail
- Banks
- Health care
- Real estate
- Food service
- Automobiles
- Radio and television stations

EARNINGS

Earnings for marketing managers range from $20,000 to $150,000 or more depending on the individual's responsibilities, education, experience, and professional reputation. Other variables affecting earnings include the specific type of industry and company as well as its size, prestige, and geographic location. Marketing managers with a great deal of responsibility working in large companies in metropolitan areas earn between $65,000 and $150,000 plus. Earnings are considerably lower for marketing managers in smaller companies or for those with less experience and responsibility.

ADVANCEMENT OPPORTUNITIES

Marketing managers may advance their careers by locating similar positions in larger or more prestigious companies.

EDUCATION AND TRAINING

A minimum of a four-year college degree is usually required for jobs in this field. A master's degree may be preferred. Good choices for majors include marketing, public relations, advertising, liberal arts, English, journalism, communications, or a related field. Seminars, courses, or workshops in promotion, public relations, marketing, communications, business, writing, sociology, research, and statistics will be useful.

EXPERIENCE AND QUALIFICATIONS

Marketing managers must have had prior experience in public relations, marketing, promotion, and advertising.

Marketing managers must have excellent writing and verbal communication skills. They must be very creative, innovative people. Knowledge of research methods and their implementation is essential.

FOR ADDITIONAL INFORMATION: Those interested in learning more about careers as marketing managers can obtain additional information by contacting the American Marketing Association (AMA), the Direct Mail/Marketing Association (DMMA), the Direct Marketing Creative Guild (DMCG), the Marketing Research Association (MRA), and the Sales and Marketing Executive International (SMEI).

TIPS

- Look for job opportunities in the classified section of newspapers under headings such as "Marketing," "Marketing Manager," or "Corporate Marketing Manager."
- Check in trade journals, company house organs, and newsletters for openings.
- Look for internships in marketing. These are often available through large corporations.
- Join relevant trade associations. They will help you locate internships, scholarships, and training programs. They also offer career guidance and support.
- Send your resume and a cover letter to the personnel directors of companies, corporations, and organizations. As there is a big turnover in this field, ask that your resume be kept on file if there are no current openings.

PLACEMENT SPECIALIST

JOB DESCRIPTION: *Arrange for clients to be interviewed on television and radio shows and in print media; develop and write letters to guest coordinators, producers, and editors.*

EARNINGS: *$18,000 to $100,000+ per year.*

RECOMMENDED EDUCATION AND TRAINING: *Educational requirements vary.*

SKILLS AND PERSONALITY TRAITS: *Excellent writing skills; verbal communication skills; aggressiveness; good phone manner.*

EXPERIENCE AND QUALIFICATIONS: *Experience requirements vary.*

JOB DESCRIPTION AND RESPONSIBILITIES

There are numerous network, regional, local, syndicated, and cable television and radio stations throughout the country. Many of these stations have talk, variety, and news programs needing a constant stream of guests. Placement specialists are responsible for placing guests on these shows. Placement specialists may represent a myriad of clients including authors, recording groups, sports stars, theatrical actors and actresses, singers, dancers, television stars, and other celebrities. The primary responsibilities of placement specialists are scheduling their clients on television and radio shows and arranging for newspaper and magazine interviews.

Placement specialists must decide what types of shows will be most effective for each client. Then they must attempt to get bookings on these shows. Network shows usually give clients the most exposure. However, it may not be easy to book every client on these national shows. Network shows are those aired on affiliate stations of networks such as ABC, CBS, NBC, and Fox. Examples might include "The Tonight Show," "David Letterman," and "Good Morning America."

Placement specialists must also determine the best market in which to obtain client exposure. Local shows are those that have a local audience. However, there is a great deal of difference between small-market local and major-market local. New York City and Los Angeles are examples of major local broadcast markets. Kingston, NY, is an example of a small local broadcast market. Although it is easier to book guests on shows in small local markets, the larger the market, the more exposure the client gains. Sometimes, the placement specialist books a client on a syndicated show. Syndicated programs are bought by local stations and may be aired at different times in different locations. Some shows are syndicated in a limited area, perhaps in three or four cities. Others, such as "Live with Regis and Kathie Lee" or "Oprah," are bought by local stations in almost every market throughout the country.

Placement specialists must determine the best places in the print media to have client stories appear. Print media includes national, regional, or local newspapers or magazines. It is essential for the placement specialist to know what cities their clients are going to be near at a given time and what radio and television shows are available in each area. The same holds true for newspapers and magazines. The placement specialist then writes cover letters to send with press information to producers, guest coordinators, editors, and reporters. Press information includes press kits, biographies, news releases, and photographs. This information is supplied to the placement specialist by the client's publicist or manager. In some instances, the placement specialist may develop the press kits, bios, or news releases for an additional fee. Once written information is sent, the placement specialist waits a few days and then begins calling the producers, guest coordinators, reporters, and editors to make a pitch for the client.

Placement specialists booking media tours must be sure that scheduling is cost effective as well as time efficient. Sometimes, the placement specialist will book radio shows from the client's home area with a telephone hookup. A satellite hookup for television is another possibility. Once shows or interviews are scheduled, the placement specialist is expected to prepare a letter for the client indicating the list of shows and interviews, times, phone numbers and addresses, and any contact names. The placement specialist may also send letters of confirmation to each program producer or reporter.

Other responsibilities of placement specialists may include:

- Accompanying clients to shows and interviews
- Preparing clients for interviews
- Writing letters of thanks to program producers and media editors for doing stories

EMPLOYMENT OPPORTUNITIES

Placement specialists often are self-employed freelancers. Some publicity, public relations, or placement firms have placement specialists on staff. Placement specialists may have various types of clients including:

- Singers
- Authors
- Comedians
- Radio personalities
- Recording groups
- Performing artists
- Dancers
- Actors and actresses
- Sports stars

EARNINGS

Earnings for placement specialists range from $18,000 to $100,000 or more depending on the type of employment situation as well as the experience, responsibilities, and professional reputation of the individual. Those working for a company receive a weekly salary. Individuals who are self-employed freelancers may be compensated in different ways. They might work on a per-project basis or on a retainer. Placement specialists might receive from $25 to $5,000 or more per placement depending on the type of program on which they place a client. They might also receive a flat fee per week, month, or city ranging from $50 to $20,000.

ADVANCEMENT OPPORTUNITIES

Placement specialists may advance their careers by building a large, prestigious client roster. This will result in increased earnings.

EDUCATION AND TRAINING

Although educational requirements vary depending on the job, a college degree in public relations, marketing, English, journalism, liberal arts, or a related field may prove very helpful. Workshops and seminars in public relations, publicity, and media placement are also useful.

EXPERIENCE AND QUALIFICATIONS

Experience requirements, like educational requirements, vary. It is essential that placement specialists either have a relationship with the media or be able to cultivate one. Placement specialists should be aggressive and have excellent writing skills and telephone manner.

FOR ADDITIONAL INFORMATION: If you are interested in learning more about a career as a placement specialist, contact the Public Relations Society of America (PRSA) or the American Publicist Guild (APG).

TIPS

- Look for classes, seminars, and workshops in media placement, publicity, and writing. These are useful for honing skills and making contacts.
- Gain experience by volunteering to place someone from a local not-for-profit event or a school or community theater group on radio shows or local TV to help publicize their event.
- Get clients by regularly placing small ads in local newspapers.
- Come up with an interesting angle to get yourself on television or radio to talk about your business.

PUBLICATIONS COORDINATOR— CORPORATE/INDUSTRY

JOB DESCRIPTION: *Develop and write internal and external corporate publications.*

EARNINGS: *$18,000 to $50,000+ per year.*

RECOMMENDED EDUCATION AND TRAINING: *Bachelor's degree in English, marketing, communications, journalism, liberal arts, or related field.*

SKILLS AND PERSONALITY TRAITS: *Writing skills; good command of the English language; organizational skills; detail orientation; understanding of graphics and layout; computer skills.*

EXPERIENCE AND QUALIFICATIONS: *Prior writing experience necessary.*

JOB DESCRIPTION AND RESPONSIBILITIES

Every corporation produces a multitude of publications, both internal and external. These include employee newsletters, stockholder reports, corporate newsletters, product information booklets, brochures, pamphlets, letters, leaflets, annual reports, and press releases. Publications coordinators are responsible for developing, writing, and editing these publications. The publications coordinator may also be referred to as publications manager or publications editor. The publications coordinator may work with other departments in the corporation such as public relations, marketing, promotion, advertising, and public and consumer affairs.

Specific responsibilities of the publications coordinator depend on the size and structure of the company. Individuals may be expected to handle the research, writing, graphics, and layout of materials by themselves or may work with copywriters, artists, computer graphics people, and so on. Publications coordinators are expected to edit copy as well as to check it for accuracy. Publications coordinators may write specific publications such as company newsletters on a regular basis. They may also be asked to develop publications for various departments in the company.

The publications coordinator is responsible for estimating budgets for each publication and then for assuring that budgets are adhered to. He or she is expected to obtain job quotes on projects to obtain the best possible prices. The publications coordinator is responsible for choosing the paper stock, type styles, and graphic format for each publication and must set realistic timetables for each project. He or she must project when graphic artists, copywriters, photographers, and printers should have their roles in the publication completed. The publications coordinator must then make sure the timetable is adhered to. Today, many publications coordinators work with computerized desktop publishing. In this way, many publications are prepared "in house" instead of at a commercial graphic design or printer shop.

Other responsibilities of publications coordinator may include:

- Choosing the size and shape of the publication
- Writing speeches
- Developing feature articles

EMPLOYMENT OPPORTUNITIES

Publications coordinators may find employment in corporations and industries throughout the country. In smaller corporations, there may be only one staff person in this position. In larger corporations, a number of different departments might have publications coordinators. These departments may include:

- Public relations
- Consumer affairs
- Promotions
- Product information

EARNINGS

Earnings for publications coordinators range from $18,000 to $50,000 or more annually depending on the size and geographic location of the specific corporation and the experience and responsibilities of the individual.

ADVANCEMENT OPPORTUNITIES

Publications coordinators may advanced their careers in different ways, depending on their career aspirations. Many find similar jobs in larger or more prestigious corporations. Others become directors of public relations or consumer affairs.

EDUCATION AND TRAINING

A minimum of a bachelor's degree is generally required for this type of position. Good majors include public relations, communications, English, journalism, liberal arts, or a related field. Seminars, conferences, and workshops in desktop publishing, graphics, layout, and writing are also useful.

EXPERIENCE AND QUALIFICATIONS

Prior writing experience is usually required. Experience working on school papers, not-for-profit group newsletters, or local newspapers will prove helpful.

Excellent writing and editing skills are essential for this job. Individuals must be able to write in a creative, clear, and concise manner. An understanding of desktop publishing, graphics, layout, and typefaces is also necessary.

FOR ADDITIONAL INFORMATION: If you are interested in learning more about careers in this field, contact the International Association of Business Communicators (IABC), Women In Communications (WIC), and the Public Relations Society of America (PRSA).

Tips

- Check for job opportunities in the classified section of newspapers under headings such as "Publications Coordinator," "Publications Manager," "Publications Editor," "Publications," "Editor," "Writer," "Communications," and "Public Relations."
- Look in trade journals for job openings.
- Look for internships and training programs in large corporations. These are valuable for the learning experience and for making important contacts.
- Get experience by volunteering to work on a local not-for-profit or civic group newsletter.

PUBLIC INFORMATION OFFICER

JOB DESCRIPTION: *Direct media relations for corporations or not-for-profit organizations; develop, write, and distribute news releases and feature articles.*

EARNINGS: *$20,000 to $75,000+ per year.*

RECOMMENDED EDUCATION AND TRAINING: *Bachelor's degree.*

SKILLS AND PERSONALITY TRAITS: *Writing skills; verbal communications skills; public speaking ability.*

EXPERIENCE AND QUALIFICATIONS: *Experience in journalism, public relations, or publicity.*

Job Description and Responsibilities

Public information officers are responsible for directing the media relations for corporations, not-for-profit organizations, trade associations, and so on. Public information officers work within the public relations departments of these companies. They act as the liaison between the media and the company they represent. Public information officers are expected to help maintain a favorable public image for their employers. As part of the job, they are expected to keep the public informed of the company's programs, accomplishments, and points of view. Public information officers are responsible for trying to keep the company's name and image in the public eye and in a positive light. They also ensure that the company receives as much positive publicity as possible. When something negative occurs regarding the company, the public information officer must attempt to handle the crisis using damage control.

Public information officers may develop and write press releases, statements, fact sheets, and feature stories regarding the company they represent. The articles must be distributed and placed in newspapers and magazines and on broadcast media. Public information officers are responsible for speaking to the media to answer questions regarding various facets of the company's business, views, and opinions. Individuals in this line of work, must constantly stay one step ahead of the media. They are expected to keep management abreast of issues that may produce questions from the media or others. Public information officers often are required to prepare statements in advance offering management's response to questions that may be asked.

If the size and structure of the company warrants it, public information officers may be expected to prepare daily news briefs on the company to distribute to the media. In other cases, individuals may handle this task on a weekly or monthly basis. A large part of the public information officer's job involves dealing with the media. He or she must have a good working relationship with the media, answering questions and requests honestly and in a timely fashion. Public information officers may develop and write press releases, fact sheets, or feature articles.

Other responsibilities of public information officers may include:

- Preparing management to handle media questions and interviews
- Writing speeches for company executives
- Preparing news bits and company information for the company's Internet Web site

EMPLOYMENT OPPORTUNITIES

Public information officers may locate jobs throughout the country. The greatest number of opportunities is found in metropolitan areas hosting large corporations. Employment settings may exist in the following:

- Corporations
- Colleges and universities
- Not-for-profit organizations
- Trade associations
- Special interest groups
- Governmental groups

EARNINGS

Annual earnings for public information officers range from $20,000 to $75,000 or more depending on the type, size, location, and prestige of the employer and the education, experience, and responsibilities of the individual.

ADVANCEMENT OPPORTUNITIES

Public information officers can climb the career ladder by locating similar positions in larger or more prestigious companies resulting in increased responsibilities and earnings. Some advance their careers by becoming director of public relations or communications director of a company.

EDUCATION AND TRAINING

A minimum of a bachelor's degree is required for most positions in this field. Good majors include communications, English, journalism, business, and liberal arts.

EXPERIENCE AND QUALIFICATIONS

Prior experience in journalism, public relations, or communications may be required or preferred by some employers. Excellent writing skills are necessary, as are good verbal communications skills. The ability to speak in front of groups is also needed. Interpersonal skills are helpful.

FOR ADDITIONAL INFORMATION: If you are interested in a career in this field, you can obtain additional information by contacting the Public Relations Society of America (PRSA).

TIPS

- Check for job opportunities in the newspaper classified section under headings such as "Public Information Officer," "Corporate Information Officer," "Trade Associations," or "Public Relations."
- Contact the Public Relations Society of America (PRSA). In addition to providing career guidance and support, this organization offers student memberships.
- Get experience by volunteering to act as the spokesperson for a local not-for-profit organization.
- Send your resume and a short cover letter to corporations, trade associations, and special interest groups. Ask that your resume be kept on file if there are no current openings.

EMPLOYEE RELATIONS COORDINATOR

JOB DESCRIPTION: *Act as liaison between corporate management and employees; create and plan employee events and functions; develop and edit employee publications.*

EARNINGS: *$25,000 to $50,000+ per year.*

RECOMMENDED EDUCATION AND TRAINING: *Bachelor's degree.*

SKILLS AND PERSONALITY TRAITS: *Communications skills; writing skills; organizational skills; detail orientation; people skills; knowledge of negotiation and arbitration.*

EXPERIENCE AND QUALIFICATIONS: *Public relations, publicity, or employee relations experience preferred.*

JOB DESCRIPTION AND RESPONSIBILITIES

Mid-size and large corporations employ many people. The employee relations coordinator works in the employee relations or human resources department of these companies making sure that employees are kept abreast of what is happening within the company and keeping them satisfied with their jobs. As part of their role, employee relations coordinators also act as liaisons between management and employees. They must bring problems of employees to the attention of management. Conversely, the employee relations coordinator is expected to explain management policies to employees. In order to do this, he or she meets with management on a regular basis to learn about new policies or changes in existing ones. The employee relations coordinator is responsible for handling staff communications by developing and writing letters, memos, flyers, posters, and employee newsletters. In some companies, the coordinator may hand some of these duties on to an assistant, taking responsibility for editing and checking the written communications.

The employee relations coordinator also develops and implements employee events. These not only boost morale but help everyone relax and get to know one another on a different level. The employee relations coordinator may, for example, develop functions such as company picnics, parties, dances, and basketball or softball games. Employee relations coordinators often make others aware of employee honors or achievements by developing and writing press releases to send to the media or may notify someone else in the public relations department to handle this task.

In unionized settings, such as at large hotels, the employee relations coordinator may be responsible for working with union representatives. He or she must attend union meetings and relay information to management. In some cases, the coordinator works with other management people negotiating union requests.

Other duties of the employee relations coordinator include:

- Conducting training seminars and workshops for employees
- Investigating and answering employee grievances
- Negotiating with employees regarding grievances

EMPLOYMENT OPPORTUNITIES

Employment opportunities for employee relations coordinators are available in mid-sized and larger companies throughout the country. Employee relations coordinators may work in corporations, hotels, or large hospitals.

EARNINGS

Employee relations coordinators earn salaries ranging from $25,000 to $50,000 annually. Factors affecting earnings include the geographic location, size, and prestige of the specific company or institution as well as the education, experience, and responsibilities of the individual. Generally, those who work in larger facilities and who are responsible for greater numbers of employees earn higher salaries.

ADVANCEMENT OPPORTUNITIES

Employee relations coordinators may advance their careers by locating similar positions in larger companies. Some climb the career ladder by being promoted to public relations director or personnel director.

EDUCATION AND TRAINING

A bachelor's degree is usually required for becoming an employee relations coordinator. A broad educational background with courses in writing, English, journalism, business, group dynamics, negotiation, arbitration, labor relations, human resources, personnel, public relations, marketing, communications, and psychology is useful.

EXPERIENCE AND QUALIFICATIONS

Experience requirements vary for employee relations coordinators. Some individuals obtain experience as employee relations assistants. Others come with experience in public relations or publicity.

Employee relations coordinators should be personable and genuinely like others. They need good communications skills and the ability to speak articulately to groups of people. They must be able to write clearly and factually. Employee relations coordinators also must have a good understanding of the attitudes of employees and of those in management. A general knowledge of group dynamics, negotiation, and arbitration is also needed.

FOR ADDITIONAL INFORMATION: If you are interested in learning more about a career as an employee relations manager, contact the Society for Human Resources Management (SHRM) or the Public Relations Society of America (PRSA).

TIPS

- Mail or fax your resume and a short cover letter to large companies and corporations. Ask if there are any openings in this area. Request that your resume be kept on file if there are no current openings.
- Check for job opportunities in the classified sections of newspapers under "Employee Relations Coordinator," "Employee Relations Manager," "Employee Relations," "Staff Relations," or "Public Relations."
- Look for an internship in the employee relations department of a large corporation. This will provide you with great on-the-job training.

PRESS SECRETARY—GOVERNMENT/POLITICS

JOB DESCRIPTION: *Handle press and media functions for an elected official.*

EARNINGS: *$25,000 to $80,000+ per year.*

RECOMMENDED EDUCATION AND TRAINING: *Bachelor's degree required.*

SKILLS AND PERSONALITY TRAITS: *Writing skills; verbal communications skills; organizational skills; political awareness; articulateness; ability to speak in front of groups.*

EXPERIENCE AND QUALIFICATIONS: *Prior experience in politics, government, journalism, or public relations necessary.*

JOB DESCRIPTION AND RESPONSIBILITIES

Press secretaries working in government represent public officials or those hoping to be elected to public office. They are responsible for handling press and media relations for those people. Press secretaries have several duties. They must keep the media well informed about the official's activities, schedules, and photo opportunities. They are also responsible for writing and distributing both routine and informational press releases. Press secretaries also must try to keep the official in the public eye in a positive light and to continually improve the official's image.

The press and other media ask a great many questions of politicians and government officials. Press secretaries are responsible for responding to these questions. Press secretaries may be responsible for responding themselves or may brief the public official on the situation so he or she can respond directly. At times, the press secretary must act as a buffer between the official and the media. This may occur, for example, when the official is not yet ready to answer questions from the media. At other times, the press secretary prepares and reads a statement to the press when the official is not available to answer questions.

One of the essential duties of the press secretary is helping the official identify relevant subjects, issues, and topics for speeches and presentations. Another important duty is scheduling press conferences and briefings. The press secretary is also responsible for developing and distributing handouts for the media at these conferences.

Other responsibilities of press secretaries may include:

- Determining effective ways to answer difficult questions
- Writing or editing speeches
- Developing feature articles

EMPLOYMENT OPPORTUNITIES

Although employment opportunities are available throughout the county, the greatest number of opportunities for press secretaries in government is located in Washington, DC, and state capitals. The press secretary to the President of the United States is the most prominent individual in this position. Other possible employers include mayors, state legislators, federal legislators, cabinet officers, federal agencies, state agencies, local agencies, and political candidates.

EARNINGS

Earnings for press secretaries range from $25,000 to $85,000 or more annually depending on the specific government official with whom the press secretary works as well as on the experience, responsibilities, and professional reputation of the individual press secretary. It should be noted that federal positions may have a maximum annual salary that can be paid to people in this position. Press secretaries working with major political candidates often earn the highest salaries in this field.

ADVANCEMENT OPPORTUNITIES

Press secretaries may advance their careers in various ways, depending on their individual aspirations. Many find similar jobs working for politicians in higher forms of government. This results in increased responsibilities and earnings. Others may be hired by major political candidates. Some go into lobbying or move into public relations jobs in agencies or large corporations.

EDUCATION AND TRAINING

A minimum of a bachelor's degree is generally required for this type of job. Good majors include public relations, communications, marketing, English, journalism, liberal arts, and political science.

EXPERIENCE AND QUALIFICATIONS

Prior experience in journalism, public relations, politics, or government is required. Press secretaries must have an understanding of politics and government. A good relationship with the media and strong interpersonal skills are essential to the success of a press secretary. Excellent communications skills, both written and verbal, are necessary. Press secretaries must be articulate and able to speak comfortably in front of groups and before television cameras.

Press secretaries need a lot of stamina. This is not a nine-to-five job. Individuals must also be able to work under great pressure and deal with stress.

FOR ADDITIONAL INFORMATION: If you are an aspiring press secretary, you can obtain additional career information by contacting the National Association of Government Communicators (NAGC), the Association of House Democratic Press Assistants (AHDPA), the Republican Communications Associations (RCA), and the Public Relations Society of America (PRSA).

TIPS

- Get involved in the political scene in your local community. Contacts help a great deal in landing a position as press secretary.
- Volunteer to work on a political campaign. Campaigns are a wonderful opportunity to network, make contacts, and get professional experience.
- Contact your county political chairperson. He or she may know of an opening or might give you some ideas on whom to contact regarding a job as press secretary.
- Seek out a political internship—this is another good method of making contacts and networking.

SPEECHWRITER—FREELANCE

JOB DESCRIPTION: *Develop and write speeches for executives, politicians, or other individuals.*

EARNINGS: *$18,000 to $100,000+ per year.*

RECOMMENDED EDUCATION AND TRAINING: *Bachelor's degree helpful.*

SKILLS AND PERSONALITY TRAITS: *Excellent writing skills; good command of the English language; research skills; knowledge of public speaking.*

EXPERIENCE AND QUALIFICATIONS: *Writing experience helpful.*

Job Description and Responsibilities

Speechwriters who work on a freelance basis are responsible for developing speeches for individuals who must appear and speak in public, give presentations, or speak at news or media conferences. Freelance speechwriters prepare speeches for people in business, industry, politics, trade associations, and not-for-profit organizations. Speechwriters may be retained for a number of reasons. Some people do not feel comfortable writing their own speeches. Others might not have the time to prepare their own speeches. Many do not have the ability to prepare a clear, concise, and interesting presentation.

Freelance speechwriters have many responsibilities. Usually they must do background work prior to writing a speech. First they must determine the subject matter and direction of the speech. The speechwriter usually discusses this directly with the speaker to get his or her ideas. Then he or she may have to research the subject. This can be accomplished by talking to others, visiting libraries, looking into trade sources, and so on. It is essential for the speechwriter to understand and become familiar with the speaker's style by looking over other speeches that person has delivered. The speechwriter must understand the speaker's personality in order to tailor the speech to the speaker. The speech must sound as if it were written by the speaker.

One of the main responsibilities of the speechwriter is making sure he or she writes the speech to get the major presentation points across. To do this, the speechwriter must know not only the topic but also the type of audience to which the speech must be geared. Different audiences require different approaches in speeches. The speechwriter must also keep in mind how long the speech will be and know how best to get the points across in the allotted time. The speechwriter develops a rough draft of the speech for the approval of the speaker. Then he or she makes changes, deletions, and additions to the copy. The speechwriter often is responsible for typing the entire speech on index cards or paper using large, easy-to-read type. Sometimes the speech is turned over to a clerical staff person who types it in to a

Teleprompter so the speaker can read it off of a monitor. When working for a seasoned speaker, the speechwriter might be responsible for giving the speaker just the key points so he or she can speak "off the cuff."

Other responsibilities of freelance speechwriters may include:

- Working with the speaker to rehearse the presentation
- Changing words or passages with which the speaker is not comfortable
- Preparing the speaker to handle questions and answers in response to the speech

EMPLOYMENT OPPORTUNITIES

Those who have a flair for speechwriting are usually in demand. Speechwriters who freelance must find clients to retain them. Those with less experience may find clients more easily in smaller areas where they are better known. Those with more experience may find success in metropolitan areas where the number of possible clients is greater. Clients may include the following:

- Corporations
- Trade associations
- Politicians
- Industry
- Not-for-profit organizations

EARNINGS

Freelance speechwriters can be compensated in different ways. Some are hired on a per-project basis. Others are retained on a monthly basis and may be responsible for writing a number of speeches for a client. Annual earnings are difficult to determine because they are based on the amount of work the individual does each year, the number of speeches he or she writes, and the number and prestige of his or her clients. Speechwriters who work fairly consistently may earn between $20,000 and $100,000 or more annually.

ADVANCEMENT OPPORTUNITIES

Freelance speechwriters may advance their careers by finding more consistent work or more prestigious clients. Some individuals become staff speechwriters for major politicians or political candidates or for large corporations. Many speechwriters move into the public relations field and become public relations directors in either industry or business.

EDUCATION AND TRAINING

As a rule, there are no educational requirements for freelance speechwriters. However, a college background and degree are useful. Good majors include public relations, communications, liberal arts, English, journalism, or political science. Workshops, seminars, and classes in speechwriting and public speaking will also be helpful.

EXPERIENCE AND QUALIFICATIONS

Those with a flair for this work usually have written speeches in high school and college. Others have had experience preparing speeches as volunteers for local political candidates or for not-for-profit organizations.

Successful freelance speechwriters must have excellent writing skills. The ability to write humorous, interesting, and stylish speeches is essential. Freelance speechwriters must also be able to work on several different speeches at one time.

FOR ADDITIONAL INFORMATION: If you are an aspiring speechwriter, you can learn more about this career by contacting the Public Relations Society of America (PRSA).

TIPS

- Consider looking for opportunities in a smaller market where you are known to more people—it's usually easier to break into the field this way. Get some experience and then move up the career ladder.
- Check for freelance positions in the newspaper classified section under headings such as "Freelance," "Part Time," "Speechwriter," and "Writer."
- Write as much as you can. The more practice you have, the more polished your writing skills and techniques will become.
- Send your resume with a short cover letter to political candidates, not-for-profit organizations, corporations, and trade associations.
- Obtain experience volunteering to write speeches for local political candidates or preparing presentations for not-for-profit organizations.
- Join community groups, civic groups, and volunteer organizations. Membership is useful for helping people know what you can do and making contacts.
- Put together a portfolio of speeches you have prepared. Make sure you bring your portfolio to interviews.
- Keep up with current affairs and news items—this is essential.

CHAPTER 6

Miscellaneous Careers for Writers

Careers in writing cover a broad spectrum. This chapter offers a number of careers that do not fit into the specific categories set up in this book.

Careers covered in this section are:

Technical Documentation Specialist   Cartoonist
Technical Writer   Journalism/Creative Writing
Theatrical Literary Agent   Teacher—Secondary School
Greeting Card Writer—Freelance   Communications Professor

TECHNICAL DOCUMENTATION SPECIALIST

JOB DESCRIPTION: *Develop and write computer hardware and software manuals.*

EARNINGS: *$25,000 to $65,000+ per year.*

RECOMMENDED EDUCATION AND TRAINING: *Bachelor's degree in computer science, English, communications, liberal arts, or a related field.*

SKILLS AND PERSONALITY TRAITS: *Excellent writing skills; ability to translate technical information into understandable language; knowledge of computers.*

EXPERIENCE AND QUALIFICATIONS: *Writing experience necessary.*

JOB DESCRIPTION AND RESPONSIBILITIES

Computer hardware and software manuals are written by technical documentation specialists. These individuals are responsible for taking information that might be hard to understand and turning it into language that can be easily followed by most people. Technical documentation specialists with good writing skills can make hardware and software easy to use.

Technical documentation specialists collaborate with programmers, engineers, and other technical people. They must learn everything there is to know about the specific software program or hardware for which they are creating the documentation. Once the specialist knows everything there is to know about the subject, he or she must write the documentation, the user's manual. The user's manual describes the features and capabilities of the program or the computer and provides step-by-step instructions for its use. Similar documentation must be written for printers, modems, scanners, and other peripheral equipment.

Other responsibilities of technical documentation specialists may include:

- Preparing copy for computer or software catalogs
- Developing sales promotion material, advertising, and marketing copy for hardware or software companies

EMPLOYMENT OPPORTUNITIES

Technical documentation specialists may work full or part time. Employment situations include:

- Hardware manufacturers
- Software manufacturers
- Self-employment
- Software developers
- Book publishers

EARNINGS

Technical documentation specialists may have earnings ranging from $25,000 to $65,000 or more annually depending on the individual specialist's experience, education, technical knowledge, and responsibilities as well as on the specific employment setting and geographic location.

ADVANCEMENT OPPORTUNITIES

There are a number of paths technical documentation specialists may take to career advancement. Some find similar positions in larger or more prestigious companies resulting in increased responsibilities and earnings. Technical documentation specialists might also become editors or managers of technical documentation projects.

EDUCATION AND TRAINING

Technical documentation specialists usually must have a college degree. Good majors for a career in this field include computer science, English, communications, or liberal arts.

EXPERIENCE AND QUALIFICATIONS

Some sort of writing experience is usually required by employers along with the absolutely obligatory technical knowledge in the computer and software field. Some documentation specialists began their careers as programmers or technicians. The ability to make technical information understandable is essential.

FOR ADDITIONAL INFORMATION: If you are interested in learning more about a career as a technical documentation specialist, contact the Society for Technical Communications (STC), the Association of Computer Programmers and Analysts (ACPA), the Association for Computing Machinery (ACM), and the Microcomputer Software Association (MSA).

TIPS

- Look in the newspaper classified section for jobs advertised under headings such as "Technical Documentation Specialist," "Technical Writer," "Freelance," "Writer," or "Documentation Specialist."
- Check for job openings advertised or listed in trade journals.
- Get lists of software companies and hardware manufacturers. Send your resume and a short cover letter asking about openings.

TECHNICAL WRITER

JOB DESCRIPTION: *Develop and write material for reports, manuals, and related technical publications; write technical and scientific information in understandable language.*

EARNINGS: *$25,000 to $65,000+ per year.*

RECOMMENDED EDUCATION AND TRAINING: *Bachelor's degree in computer science, science, engineering, English, communications, liberal arts, or a related field.*

SKILLS AND PERSONALITY TRAITS: *Excellent writing skills; good command of the English language; ability to translate technical information into understandable language.*

EXPERIENCE AND QUALIFICATIONS: *Writing experience necessary.*

JOB DESCRIPTION AND RESPONSIBILITIES

Technical writers take scientific and technical information and put it into easy-to-understand language, making it possible for the nonspecialist to follow it. Technical writers collaborate with other technical people such as engineers, programmers, and scientists. They must learn everything there is to know about the specific area for which they are writing. Technical writers develop user's manuals, equipment specifications, and instructional materials. They may also develop reports on scientific or health-related research. Some technical writers prepare papers for engineers or scientists. Others write articles for technical publications. In some cases, technical writers develop corporate annual reports for companies dealing with technical information.

Other responsibilities of technical writers may include:

- Overseeing preparation of technical or scientific illustrations, photographs, diagrams, and charts
- Developing sales promotion material, advertising, and marketing copy for hardware, software, or electronic companies or catalogs

EMPLOYMENT OPPORTUNITIES

Technical writers may work full or part time. Employment situations include:

- Electronics manufacturers
- Hardware manufacturers
- Health-related companies
- Software manufacturers
- Federal government
- Self-employment
- Scientific journals
- Pharmaceutical companies
- Software developers
- Book publishers
- Research laboratories

EARNINGS

Technical writers may have earnings ranging from $25,000 to $65,000 or more annually. Factors affecting earnings include the experience, education, technical knowledge, and responsibilities of the individual as well as the specific employment setting and geographic location. Earnings for the freelance technical writer depend on the amount of work the individual does during the year and his or her expertise in a specific field.

ADVANCEMENT OPPORTUNITIES

Technical writers can advance their careers in a number of ways. Some find similar positions in larger or more prestigious companies resulting in increased responsibilities and earnings. Others become editors or managers of technical publications.

EDUCATION AND TRAINING

A technical writer must have a college degree. Good majors for a career in this field include computer science, science, engineering, technical communications, English, communications, and liberal arts.

EXPERIENCE AND QUALIFICATIONS

Employers require some writing experience as well as technical knowledge in the area the writer will be concerned with. Technical writers often have had prior experience as research assistants. Others may have worked in technical or scientific fields in various capacities. Excellent writing skills are mandatory for this work. The ability to make technical information understandable is essential.

FOR ADDITIONAL INFORMATION: If you are interested in learning more about a career as a technical writer, you can obtain additional information by contacting the Society for Technical Communications (STC) and the National Association of Science Writers, Inc. (NASW).

TIPS

- Look in the classified section of newspapers under headings such as "Technical Writer," "Scientific Writer," "Technical Documentation Specialist," "Freelance," "Writer," or "Documentation Specialist."
- Check for job openings advertised or listed in trade journals.
- Get lists of software and electronics companies and hardware manufacturers as well as pharmaceutical companies. Send your resume and a short cover letter asking about openings.

THEATRICAL LITERARY AGENT

JOB DESCRIPTION: *Market and sell playwrights' scripts to producers.*

EARNINGS: *$15,000 to $500,000+ per year.*

RECOMMENDED EDUCATION AND TRAINING: *Educational requirements vary.*

SKILLS AND PERSONALITY TRAITS: *Written and verbal communication skills; ability to see raw talent; contacts in theatrical industry.*

EXPERIENCE AND QUALIFICATIONS: *Prior experience working in publishing or theater useful; experience writing scripts helpful.*

JOB DESCRIPTION AND RESPONSIBILITIES

Once a playwright completes a script, he or she needs to find a way to market it. The playwright must either sell the script himself or herself or find someone else to handle the task. Literary agents are the people who help playwrights market and sell their work.

There are a couple of ways literary agents may sell a script. They may sell a script outright, meaning that the playwright is paid a one-time fee for the use of the script. Sometimes literary agents sell limited rights or options. With limited rights or options, the buyer has the exclusive right to use the script for a specified period of time.

Literary agents find clients in a number of ways. Sometimes they actively seek out playwrights. In other cases, playwrights seek out agents by sending them scripts to read. Literary agents are responsible for reading scripts. They may read hundreds of them until they find one that shows promise. A successful theatrical literary agent is able to recognize potential in raw material. If the literary agent thinks a particular script or its writer has talent and potential, he or she attempts to acquire the playwright as a client.

Once the theatrical literary agent has a playwright under contract, he or she is responsible for marketing that client's scripts. The agent must bring the script to the attention of theatrical producers. This may be done through phone calls, meetings, etc. Agents also socialize with producers and others in the theatrical industry in order to make contacts and to market their clients' scripts. Sometimes a producer is searching for a specific type of script. The producer then may contact literary agents to see if any of their clients have the type of script desired. At other times, producers may be looking for playwrights to write specific scripts. The agent brings together the writers and the users to everyone's benefit.

Other responsibilities of theatrical literary agents may include:

- Suggesting revisions in scripts
- Negotiating contracts on behalf of clients

EMPLOYMENT OPPORTUNITIES

The greatest number of opportunities for theatrical literary agents are located in New York City. Other culturally active cities may also offer opportunities. Theatrical literary agents may work in the following settings:

- Literary agencies
- Talent agencies
- Theatrical agencies
- Self-employment

EARNINGS

Earnings for theatrical literary agents can range dramatically. Some agents earn approximately $15,000 a year. Others can earn $500,000 or more. Factors affecting earnings include the specific employment situation as well as the experience, quality of contacts, and professional reputation of the agent. Theatrical literary agents working for an agency may earn a salary plus a commission for each new client brought in. They may also receive a percentage of any deals they negotiate. Literary agents working on their own are usually paid a percentage of any monies earned by their clients.

ADVANCEMENT OPPORTUNITIES

Theatrical literary agents can advance their careers in a number of ways. Some locate similar positions in larger or more prestigious literary agencies. Others are assigned more prestigious clients or projects. Some literary agents climb the career ladder by striking out on their own.

EDUCATION AND TRAINING

Although educational requirements vary depending on the job, a college degree in theater arts, arts management, English, marketing, public relations, or a related field is recommended. Classes and seminars on script writing, theater, and marketing are also useful.

EXPERIENCE AND QUALIFICATIONS

One must have had some sort of related experience before becoming a theatrical literary agent. Often a theatrical literary agent was once a playwright. Other theatrical literary agents have gained their experience by working as assistants to other agents in the theatrical world, publishing, or a related industry. Some theatrical literary agents first obtained experience as writers or editors.

Theatrical literary agents need contacts in the theatrical world. Marketing skills are a must. Communication skills, both written and verbal, are essential. The ability to recognize unpolished talent and to envision a production when reading a script are also critical skills.

FOR ADDITIONAL INFORMATION: If you are interested in learning more about a career as a theatrical literary agent, contact the Authors Guild (AG) or the Association of Authors' Representatives (AAR).

Tips

- Look for classes, seminars, and workshops in playwriting, publishing, marketing, and theater. These are useful for honing skills and making contacts.
- If you can't find a job as a theatrical literary agent right away, consider a position as an editor or assistant editor with a book publishing company.
- Also consider a job as an administrative assistant or secretary to a producer. It will give you the opportunity to meet people in the theatrical world. You will probably also meet other literary agents who are trying to contact that producer.
- Look for an internship with a literary agency—it's one of the best ways to get experience and get your foot in the door of this industry.

GREETING CARD WRITER—FREELANCE

JOB DESCRIPTION: *Develop ideas for greeting cards; write the wording for cards.*

EARNINGS: *$50 to $350+ per card.*

RECOMMENDED EDUCATION AND TRAINING: *No formal educational requirements or training required.*

SKILLS AND PERSONALITY TRAITS: *Writing skills; creativity; imagination; communication skills; selling skills; articulateness.*

EXPERIENCE AND QUALIFICATIONS: *Writing experience helpful but not required.*

Job Description and Responsibilities

Greeting cards are created for every occasion. These include birthdays, anniversaries, weddings, divorces, Mother's Day, Father's Day, and no reason at all. Freelance greeting card writers develop the ideas for the wording on cards and then sell them to greeting card companies. People in this line of work must not only come up with creative, unique, imaginative lines but must write them in creative, unique, imaginative ways. They then send them off to greeting card editors. Greeting card editors purchase the writing that appeals to them.

Some freelance greeting card writers work by waiting for inspiration to hit them and then write a great many ideas at one time. Others sit down for a specified period of time each day and write. Each greeting card writer has his or her own writing style. Some write poetically. Others write humorous cards, serious cards, or cards with a specific theme.

Additional responsibilities of greeting card writers may include:

- Suggesting graphic ideas for greeting card images
- Calling greeting card editors to see what types of cards they are seeking

EMPLOYMENT OPPORTUNITIES

Greeting card writers who freelance can do so anyplace in the country, or the world for that matter. Many companies utilize freelancers in addition to staff writers. Larger companies include:

- Hallmark
- United Greeting Card
- American Greeting Cards

EARNINGS

Earnings for freelance greeting card writers range from $50 to $350 or more per card idea. Annual earnings depend on the number of cards the writer sells each year.

ADVANCEMENT OPPORTUNITIES

Greeting card writers can advance their careers by selling more card ideas, thereby generating larger incomes. Some freelancers decide they would rather work for a card company on-staff instead.

EDUCATION AND TRAINING

There is no formal educational requirement for freelance greeting card writers. Courses, seminars, and workshops in various facets of writing may be helpful. Continuing education programs sometimes offer courses in greeting card writing.

EXPERIENCE AND QUALIFICATIONS

Greeting card writers should be creative, clever people with an imaginative way of looking at things. A good writing style is necessary. Freelance greeting card writers must also have the salesmanship to sell their work. They may sell over the phone, in person, or in writing. Freelance greeting card writers should be personable and be able to cultivate good relationships with greeting card editors. The ability to deal with inevitable rejection is critical.

FOR ADDITIONAL INFORMATION: If you are interested in pursuing a career as a greeting card writer, contact major greeting card companies for additional information.

TIPS

- Go into card shops and look at a variety of cards. This will give you an idea of what types of text card companies use.
- Many card companies will send you writers' guidelines, and some will send samples of their lines.
- When submitting ideas, submit an idea to only one company at a time.
- Contact greeting card editors and tell them you are freelancing. Ask if they have any procedures you should follow for submitting ideas.
- Try to build rapport with these editors. Be pleasant and accommodating.
- Contact greeting card editors and find out if they have a list of card ideas they might need.

CARTOONIST

JOB DESCRIPTION: *Create the idea or story for cartoons; write cartoon captions; draw cartoons.*

EARNINGS: *$20,000 to $200,000+ per year.*

RECOMMENDED EDUCATION AND TRAINING: *No formal education or training requirements.*

SKILLS AND PERSONALITY TRAITS: *Writing skills; imagination; drawing skills; creativity; sense of humor; self motivation.*

EXPERIENCE AND QUALIFICATIONS: *Prior writing and/or drawing experience helpful.*

JOB DESCRIPTION AND RESPONSIBILITIES

Comic strips are, perhaps, the best known and most popular of cartoon styles. These strips look at life, people, politics, and events in a humorous manner. Cartoons may be used to amuse readers or to interpret or illustrate news highlights. Sometimes cartoons are also used to illustrate advertisements, stories, or feature articles.

Depending on his or her skills, a cartoonist might create the idea or story for the cartoon, write the caption, draw the cartoon, or do all three. Cartoonists who draw cartoons are visual artists. Cartoons are sketched drawings. Some are simply line drawings in black and white; others are drawn in full color. The cartoonist must have an idea of the story he or she will tell before drawing the cartoon. Cartoonists who write the captions must be very creative people. They need to tell the story with very few words.

Other responsibilities of cartoonists may include:

- Making revisions in wording at the request of editors or publishers
- Keeping abreast of current events and issues to develop ideas for cartoons

EMPLOYMENT OPPORTUNITIES

Cartoonists may be employed in the following settings:

- On-staff cartoonists at newspapers or magazines
- Freelance cartoonists
- Syndicated cartoonists
- Advertising agencies

EARNINGS

Cartoonists who are on staff at newspapers or magazines earn between $20,000 and $55,000 or more. Earnings for individuals who freelance are dependent on the number of cartoons they sell. Earnings for cartoonists who sell to syndicates depend on the number of papers or other publications that buy the cartoon. Highly successful cartoonists may earn up to $200,000 or more.

ADVANCEMENT OPPORTUNITIES

Cartoonists advance their careers by attaining recognition in the field. The top rung of the ladder for most cartoonists is having their cartoons syndicated nationally in a great many newspapers.

EDUCATION AND TRAINING

There are no formal education or training requirements for becoming a cartoonist. However, a college background is often helpful. Good majors include communications, English, liberal arts, or a related field. Art and drawing courses as well as writing courses are useful.

EXPERIENCE AND QUALIFICATIONS

Talent and skills needed to either write or draw cartoons is more important than experience in this field. A portfolio of samples of cartoons is essential.

A cartoonist must have a sense of humor. Good writing skills are necessary. The ability to convey an idea in a few short words is mandatory. Drawing and sketching skills are also needed if the cartoonist is drawing his or her own cartoons.

FOR ADDITIONAL INFORMATION: Aspiring cartoonists may learn more about this career by contacting syndicates such as Cartoon Express Syndications, Los Angeles Times Syndicate, United Features Syndicate, and United Cartoonist Syndicate.

TIPS

- Write to the various syndicates to ask about their rules for submissions of cartoons.
- Consult *Writers Digest*, which prints lists of syndicates with names, addresses, and phone numbers.
- Gain experience preparing cartoons for your school or local newspaper. This is a good way to hone skills, develop your craft, and get samples for your portfolio.

- Don't worry if you can't draw well. You can always find another cartoonist to collaborate with.

JOURNALISM/CREATIVE WRITING TEACHER— SECONDARY SCHOOL

JOB DESCRIPTION: *Teach secondary students journalism and creative writing; develop ideas for classes.*

EARNINGS: *$20,000 to $55,000+ per year.*

RECOMMENDED EDUCATION AND TRAINING: *Bachelor's degree in education; some schools require additional education for permanent certification.*

SKILLS AND PERSONALITY TRAITS: *Enjoyment of working with young people; teaching ability; communications skills; writing skills; patience; creativity; organizational skills.*

EXPERIENCE AND QUALIFICATIONS: *Student teaching and certification usually required.*

JOB DESCRIPTION AND RESPONSIBILITIES

Secondary school journalism/creative writing teachers instruct junior high or high school students in various writing skills. Teachers in this area are usually part of the English department. They teach students journalism and creative writing skills. They may also teach students other facets of writing, such as poetry. Specific duties vary depending on the school and the size of that department. Although teachers usually follow a mandated curriculum, they are required to develop activities for each class and to decide how to teach each subject. It is essential that they plan interesting, inspiring lessons to make learning a positive experience.

Journalism/creative writing teachers first must instruct students in word usage, sentence structure, grammar, etc. They may then instruct students in methods of gathering news and of writing and editing stories for newspapers, magazines, or other publications. Most writing classes in secondary schools involve students in hands-on writing activities. This means the teacher must develop a variety of journalism and creative writing projects. In many schools, the writing teacher is responsible for coordinating student publications such as newspapers, magazines, and other creative writing projects. Journalism/creative writing teachers may plan field trips to local newspapers or magazines. They may also invite established journalists, poets, and writers to be guest speakers for their classes.

Teachers are usually evaluated after a certain number of years of work in a specific school system. If the school believes the teacher is good, he or she receives tenure. This means that the teacher cannot be fired from the school system under normal circumstances.

Other responsibilities of secondary school journalism/creative writing teachers may include:

- Teaching other English classes
- Nurturing special talent in students
- Grading work

EMPLOYMENT OPPORTUNITIES

Employment Opportunities for secondary school journalism/creative writing teachers are located throughout the country. A teacher may, however, have to relocate to obtain a job. Employment settings exist in public, private, and parochial schools.

EARNINGS

Teachers in this field may earn between $20,000 and $55,000 or more annually depending on the type, size, location, and prestige of the school as well as on the education, experience, and responsibilities of the teacher.

ADVANCEMENT OPPORTUNITIES

Journalism/creative writing teachers may advance their careers in a number of ways. A monetary increase is usually given as teachers obtain more experience and education. Some teachers find similar positions in larger or more prestigious school districts. Others advance their careers by becoming department heads.

EDUCATION AND TRAINING

A minimum of a bachelor's degree is required to teach. Usually individuals must take a semester of student teaching while still in school. Many school districts require their teachers to have or to obtain a master's degree.

While still in college, aspiring teachers learn many of the teaching methods they will use in class when they are student teaching. Student teaching gives them a chance to obtain hands-on training with supervision.

EXPERIENCE AND QUALIFICATIONS

Teachers working in public schools are generally required to be certified or licensed in the state in which they work. Journalism/creative writing teachers should enjoy working with young people. The ability to teach is mandatory. Writing teachers must be creative, innovative, and imaginative people with good writing skills and a complete knowledge of word usage, grammar, and sentence structure.

FOR ADDITIONAL INFORMATION: Those seeking a career in this field may obtain additional information from the National Educators Association (NEA) or the National Federation of Teachers (NFT).

TIPS

- Look in the newspaper classified section under headings such as "Teacher," "English Teacher," "Secondary School Teacher," "Journalism Teacher," "Creative Writing Teacher," or "Education."
- Check with your college placement office for notices of openings for teachers at schools.
- Obtain letters of recommendation from several of your professors at school as well as from your student teaching supervisor.
- Search for summer school teaching positions. They can help get your foot in the door.

COMMUNICATIONS PROFESSOR

JOB DESCRIPTION: *Teach college-level classes in writing, journalism, and other communications areas.*

EARNINGS: *$25,000 to $65,000+ per year.*

RECOMMENDED EDUCATION AND TRAINING: *Minimum of master's degree required; many positions may prefer Ph.D.*

SKILLS AND PERSONALITY TRAITS: *Teaching ability; communications skill; writing skills; organizational skills; ability to speak in front of others.*

EXPERIENCE AND QUALIFICATIONS: *Experience in journalism, writing, public relations, or advertising.*

JOB DESCRIPTION AND RESPONSIBILITIES

Those aspiring to be writers, journalists, public relations counselors, and so on usually must go to college to learn these skills. College and university communications professors are expected to teach a variety of classes in communications, writing, journalism, and related fields. Depending on the specific school and its structure, a communications professor may be part of the English department, journalism department, or communications department. Communications professors may specialize in one area such as journalism, public relations, or advertising or may be expected to teach courses in a variety of related fields. They may teach students in introductory classes as well as in-depth specialized classes in various subjects.

As part of their duties, professors must develop course outlines, choose textbooks, develop methods of teaching, and grade student work. Professors usually lecture to students regarding the specific subject matter. They must also assign term papers, projects, and reading material. These professors are usually expected to develop, administer, and grade quizzes, tests, midterms, and finals. It is essential to a positive learning experience that college professors plan interesting, inspiring lessons. Sometimes, a professor may plan field trips to local newspapers or magazines or may invite established journalists, poets, and writers to be guest speakers for classes.

Other responsibilities of communications professors in colleges and universities may include:

- Holding office hours to consult and advise students
- Assisting students in career preparation
- Supervising intern programs

EMPLOYMENT OPPORTUNITIES

Employment Opportunities for communications professors can be located in institutions of higher learning throughout the country. Professors may have to relocate to obtain a job where there is an opening.

Employment settings may exist in:

- Junior colleges
- Community colleges
- State colleges and universities
- Private colleges and universities

EARNINGS

College professors may earn between $25,000 and $65,000 or more annually depending on the type, size, location, and prestige of the specific college and university and on the education, experience, and responsibilities of the professor.

ADVANCEMENT OPPORTUNITIES

Assistant professors, the entry-level position, may advance to become associate professors and full professors. They may also climb the career ladder by becoming department chairpersons or by locating similar positions in larger, more prestigious colleges and universities.

EDUCATION AND TRAINING

A minimum of a master's degree is required to teach in a college or university. Majors might be in communications, English, journalism, or liberal arts. Most schools prefer applicants to hold doctorates.

EXPERIENCE AND QUALIFICATIONS

Prior experience in journalism, public relations, advertising, or communications is often required or preferred for these types of positions.

The ability to teach is mandatory. Communications professors must be creative, innovative, and imaginative people with good writing skills. The ability to speak in front of groups of people is essential.

FOR ADDITIONAL INFORMATION: Those seeking a career in this field may obtain additional information from the American Association of University Professors and National Education Association (AAUPNEA).

TIPS

- Positions are often advertised in the newspaper classified section under headings such as "Professor," "Instructor," "College," "University," "Community College," or "Junior College."
- There are newspapers dedicated exclusively to the educational field. Newspapers such as *The Chronicle of Higher Education*, for example, list professional educational opportunities at colleges and universities nationwide and worldwide.
- College placement offices receive notices of openings; check with them regularly.
- A part-time job teaching one or two classes is often a good way to get your foot in the door.
- Send your resume and a short cover letter to colleges and universities where you are interested in working.

CHAPTER 7

Careers for Artists in Theater

No one more firmly believes the familiar line, "There's no business like show business," than the people who work in theater. For those who enjoy the theater, or just being around it, a career in this field can turn an avocation into a lifelong vocation.

Individuals interested in working in this area of entertainment do not necessarily have to work on Broadway to enjoy satisfying careers. Jobs in theater are located from coast to coast and around the world. In addition to Broadway theater, there are opportunities in a broad spectrum of theatrical arenas including stock productions, dinner theaters, regional theaters, road companies, and cabarets.

In addition to employing performers, the theatrical industry encompasses careers for other creative people such as designers and artists.

Space restrictions make it impossible for this chapter to discuss all possible opportunities. The chapter covers the following jobs:

Scenic Designer—Theater   Theatrical Costume Designer
Lighting Designer—Theater   Theatrical Makeup Artist

Individuals interested in careers in theater should also review the entries in Chapter 2, "Careers for Writers in the Entertainment and Sports Industries."

SCENIC DESIGNER—THEATER

JOB DESCRIPTION: *Develop and create set designs for theatrical productions.*

EARNINGS: *$500 to $150,000+ per production.*

RECOMMENDED EDUCATION AND TRAINING: *Bachelor's degree in theater arts or design.*

SKILLS AND PERSONALITY TRAITS: *Drawing and painting skills; ability to conceptualize; creativity.*

EXPERIENCE AND QUALIFICATIONS: *Work in theater; apprenticeships or internships are helpful.*

Job Description and Responsibilities

Without sets in theatrical productions, the stage would be bare and most likely uninteresting. Sets may include backdrops, props, furniture, and lighting. Scenic designers create the stage sets for theatrical productions. A creative artistic designer can transform a stage into a set that the audience remembers long after the production has concluded.

Designers create sets for the main productions of shows and sets to be used for road productions. Scenic designers work under the direction of a production director. Their job begins before the production goes into rehearsal, and usually ends on opening night.

Scenic designers might create elaborate or simple sets depending on the specific show and its requirements. Each set must visually illustrate for the audience where a scene is taking place. Some productions require scenic designers to create multiple sets to illustrate various scenes, such as different rooms or locations. Scenic designers define the look and essence of a production. The scenic designer is expected to meet with the show's director and lighting designer. The designer must determine the director's thoughts concerning the sets and must find out what specific effects the director desires. The scenic designer must also gather special information such as the time period in which the production is set. With all this in mind, the scenic designer is responsible for developing sketches and models for the director's approval. After the director approves a model, the scenic designer summarizes the information in writing. He or she details the plans, ideas, equipment, props, and backdrops required. The scenic designer is expected to solicit bids from scenery shops to build the sets. The designer must then make sure that the shop builds the sets to specification, on time, and within budget. The scenic designer must also make sure that after the shop completes the sets, they fit on stage where needed and can be changed quickly, smoothly, and easily when required.

Other responsibilities of the scenic designer might include the following:

- Creating models of each set
- Working with the lighting designer to make sure that lighting is correct for each set

EMPLOYMENT OPPORTUNITIES

Although scenic designers can find employment in any area hosting theatrical productions, the most opportunities exist in large, culturally active cities. These include New York, Los Angeles, Atlanta, Chicago, Philadelphia, and Washington, DC. Theatrical productions requiring the services of scenic designers include the following:

- Broadway plays
- Road shows
- Cabaret theater productions
- Stock productions
- Operatic productions

- Off-Broadway and off-off-Broadway plays
- Dinner theater productions
- Regional theater productions
- Ballet productions

EARNINGS

Because of the nature of the job, determining the actual earnings of scenic designers is difficult, if not impossible. Scenic designers are usually paid a fee for services. This may be a straight fee for each production or may include a percentage of profits in addition to the base fee. In some situations, the scenic designer might be paid a percentage of profits rather than a set fee.

Factors affecting earnings include the scenic designer's experience, expertise, and professional reputation. Other factors include the geographic location, type of theater, specific production, and number of sets required. Designers working in unionized theaters have minimum fees negotiated for them by the United Scenic Artists (USA) union. Scenic designers working for a Broadway multiset musical may earn a minimum of approximately $18,000 to $20,000 plus royalties, as well as monies for pension and welfare funds. Creative, talented scenic designers who have built a reputation in the field might earn $150,000 or more per production for a Broadway show if they have negotiated a substantial percentage of the production's profits for themselves. Scenic designers working in nonunionized theaters might receive fees ranging from $500 to $20,000 or more for production sets.

ADVANCEMENT OPPORTUNITIES

Advancement opportunities for scenic designers depend on several factors, including talent, creativity, determination, and luck. For some, just being employed fairly regularly in this field is good enough. For others, the next rung on the career ladder might be designing sets for better types of productions. For many scenic designers, their career highlight is to design sets for Broadway shows; others go on to design sets for films or television.

EDUCATION AND TRAINING

The recommended education for a job in this field is a bachelor's degree with a major in theater arts or design. A degree does not guarantee a job as a scenic designer. A college background, however, helps individuals develop contacts and obtain hands-on experience. Seminars, workshops, and classes in scenic design, lighting, architecture, stagecraft, theater arts, art history, and drawing are useful.

EXPERIENCE AND QUALIFICATIONS

Scenic designers should obtain as much hands-on experience as possible. This might include internships, apprenticeships, and experience in theater-related situations.

Scenic designers must be talented, creative, and artistic, and have the insight and ability to turn ideas into actual sets.

FOR ADDITIONAL INFORMATION: If you are interested in learning more about a career as a scenic designer, contact the United Scenic Designers (USA).

TIPS

- Look for apprenticeships and internships with theaters, opera, and ballet companies.
- Contact the Actors' Equity Association (AEA) and ask for lists of resident, stock, dinner, Broadway, and off-Broadway theaters. These are helpful in locating internships, apprenticeships, and jobs.
- Get experience by volunteering to design sets for your local community theater, school, or college production.
- Part-time and summer jobs are often available at theaters, ballet, and opera companies. These jobs are useful for honing skills and making important contacts.

LIGHTING DESIGNER—THEATER

JOB DESCRIPTION: *Develop and coordinate stage lighting for theatrical productions.*

EARNINGS: *$500 to $150,000+ per production.*

RECOMMENDED EDUCATION AND TRAINING: *Hands-on training; a bachelor's degree is useful.*

SKILLS AND PERSONALITY TRAITS: *Electrician skills; ability to conceptualize; creativity.*

EXPERIENCE AND QUALIFICATIONS: *Experience as an electrician.*

JOB DESCRIPTION AND RESPONSIBILITIES

Actors and actresses in theatrical productions are a distance from the audience. Lighting is vital for the audience to see cast members' faces, expressions, and movements. Productions also use lighting to set mood and locale and to suggest the time of day. The person responsible for handling the lighting needs of a theatrical production is called the lighting designer. He or she is responsible for coordinating all aspects of the stage lighting.

The lighting designer first must meet with the production's director and scenic designer. The lighting designer gets ideas from these colleagues. He or she then must come up with ways to achieve the results that the director and scenic designer have conceptualized. The lighting designer helps communicate the production's mood to the audience. This responsibility might entail making the stage resemble a moonlit night or a foggy day. To accomplish these effects, a lighting designer uses different lights, filters, and colors. He or she also places lights in various places to produce specific effects.

The lighting designer is expected to create a detailed plan documenting the lighting information needed to create the specific effects for the production. The plan must include the procedures and equipment that the production is to use. It must also include a lighting schedule so that the lighting crew knows when to turn each light on or off. The lighting designer creates a chart detailing each individual knob on the light board and the light in the theater that the knob controls. The lighting designer also creates charts that include information about the wattage that each light in the theater draws. The lighting designer works with a master electrician on the technical end. In this way, he or she can be sure that each light is the correct color and is properly placed and focused. In smaller productions, the lighting designer might also work as the master electrician.

The lighting designer's job is over on opening night. Afterward, he or she turns over the responsibilities of the lighting to the individual who handles the light board.

Other responsibilities of lighting designers working in theater include the following:

- Explaining the implementation of lighting requirements to the people handling the light board and to the electricians
- Checking and adjusting lighting though dress rehearsals

EMPLOYMENT OPPORTUNITIES

The greatest number of employment opportunities are located in culturally active cities such as New York, Los Angeles, Philadelphia, Washington, DC, Chicago, and Atlanta. Positions are usually freelance. However, several staff positions are available at universities, colleges, and regional theaters. Employment might be available in theaters or production companies, including those that present the following:

- Broadway plays
- Off-off-Broadway plays
- Regional theater productions
- Road company productions
- Ballet productions
- Off-Broadway plays
- Cabaret theater productions
- Stock productions
- Dinner theater productions
- Operatic productions

EARNINGS

Theatrical lighting designers are compensated in several different ways. Some receive a fee for each production in which they handle the lighting requirements, a percentage of the profits, or a combination of the two. Sometimes successful designers negotiate a percentage of the box-office gross in addition to their set fees.

Many variables affect the earnings of lighting designers. These include the number of performances and the type and the prestige of the production. Other factors might include the designer's experience and professional reputation. Lighting designers might earn between $500 and $150,000 or more per production. Those who work in unionized theaters have their minimum fees negotiated and set by the United Scenic Artists (USA) union. Minimum fees for designing the lighting for Broadway shows can range from approximately $5,000. Some individuals with an excellent reputation in the field can earn $150,000 or more. Those who work in nonunionized settings might receive fees ranging from $500 to $5,000 per production.

ADVANCEMENT OPPORTUNITIES

Lighting designers climb the career ladder by handling the lighting design for a larger number of productions or for more prestigious ones. Designing the lighting for a major Broadway show is the career highlight for many lighting designers.

EDUCATION AND TRAINING

There are no formal educational requirements to become a lighting designer. A four-year degree in theater or theater arts is helpful, however, to obtain training, opportunities, and experience that might not be available to others. Internships, apprenticeships, or positions assisting other lighting designers or electricians are also helpful in learning skills necessary for a career in this field.

EXPERIENCE AND QUALIFICATIONS

Lighting designers must have prior experience as electricians. Any other experience in theater is also helpful.

Lighting designers should have a good knowledge of theater, staging, and color. They need the ability to conceptualize the ideas of others as well as to turn those ideas into reality.

FOR ADDITIONAL INFORMATION: Aspiring theatrical lighting designers can obtain additional information by contacting the United Scenic Artists (USA), the International Brotherhood of Electrical Workers (IBEW), or the International Alliance of Theatrical Stage Employees (IATSE).

TIPS

- Contact schools, colleges, universities, theater groups, and performing arts centers to look for internships. These are important for honing skills and making contacts.
- Get experience by volunteering to handle the lighting requirements of a school or community theater production.
- Obtain apprenticeships, which are also a valuable way to learn skills. Contact the USA, IBEW, and IATSE.
- Look for books on theatrical lighting to learn about various lighting techniques and styles.
- Make sure that you contact the Actors' Equity Association (AEA) to get lists of resident, stock, dinner, Broadway, off-Broadway, and off-off-Broadway theaters throughout the country. These lists are useful to find places to write to inquire about internships or job possibilities.

THEATRICAL COSTUME DESIGNER

JOB DESCRIPTION: *Design and create costumes for theatrical productions.*

EARNINGS: *$500 to 100,000+ per production.*

RECOMMENDED EDUCATION AND TRAINING: *A bachelor's degree in fashion, costume design, theater, or theater arts is helpful.*

SKILLS AND PERSONALITY TRAITS: *Drawing and sketching skills; sewing skills; fashion drawing; artistic flair; creativity; ability to bring an idea from concept to reality; imagination.*

EXPERIENCE AND QUALIFICATIONS: *Experience in clothing or costume design.*

JOB DESCRIPTION AND RESPONSIBILITIES

Theatrical costume designers are responsible for developing and creating the costumes for theatrical productions. Costumes add to the allure of the stage and help bring characters to life.

The costume designer starts the job by reading the script. He or she then meets with the director, scenic designer, lighting designer, and so on. From this meeting, the costume designer determines the number of costumes that each actor and actress in the production needs. The costume designer also discusses other costuming requirements. The costume designer learns about the characters in the production and the time period in which the action is taking place. The costume designer might do research on the specific time period by looking through books and magazines, watching television and movies, and visiting museums. In this way, he or she can make sure that the costumes match the particular time period in which the production is set. After the costume designer determines all the requirements, he or she must begin developing ideas for costumes. The designer is responsible for costuming the entire cast, including the lead characters, supporting actors, and extras.

To do the actual designing of the costumes, the costume designer must put together sketches and drawings of ideas. The designer might also photograph samples and create sample models. The designer must also choose fabrics and colors for each costume. Then the costume designer brings the samples to the director, who approves them or asks for changes. If the director approves the sketches, the designer must have the costumes constructed. If the director does not approve the first designs, the designer must go back to the drawing board and create new ideas. The designer might construct the costumes with or without the help of assistants. Others might also construct the costumes working under the designer's direction and supervision. In elaborate productions, the costume designer might send the costume requirements to outside companies specializing in the manufacturing of costumes. After construction, the costumes must be fitted to each actor and actress.

When all costumes have been completed, a dress parade is held. This event is similar to a dress rehearsal. At the dress parade, all the actors and actresses try their costumes on and walk across the stage. This is done to make sure that costumes fit properly and that they work with the lights, sets, and movements. After everything is satisfactory, the costumes are turned over to the wardrobe department. The job of the costume designer is then completed for that production.

Other responsibilities of theatrical costume designers might include the following:

- Designing, selecting, and locating accessories for actors and actresses to wear with each costume
- Redesigning costumes
- Supervising assistants in costume alteration, fitting, changes, and repairs

Employment Opportunities

The greatest number of opportunities for theatrical costume designers exists in culturally active cities. These include New York City, Los Angeles, Washington, DC, Philadelphia, Atlanta, Chicago, and Seattle. Costume designers might work on staff at theaters or might freelance. Employment opportunities include the following:

- Stock theater productions
- Regional theater productions
- Off-Broadway plays
- Cabaret productions
- Operas
- Dinner theater productions
- Broadway plays
- Off-off-Broadway plays
- Ballets
- Road company productions

Earnings

The United Scenic Artists (USA) union sets the minimum fees for costume designers working in unionized theaters. Designers working in nonunionized theaters must negotiate their own fees. Because of the nature of the job, determining the annual earnings of costume designers is difficult. Factors affecting earnings include the designer's experience, responsibilities, and professional reputation. Other factors include the type, location, and prestige of the particular production.

Costume designers freelancing in nonunionized situations earn $500 to $3,500 per production. Those working on staff might earn from $350 to $750 or more per week. Costume designers responsible for the costuming requirements for a Broadway musical can have earnings starting at approximately $15,000 per production. However, those with a reputation for success in this field can earn $100,000 or more per production.

ADVANCEMENT OPPORTUNITIES

Costume designers climb the career ladder by locating more prestigious projects. The high point for a costume designer in theater is to design the costumes for a major Broadway production.

EDUCATION AND TRAINING

There are no formal educational requirements to become a theatrical costume designer. A college degree can give an aspiring designer opportunities and experience that he or she might not otherwise have. Good majors include theater, costume design, or fashion. Courses and workshops in fashion design, costuming, drawing, sketching, theater arts, design, history, sewing, and staging are also useful.

EXPERIENCE AND QUALIFICATIONS

Experience in clothing design is necessary for costume designers working in theaters. Designers should also have knowledge and understanding of theater.

Theatrical costume designers must be able to sew, sketch, and draw.

FOR ADDITIONAL INFORMATION: To learn more about careers in this field, contact the United Scenic Artists (USA) and the Costume Designer's Guild (CDG).

TIPS

- Look for apprenticeships and internships to get hands-on experience and on-the-job training. You can often find these opportunities by contacting theaters, production companies, colleges, universities, or costume designers.
- Contact the Actors' Equity Association (AEA) to get its lists of resident, stock, dinner, Broadway, off-Broadway, and off-off-Broadway theaters. These lists are useful to get the names and addresses to which to write to learn about internships or job possibilities.
- Get experience by designing costumes for local school and community theater groups.
- Contact museums in your area to see if they have exhibits on costumes or fashions from other time periods.
- Do not turn down any opportunity to get experience, even if the compensation is low or nonexistent. Remember that any production that you work on will be useful for listing on your resume.
- Put together a portfolio of sketches. Try to have a varied collection illustrating your skill at designing for various situations.

- Attend as many plays, ballets, and operas as you can to see their costume designs.
- Take classes, workshops and seminars in fashion design, theater, and costuming. These are excellent ways to hone skills, get new ideas, and make important contacts.

THEATRICAL MAKEUP ARTIST

JOB DESCRIPTION: *Develop and create the appearance and physical personality of actors and actresses through the use of makeup.*

EARNINGS: *$15,000 to $75,000+ per year.*

RECOMMENDED EDUCATION AND TRAINING: *Training requirements vary.*

SKILLS AND PERSONALITY TRAITS: *Creativity; cosmetology, theatrical makeup, and hairstyling skills.*

EXPERIENCE AND QUALIFICATIONS: *Experience working with theatrical makeup.*

JOB DESCRIPTION AND RESPONSIBILITIES

Theatrical makeup is used to help convey to the audience the personality of the characters in a production. Theatrical makeup artists are responsible for utilizing makeup so that the audience can clearly view the faces and expressions of actors and actresses while they are on stage.

Theatrical makeup artists have varied responsibilities depending on the specific production. Theatrical makeup artists must apply makeup skillfully and creatively. They might, for example, be responsible for making actors or actresses appear older or less attractive. Theatrical makeup is usually heavier and more pronounced than street makeup. The size and lighting of the theater and stage determines the makeup's application. The theatrical makeup artist must have a complete knowledge of the lighting, staging, and costume design that the production will use. The makeup artist must determine the "look" the director is striving for the character to have. The makeup artist works with the costume designers and production hairstylist to coordinate colors of makeup with the character's costumes, hair color, and style. The theatrical makeup artist is responsible for applying the makeup to the actors and actresses in the production, usually immediately before each performance. The makeup artist is additionally responsible for making changes, touching up, and so on for actors and actresses during each performance.

Other responsibilities of the theatrical makeup artist might include the following:

- Functioning as the production hairstylist
- Keeping necessary makeup and supplies stocked for performances

EMPLOYMENT OPPORTUNITIES

Although theatrical makeup artists can find employment in any area hosting theatrical productions, the most opportunities exist in large, culturally active cities. These include New York, Los Angeles, Atlanta, Chicago, Philadelphia, and Washington, DC. Theatrical productions requiring the services of theatrical makeup artists include the following:

- Broadway plays
- Road shows
- Cabaret theater productions
- Stock productions
- Operatic productions

- Off-Broadway and off-off-Broadway plays
- Dinner theater productions
- Regional theater productions
- Ballet productions

EARNINGS

Earnings for theatrical makeup artists can vary greatly depending on the makeup artist's experience, expertise, responsibilities, and professional reputation, the specific type of production, and the amount of work performed annually. Theatrical makeup artists may be paid weekly salaries or may be compensated by the performance. Theatrical makeup artists can earn $15,000 to $75,000 or more annually. The International Alliance of Theatrical Stage Employees (IATSE) local union sets the minimum earnings for theatrical makeup artists working on Broadway productions.

ADVANCEMENT OPPORTUNITIES

Advancement opportunities for theatrical makeup artists depend on several factors, including talent, creativity, determination, and luck. Theatrical makeup artists climb the career ladder by working in larger or more prestigious productions. The career highlight of a theatrical makeup artist is to work on successful Broadway shows. Some artists go into handling the makeup for actors in films or television.

EDUCATION AND TRAINING

Training requirements for theatrical makeup artists vary from a college degree with a major in theater arts, to internships, apprenticeships, or on-the-job training. Workshops and seminars in theatrical makeup, hairstyling, staging, lighting, and costuming are also helpful. In some situations, theatrical makeup artists attend a licensed school of cosmetology and hairstyling to obtain basic training.

EXPERIENCE AND QUALIFICATIONS

A theatrical makeup artist must obtain as much hands-on experience as possible. The artist can get such experience through apprenticeships, internships, volunteer opportunities, and experience in other theater-related situations.

Makeup artists working in unionized situations might be required to be members of IATSE. To become a member, a theatrical makeup artist usually must take and pass a practical exam demonstrating competence with various theatrical makeup techniques.

FOR ADDITIONAL INFORMATION: To learn more about a career as a theatrical makeup artist, contact the International Association of Theatrical Stage Employees (IATSE) or the National Hairdressers and Cosmetologists Association (NHCA).

TIPS

- Get experience by volunteering to handle the makeup requirements for local community theater, school, or college productions.
- Look for apprenticeships and internships with theaters and with opera and ballet companies.
- Contact the Actors' Equity Association (AEA) and ask for lists of resident, stock, dinner, Broadway, and off-Broadway theaters. These lists are helpful in locating internships, apprenticeships, and jobs.
- Seek the part-time and summer jobs that often are available at theaters and with ballet and opera companies. These jobs are useful in honing skills and making important contacts.
- Try to attend a variety of theatrical productions, operas, and ballets to see and study the makeup and appearance of the various actors and actresses. Such productions provide examples of how makeup is used to create characters.
- Contact IATSE and NHCA to learn what their membership requirements are and what seminars, conferences, and classes they provide.
- Look for a theatrical makeup artist who is willing to let you apprentice with him or her. This is an excellent way to learn the craft of theatrical makeup.

CHAPTER 8

Careers for Artists in Design

Design is not one but several different fields. Designers organize and design articles, products, and materials so that they not only serve the purpose for which they were intended but are visually pleasing as well. Designers can create pleasant surroundings, beautiful clothes, attractive floral arrangements, and eye-catching products and packages.

Space restrictions make it impossible for this chapter to discuss all possible opportunities. The chapter covers the following jobs:

Fashion Designer	Record Label Graphic Designer
Interior Designer	Floral Designer
Package Designer	Textile Designer
Exhibit Designer—Museum	Window Dresser

If you are interested in a career in design, you should also review entries in Chapter 7, "Careers for Artists in Theater"; Chapter 9, "Careers for Artists in Television, Film & Video"; and Chapter 10, "Careers for Artists in Advertising and Graphic Design."

FASHION DESIGNER

JOB DESCRIPTION: *Design clothing and accessories.*

EARNINGS: *$16,000 to $100,000+ per year.*

RECOMMENDED EDUCATION AND TRAINING: *Educational requirements vary.*

SKILLS AND PERSONALITY TRAITS: *Drawing and sketching skills; sewing skills; fashion drawing; artistic creativity; the ability to bring an idea from concept to reality; imagination.*

EXPERIENCE AND QUALIFICATIONS: *Experience requirements vary.*

JOB DESCRIPTION AND RESPONSIBILITIES

Fashion designers are the individuals who design the clothing and accessories that we all wear. Fashion designers might design original garments or design garments following current fashion trends.

Fashion designers might specialize in designing garments for men, women, or children. Some designers specialize in a specific type of garment such as outerwear, lingerie, swimwear, careerwear, or eveningwear. Others design accessories such as belts, handbags, or shoes. When designing garments, fashion designers must first sketch their ideas. These sketches illustrate the colors or patterns as well as trimmings to be used in the final design. Sketches are then used to create patterns and make samples. When creating designs, fashion designers often combine several principles of dressmaking with flat pattern design and draping. Some fashion designers are required to have their designs approved by supervisors or clients before moving forward. Some fashion designers have showings of their designs. The most well-known designers might then have their designs "knocked off" or copied throughout the world.

Other responsibilities of fashion designers might include the following:

- Designing, selecting, and locating ornaments (buttons, ribbons, threads, and so on) for fashions
- Fitting finished garments
- Keeping up on fashion trends

EMPLOYMENT OPPORTUNITIES

Fashion designers can find employment throughout the country. The greatest number of opportunities can be located in large metropolitan areas where there is a greater number of apparel manufacturers. Fashion designers might freelance, be self-employed, or work on staff in a number of settings, including the following:

- Apparel manufacturers
- Dressmaking companies
- Department stores
- Theatrical companies
- Custom dress shops
- Design studios
- Pattern houses

EARNINGS

Fashion designers can earn between $16,000 and $100,000 or more per year. Factors affecting earnings include the designer's talent, training, experience, responsibilities, and professional reputation. Other variables include the employer's size, type, and prestige. Earnings of self-employed fashion designers also depend on their business ability, clientele, and geographic location.

ADVANCEMENT OPPORTUNITIES

Fashion designers often begin their careers as assistant designers or as trainees in design departments. They then can advance their careers by becoming full-fledged designers. As designers obtain experience, they often find similar positions in more prestigious companies. Fashion designers can also advance their careers by becoming self-employed.

EDUCATION AND TRAINING

Educational requirements vary from job to job. Although some fashion designers have had no formal education, such education is recommended. Two- and four-year programs in fashion and costume design are available in colleges and universities throughout the country. Also, vocational, technical, and trade schools offer programs in the fundamentals of fashion design.

EXPERIENCE AND QUALIFICATIONS

Employers might require various degrees of experience for fashion designers. Fashion designers must be able to sew, sketch, and draw. They must be artistic, creative people. Designers must also understand textiles, fabrics, and ornamentation and have a sense of style and trends.

FOR ADDITIONAL INFORMATION: To learn more about careers in this field, contact the Costume Designer's Guild (CDG) and the Council of Fashion Designers of America (CFDA).

TIPS

- Look for apprenticeships and internships to get hands-on experience and on-the-job training. You can often find apprenticeships and internships by contacting clothing manufacturers, theaters, production companies, colleges, universities, or costume designers.

- Contact museums in your area to see whether they have exhibits on costumes or fashions from other time periods.

- Put together a portfolio of sketches. Try to have a varied collection illustrating your skill at designing for various situations.

- Take classes, workshops, and seminars in fashion design, theater, and costuming. These are excellent ways to hone skills, get new ideas, and make important contacts.

- Make sure that you register with your school's job placement office.

- Check trade journals or the newspapers' classified section for advertised job openings. Look under such headings as "Fashion Designer," "Fashion," "Design Studio," and "Pattern Houses."

- Send your resume with a short cover letter to pattern houses, custom dress stores, design studios, clothing manufacturers, and dressmaking companies.

INTERIOR DESIGNER

JOB DESCRIPTION: *Plan, develop, and create the design, decoration, and function of residential or commercial spaces.*

EARNINGS: *$15,000 to $100,000+ per year.*

RECOMMENDED EDUCATION AND TRAINING: *Training requirements vary.*

SKILLS AND PERSONALITY TRAITS: *Creativity; imagination; a sense of color; an eye for detail.*

EXPERIENCE AND QUALIFICATIONS: *Experience in interior design is necessary; state licensing might be required.*

JOB DESCRIPTION AND RESPONSIBILITIES

Interior designers are responsible for planning the space and furnishing the interiors of private homes, public buildings, and commercial establishments. These might include offices, hospitals, hotels, restaurants, and theaters. In some situations, interior designers start from scratch, before construction even begins. In other circumstances, they are called in when people renovate or plan additions.

Interior designers must meet with clients to determine their needs, tastes, preferences, and budgets. The designers then are expected to develop designs for the necessary spaces. As part of their jobs, interior designers are expected to develop detailed drawings that clarify specifications for interior construction. These drawings show the proposed furnishings, floor coverings, accessories, lighting, and other finishes. Interior designers are expected to choose furnishings, floor coverings, window treatments, and coordinating colors. Drawings and sketches are given to clients for approval. In addition to providing scaled floor plans, interior designers are expected to hand clients color charts and samples of upholstery and drapery fabrics, wallcoverings, carpeting, and so on. The designer might produce the drawings mechanically; however, many interior designers currently are beginning to use computers to prepare these plans. With the use of computers and special layout software, designers can change their designs quickly to accommodate clients' needs and preferences.

Other responsibilities of interior designers might include the following:

- Estimating costs of products and installation
- Looking for and ordering furnishings and accessories
- Hiring and supervising contractors and craft workers

EMPLOYMENT OPPORTUNITIES

Although interior designers can find employment throughout the country, the greatest number of employment opportunities for interior designers exists in large metropolitan areas. Interior designers might work in the following settings:

- Design firms
- Retail office-furnishings stores
- Freelance or self-employment
- Retail furnishings stores
- Architectural firms
- The design department of large corporations, businesses, or institutions

EARNINGS

Earnings for an interior designer range from $15,000 to $100,000 or more depending on the designer's experience, expertise, responsibilities, and professional reputation. Other factors include the type, size, and complexity of the design projects. Interior designers might be paid a salary, a commission, or a combination of the two. Independent or self-employed designers may also be paid on a per-project basis.

ADVANCEMENT OPPORTUNITIES

Advancement opportunities are based on a combination of experience, talent, hard work, and luck. Some individuals climb the career ladder by striking out on their own and going into business for themselves. Others advance by promotion to more complex projects with larger budgets with resultant increased responsibilities and earnings.

EDUCATION AND TRAINING

Aspiring interior designers should attend a college, university, or professional school of interior design accredited by the Foundation for Interior Design Education Research (IDER). Courses include principles of design, basic architecture, history, art, and drawing and sketching. Continuing education is helpful.

EXPERIENCE AND QUALIFICATIONS

Interior designers must have professional experience. A designer might obtain such experience through internships or as an assistant to other interior designers.

Certain positions might require federal licensing. Licensing is available through the National Council For Interior Design (NCID). To become licensed, designers must take and pass a qualifying examination. Interior designers must be creative, imaginative people with a sense of style and color and an eye for detail. Designers must further be knowledgeable regarding federal, state, and local codes as well as the toxicity and flammability standards for both furniture and furnishings.

FOR ADDITIONAL INFORMATION: If you are interested in learning more about a career as an interior designer, you should contact the Foundation for Interior Design Education Research (IDER) and the American Society for Interior Designers (ASID).

TIPS

- Develop a portfolio showcasing your best work. A portfolio is essential for locating employment in this profession.
- Look for internships in interior design studios, retail or office furnishing stores, architectural firms, or the design departments of large corporations and institutions.
- Find an interior designer willing to let you apprentice with him or her. This is an excellent way to learn the craft.
- Join professional trade associations.
- Seek state licensing. Such licensing is not always necessary, but might give you an edge over others.
- Contact the placement offices of schools of interior design.
- Get experience working in the furniture departments of retail stores.

PACKAGE DESIGNER

JOB DESCRIPTION: *Design containers for products; sketch designs of containers.*

EARNINGS: *$20,000 to $65,000+ per year.*

RECOMMENDED EDUCATION AND TRAINING: *Educational requirements vary.*

SKILLS AND PERSONALITY TRAITS: *Creativity; artistic ability; a sense of color; an eye for detail; sketching ability.*

EXPERIENCE AND QUALIFICATIONS: *Experience requirements vary.*

JOB DESCRIPTION AND RESPONSIBILITIES

Package designers develop and design containers for products. These containers include those for such items as food, beverages, toiletries, cigarettes, computers, medicine, and equipment of all types.

In developing a new design or altering an existing one, product designers must first determine the needs of their client and of potential users. Package designers must consider the product's size, shape, weight, and color, the materials used to create the product, and the way that the product functions. The designer must also keep in mind how the packaging can make the produce easy and convenient for the consumer to use, maintain, handle, and store. Other important factors include the design's safety and cost. When developing a package design, the designer must make it distinctive so that consumers can easily identify the product.

Package designers begin by designing sketches of several concepts. The designer might prepare these sketches by hand or with a computer-aided design program. Sketches must include exterior markings and labels. The designer presents sketches of possible package designs, from which the product development team or design directors choose the best design. Finally, the package designer is expected to create a model, prototype, or detailed plan drawn to scale.

Other responsibilities of package designers might include the following:

- Comparing similar or competitive package designs
- Making changes or modifications in package design

EMPLOYMENT OPPORTUNITIES

Package designers can find employment opportunities throughout the country. The greatest number of opportunities is located in large metropolitan areas where there are more large corporations and design firms. Possible employment settings include the following:

- Manufacturing establishments
- Self-employment
- Advertising agencies
- Design firms
- Corporations

EARNINGS

Package designers can earn between $20,000 and $65,000 or more. Factors affecting earnings include the designer's experience, expertise, and talent, as well as the size, location, and prestige of the company for which the designer works. Package designers who freelance might be compensated by the project.

ADVANCEMENT OPPORTUNITIES

Advancement depends to a great extent on the designer's talent and creativity. Package designers can advance their careers by locating similar positions in larger or more prestigious companies or settings. Others climb the career ladder by striking out on their own, building a customer base, and freelancing.

EDUCATION AND TRAINING

Educational requirements vary from job to job. Most companies require or prefer package designers to hold a college degree. Good majors include fine arts or commercial art. Courses in advertising, communications, marketing, graphic art, and computer graphics are also useful.

EXPERIENCE AND QUALIFICATIONS

Usually package designers must have had prior experience or at least have a portfolio of designs. They should have a good understanding of design, including a sense of color and balance and an eye for detail.

Package designers should be creative and artistic. Drawing, sketching, and illustration skills are necessary. A working knowledge of CAD (computer-aided design) programs is helpful.

FOR ADDITIONAL INFORMATION: Aspiring package designers can obtain more career information by contacting the American Advertising Federation (AAF), the Society of Illustrators (SOI), and the National Association of Schools of Art and Design (NASAD).

TIPS

- Look for positions advertised in the classified section of newspapers under such headings as "Package Designer" or "Designer."
- Develop a really good, creative portfolio demonstrating your best work. Include diverse work to show your various talents.
- Look for internships at design firms, corporations, and manufacturing companies.

EXHIBIT DESIGNER—MUSEUM

JOB DESCRIPTION: *Design the installation of exhibitions in museums and in temporary locations.*

EARNINGS: *$20,000 to $60,000+ per year.*

RECOMMENDED EDUCATION AND TRAINING: *Requirements vary.*

SKILLS AND PERSONALITY TRAITS: *Knowledge of design and balance; aesthetic judgment; communications skills; creativity; artistic ability.*

EXPERIENCE AND QUALIFICATIONS: *Prior experience in exhibit design.*

JOB DESCRIPTION AND RESPONSIBILITIES

Every museum exhibit must be carefully planned. Exhibit designers determine where and how to display art objects, photographs, pictures, and other pieces. Exhibit designers are ultimately responsible for the way that an exhibition looks and how the public receives it.

Sometimes an exhibit designer works on permanent exhibits. In other situations, he or she designs temporary exhibits. Some exhibit designers specialize in traveling exhibits that tour the country or the world. The design of such exhibits can be more difficult because exhibition areas might not present the same conditions as museums. Exhibit designers usually work closely with museum curators to get the curators' ideas of how they want exhibits to look. They must then translate these ideas into gallery installations.

Sometimes exhibit design is based on a specific order. For example, an exhibit might require that items be arranged historically or chronologically. The exhibit designer must also determine where and how to place the documentation describing the specific items. Exhibit designers are expected to create floorplans, renderings, and scale models to illustrate where and how to exhibit objects. These plans might show the placement of art on the wall or illustrate placement of display cases or pedestals that might be needed. Everything is important when designing exhibits. In addition to the placement of objects, exhibit designers are expected to determine the proper lighting to obtain desired effects and to maintain all safety precautions. To display the exhibit most effectively, the exhibit designer must also choose colors for the walls and cases.

Other responsibilities of exhibit designers might include the following:

- Supervising the exhibit installation crew
- Creating exhibition cases and cabinets
- Working with graphic designs for the exhibit's signs

EMPLOYMENT OPPORTUNITIES

Exhibit designers may either work on staff at museums or on a freelance basis. Full and part-time positions may be available. Some exhibit designers specialize in the design of traveling exhibits. Not every museum employs full-time exhibit designers. Smaller facilities might utilize the services of freelance designers. Designers can find the greatest number of opportunities in culturally active cities that have many museums. Such cities include New York City, Los Angeles, Boston, Seattle, Washington, DC, and Atlanta.

EARNINGS

Earnings for exhibit designers can range from approximately $20,000 to $60,000 or more, depending on the designer's experience, training, responsibilities, and professional reputation. Other factors affecting earnings include the specific employment setting, the size of the exhibit, the prestige of the institution, and geographic location.

ADVANCEMENT OPPORTUNITIES

Exhibit designers can advance their careers by obtaining similar positions in larger or more prestigious museums. Others strike out on their own and freelance. Depending on career aspirations and training, exhibit designers can also climb the career ladder by becoming museum curators.

EDUCATION AND TRAINING

Educational requirements vary from job to job. Usually, the larger and more prestigious the facility, the more education required. Some type of formal education or training is almost always preferred. Degree or certificate programs in architecture, commercial art, industrial design, or graphic design are good choices.

EXPERIENCE AND QUALIFICATIONS

Prior experience working in exhibit design is usually required. You can usually obtain such experience through internships or in jobs as an assistant exhibit designer or on an exhibition installation crew. You can also obtain experience by planning exhibits as a museum curator in smaller museums.

Exhibit designers should be creative and artistic with knowledge of graphic design and balance. Aesthetic judgment is essential. Familiarity with conservation principles is necessary. You also need to be able to bring a concept to fruition.

FOR ADDITIONAL INFORMATION: If you are interested in a career as an exhibit designer, you can obtain additional information by contacting the American Institute for Conservation of Historic and Artistic Works (AICHAW).

TIPS

- Visit a variety of museums, galleries, and traveling exhibitions to see various exhibit designs.
- Check the classified section of newspapers for jobs advertised under such headings as "Museums," "Art Museums," "Traveling Exhibits," "Exhibitions," "Exhibit Designer," or "Art Gallery."
- Look in trade journals for advertised openings.
- Send a short cover letter and your resume to museums, galleries, and not-for-profit groups hosting exhibits.

RECORD LABEL GRAPHIC DESIGNER

JOB DESCRIPTION: *Design and develop graphics for CD, cassette, and album covers.*

EARNINGS: *$18,000 to $45,000+ per year.*

RECOMMENDED EDUCATION AND TRAINING: *Educational requirements vary.*

SKILLS AND PERSONALITY TRAITS: *Creativity; knowledge of pasteup, mechanicals, color, and photography; artistic ability; drawing and illustration skills.*

EXPERIENCE AND QUALIFICATIONS: *Experience requirements vary.*

JOB DESCRIPTION AND RESPONSIBILITIES

The music business is both glitzy and glamorous. It is essential therefore, that the packaging surrounding CDs, cassettes, and albums be attractive, be distinctive, and create an identifiable graphic image. Record label graphic designers are responsible for handling this task. Record label designers must develop creative, innovative, and memorable graphics for a variety of purposes.

Each album must have a distinctive cover identifying the artist and the product. This cover is often shown whenever the artist appears on television as well as in advertisements and in reviews of the CD. It is also visible in hundreds, if not thousands, of record stores throughout the country and often the world. Record label graphic designers might also design point-of-purchase displays, signs, display racks, shelving, and more, for record stores. These designers also might be expected to design the graphics for company logos, stationery, envelopes, order forms, labels, and so on. Some designers also handle the designs for company publications and packaging. The record label graphic designer must keep the company's image prominently identified, by keeping the design of all product names, graphics, logos, and product packages closely tied together. Then customers will relate the image to the company.

Other responsibilities of record label graphic designers might include the following:

- Developing designs for cover notes and other information placed inside CD packaging
- Developing the art used in advertisements to sell CDs
- Acting as the label art director

EMPLOYMENT OPPORTUNITIES

The greatest number of employment opportunities for record label graphic designers are located in areas hosting large record labels. These include New York City, Los Angeles, and Nashville.

EARNINGS

Earnings for record label graphic designers can range from approximately $18,000 to $45,000 or more annually depending on a number of variables. These variables include the record label's size, location, and prestige as well as the designer's experience, expertise, responsibilities, and professional reputation.

ADVANCEMENT OPPORTUNITIES

Advancement depends to a great extent on the designer's talent and creativity. Some record label graphic designers move up the career ladder by locating similar positions in larger or more prestigious labels or other industries. Other designers climb the career ladder by becoming the assistant art directors in the label's advertising department.

EDUCATION AND TRAINING

Educational requirements vary from job to job. Most labels prefer or require a designer to hold a college degree, although some take talented people with art school training. Good majors include fine arts or commercial art. Other majors might include advertising, communications, or marketing, with courses in commercial and graphic art and computer graphics. Seminars, workshops, and classes in these areas are also helpful.

EXPERIENCE AND QUALIFICATIONS

In this industry, the ability to demonstrate talent and creativity can often take the place of experience. You can demonstrate talent and creativity by maintaining an excellent portfolio.

Record label designers should be creative and imaginative and understand advertising, pasteups, mechanicals, typography, color, and photography. They should also be skilled at drawing, sketching, and other artistic activities. An understanding of the music and record industry is helpful in creating packaging that is eye-catching for the audience.

FOR ADDITIONAL INFORMATION: If you are interested in a career as a record label graphic artist, you can obtain more information by contacting the American Advertising Federation (AAF), the Society of Illustrators, and the American Institute of Graphic Arts (AIGA).

TIPS

- Send your resume with a short cover letter to record companies. Ask if they have any openings and request an opportunity to show your portfolio.
- Check the classified section of newspapers in areas hosting the record industry for jobs advertised under such headings as "Record Label Graphic Designer," "Record Jacket Designer," "Designer," "Graphic Designer," "Corporate Graphic Designer," or "Music."
- Prepare to demonstrate your skills. This is the type of job that you can secure by demonstrating that you have the skills, even if you lack experience.
- Put together the very best portfolio that you can to demonstrate your creativity and imagination.

- Look for internships in the design departments of record companies or large corporations. This is an excellent way to obtain on-the-job experience and training and make important contacts.
- Get experience and samples for your portfolio by doing some freelance assignments for music artists who are just starting out.

FLORAL DESIGNER

JOB DESCRIPTION: *Arrange fresh, dried, or artificial flowers in an artistically attractive manner.*

EARNINGS: *$5.50 to $11.00+ per hour.*

RECOMMENDED EDUCATION AND TRAINING: *Training requirements vary.*

SKILLS AND PERSONALITY TRAITS: *Creativity; imagination; a sense of style, balance, and color.*

EXPERIENCE AND QUALIFICATIONS: *Experience requirements vary.*

JOB DESCRIPTION AND RESPONSIBILITIES

Floral designers work with fresh, dried, silk, or other artificial flowers and foliage. They are responsible for cutting and arranging these flowers into attractive arrangements. Floral designers arrange flowers into bouquets, sprays, and wreaths. They put together arrangements in vases, mugs, or other containers. Floral designers might also be expected to create dish gardens out of plants. In many cases, designers arrange plants attractively in baskets, planters, or interesting or unique pots. When planning arrangements, designers must first establish the customer's tastes, preferences, and budget. Depending on the specific employment situations, the designer might determine this information from a written work order or from conversations directly with customers. The end product of the efforts of floral designers can be seen at events such as weddings and special programs and as decoration in homes, offices, businesses, and buildings. The floral designer's work is guided by any specific types of flowers or colors that the customer requests as well as the date, time, and place that the floral arrangement or plant is to be delivered.

Floral designers working in certain types of retail outlets, such as the craft departments in department stores, might be expected to arrange dried or silk flowers that customers have chosen. Responsibilities of floral designers in small shops may be more general than of those working in larger operations. In smaller shops, floral designers may perform additional duties such as growing flowers, keeping books, and taking cash or charges. In larger shops, the floral designer might exclusively handle the arrangement of flowers.

Other responsibilities of floral designers might include the following:

- Estimating costs of arrangements
- Decorating floral arrangements and plants with balloons, ribbons, bows, or other ornaments
- Creating centerpieces for events
- Handling the floral arrangements for wedding parties

EMPLOYMENT OPPORTUNITIES

Employment opportunities for floral designers are located throughout the country. Designers work in the following settings:

- Florist shops
- Craft shops
- Freelance or self-employment
- Floral departments in retail outlets
- Craft departments of retail outlets

EARNINGS

Floral designers might be paid an hourly rate or be on salary. Earnings can range from $5.50 to $11.00 or more per hour depending on experience, expertise, responsibilities, and professional reputation. Independent or self-employed designers might also be paid on a per-project basis.

ADVANCEMENT OPPORTUNITIES

Floral designers can advance their careers by locating similar jobs in larger or more prestigious shops. Designers can also become managers of floral shops or departments. Some floral designers climb the career ladder by striking out on their own and going into business for themselves.

EDUCATION AND TRAINING

Training requirements for floral designers vary. Many designers learn on the job. Formal training is available throughout the country in vocational and technical schools. College programs in floral design, ornamental horticulture, and floriculture are also offered at community and junior colleges as well as at four-year colleges and universities.

EXPERIENCE AND QUALIFICATIONS

Experience requirements vary depending on the specific job. Some employers do not require any experience at all, as long as employees show a desire to learn the craft. Other positions might require different degrees of experience.

Floral designers must be creative and have a sense of style, balance, and color.

FOR ADDITIONAL INFORMATION: Aspiring floral designers can learn more about the career by contacting the Society of American Florists (SAF).

TIPS

- Maintain a portfolio of floral designs. Such a portfolio can be helpful when looking for a job.
- Look for jobs advertised in the newspaper classified section under such headings as "Floral Designer," "Florist," and "Floral Arranging."
- Get experience working in the dried or silk flower department of a craft store.
- Look for continuing education classes at local high schools, community colleges, or vocational technical schools. These will help you learn more about the craft and get new ideas.

TEXTILE DESIGNER

JOB DESCRIPTION: *Design textiles for apparel, home furnishings, and accessories.*

EARNINGS: *$20,000 to $75,000+ per year.*

RECOMMENDED EDUCATION AND TRAINING: *Educational requirements vary.*

SKILLS AND PERSONALITY TRAITS: *Drawing and sketching skills; artistic flair; creativity; imagination; the ability to bring an idea from concept to reality.*

EXPERIENCE AND QUALIFICATIONS: *Experience requirements vary.*

JOB DESCRIPTION AND RESPONSIBILITIES

Textile designers design the cloth and textiles for various products such as apparel, furniture, linens, and rugs. Textile designers might design original textiles or design cloth following current trends.

Some textile designers specialize in creating designs for specific types of fabrics such as cottons, linens, lycra, wools, or silks. They might design fabrics that have their designs woven in or fabrics with designs and colors painted on. Some textile designers develop fabrics with added ornamentation such as sequins, glitter, or appliques.

Textile designers originate designs for fabric by developing the weave pattern, color, and gage of thread. They might create fabrics for either functional or decorative purposes. Colors, textiles, and fabric types often change seasonally to reflect fashion trends and customer preference. Textile designers use their creative and artistic skills to develop new fabrics or to make changes in current fabrics.

Textile designers first sketch their ideas. These sketches illustrate the colors or patterns that the final design will incorporate. Samples are then made based on the sketches. Sometimes textile designers sketch ideas by hand using graph paper, water colors, brushes, pens, and rules. Others design textiles using computers and special software.

Other responsibilities of textile designers might include the following:

- Preparing written instructions to the manufacturer, specifying details such as finish, color, and construction of fabric
- Examining fabricated samples on looms
- Modifying designs
- Keeping up with trends

EMPLOYMENT OPPORTUNITIES

Most opportunities for textile designers are located in large metropolitan areas where there are a great number of textile, apparel, or home furnishing manufacturers. Fashion designers might freelance or be on staff in a number of settings, including the following:

- Textile manufacturers
- Apparel manufacturers
- Manufacturers of linens and other bedding
- Upholstery fabric manufacturers

EARNINGS

Textile designers can earn between $20,000 and $75,000 or more per year. Factors affecting earnings include the designer's talent, training, experience, responsibilities, and professional reputation. Other variables include the employer's size, type, and prestige.

ADVANCEMENT OPPORTUNITIES

Textile designers often begin their careers as assistant or apprentice designers or trainees. They then can advance their careers by becoming full-fledged designers. As designers gain experience, they often find similar positions in more prestigious companies.

EDUCATION AND TRAINING

Educational requirements vary from job to job. Although some textile designers lack formal education, such education is recommended. Two- and four-year programs in textile or fashion design are available in colleges and universities throughout the country. Vocational, technical, and trade schools offer programs in the fundamentals of textile design.

EXPERIENCE AND QUALIFICATIONS

Employers might require various degrees of experience for textile designers. Textile designers must be able to sketch and draw. Computer capability is also useful. Successful textile designers are artistic, creative people with a sense of color and design. They also must understand and appreciate style and trends.

FOR ADDITIONAL INFORMATION: To learn more about careers in this field, contact The Fashion Association (TFA), the Council of Fashion Designers of America (CFDA), and the American Apparel Manufacturers Association (AAMA).

TIPS

- Look for apprenticeships and internships to get hands-on experience and on-the-job training. You can often find these by contacting textile manufacturing companies.
- Put together a portfolio of sketches and samples. Try to maintain a varied collection demonstrating your skill at designing for various fabrics.
- Take classes, workshops, and seminars in fashion and textiles. These are excellent ways to hone skills, get new ideas, and make important contacts.
- Make sure that you register with your school's job placement office.
- Check trade journals or the classified section of newspapers for advertised job openings. Look under such headings as "Textile Designer," "Fashion," "Design Studio," or "Textiles."

WINDOW DRESSER

JOB DESCRIPTION: *Display merchandise in retail stores' windows, showcases, and so on.*

EARNINGS: *$20,000 to $55,000+ per year.*

RECOMMENDED EDUCATION AND TRAINING: *Educational requirements vary.*

SKILLS AND PERSONALITY TRAITS: *Creativity; artistic flair; sense of color and balance; an eye for detail; aesthetic judgment; communications skills.*

EXPERIENCE AND QUALIFICATIONS: *Experience requirements vary.*

Job Description and Responsibilities

Retail stores use display windows and showcases to attract the attention of prospective customers. Window dressers develop and design these windows and showcases. They create displays of clothing, accessories, furniture, tools, books, cosmetics, food items, and so on, depending on the specific type of store.

In developing the design of windows, dressers must determine the client's needs and the best way to display the items that the client wants to highlight. Often, the client asks the window dresser to showcase products that are on sale or that are unique to the particular store. The window dresser must consider the size, shape, weight, and color of the products to be used in the display. The window dresser might be responsible for constructing or assembling prefabricated displays for the products being sold. These displays might be constructed of such materials as wood, fabric, glass, paper, and plastics.

Clients might expect a window dresser to design sketches of several concepts before actually putting the window display together. The dresser might produce these sketches by hand or with a computer-aided design program. The dresser presents these designs to store or display managers to determine which ideas they like best and to obtain their approval.

Other responsibilities of window dressers might include the following:

- Dressing mannequins for use in the displays
- Making changes or modifications in window displays
- Placing prices and descriptive signs on backdrops, fixtures, and merchandise

Employment Opportunities

Window dressers can find employment opportunities throughout the country. Most opportunities are located in large metropolitan areas where there are more large retail stores. Smaller shops often design and dress their own windows. Window dressers might be employed on staff or might freelance. Possible employment settings include the following:

- Department stores
- Gift shops
- Clothing stores
- Gourmet food stores
- Furniture stores

EARNINGS

A window dresser can earn between $20,000 and $55,000 or more, depending on the dresser's experience, expertise, and talent as well as the employer's size, location, and prestige. Freelance window dressers might be compensated per project.

ADVANCEMENT OPPORTUNITIES

Advancement depends to a great extent on the dresser's talent and creativity. Some advance their careers by locating similar positions in larger or more active settings. Others strike out on their own, building a customer base, and freelancing.

EDUCATION AND TRAINING

Educational requirements vary from job to job. Some employers require or prefer a college degree. Good majors include fine arts, commercial art, or design.

EXPERIENCE AND QUALIFICATIONS

Window dressers can acquire experience by working in retail stores and handling their window and showcase displays. Dressers should have a good understanding of design, including a sense of color and balance and an eye for detail. Window dressers should be creative and artistic. Drawing, sketching, and illustration skills are helpful.

FOR ADDITIONAL INFORMATION: You can obtain more information by contacting the American Advertising Federation (AAF), the Society of Illustrators (SOI), and the National Association of Schools of Art and Design (NASAD).

TIPS

- Check the classified section of newspapers for advertised positions under such headings as "Window Dresser," "Window Designer," "Window Display Designer," or "Designer."
- Develop a good, creative portfolio demonstrating your best work. Maintain a diverse portfolio to show your various talents.
- Look for internships at design firms, interior design firms, department stores, and large retail outlets.

CHAPTER 9

Careers for Artists in Television, Film & Video

When television sets were first manufactured, they were a luxury few could afford. Today, there are few households without at least one television set. The television, film, and video industries are profoundly influential and are still growing rapidly. Feature films are released in theaters and are soon after put out on video.

Television and film productions require the talents of many skilled professionals. Careers in this field are wide ranging. Many talents, skills, educational backgrounds, and experience levels are required.

In addition to employing performers, the television and film industries offer careers for other creative people, such as designers and artists. These people help create the illusions, moods, and settings that you see on film.

Space restrictions make it impossible for this chapter to discuss all possible opportunities. This chapter covers the following careers:

> Costume Designer—Television/Film
> Makeup Artist—Television/Film
> Set Designer—Television/Film/Video
> Animator

If you are interested in careers in television and video, you should also review entries in other chapters of this book. Chapter 1, "Careers for Writers in Radio, Television & Film," discusses related opportunities.

COSTUME DESIGNER—TELEVISION/FILM

JOB DESCRIPTION: *Develop and design costumes for television, films, and videos.*

EARNINGS: *$22,000 to $85,000+ per year.*

RECOMMENDED EDUCATION AND TRAINING: *A bachelor's degree in fashion or costume design is helpful, but not always required.*

SKILLS AND PERSONALITY TRAITS: *Drawing and sketching skills; sewing skills; artistic flair; creativity; the ability to bring an idea from concept to reality; imagination; a sense of style.*

EXPERIENCE AND QUALIFICATIONS: *Experience in costume design.*

JOB DESCRIPTION AND RESPONSIBILITIES

Costume designers develop and create the costumes, clothing, and accessories that dress the casts of television shows and film productions. Costume designers might actually design the clothing of the cast or be responsible for renting or purchasing the needed outfits.

To determine the costuming requirements, costume designers read the script of the particular television show or film and talk to the director. Costume designers must learn about the characters and the time period in which the film or show is set. Costume designers might be expected to do research on the specific time period by looking through books or magazines, visiting museums, and so on. After compiling all the required information, costume designers must begin developing ideas for costumes. The designer might be responsible for costuming the entire cast—the lead characters, supporting actors, and extras.

One of the most exciting parts of a costume designer's job is the actual designing of the costumes. The designer is expected to create sketches and drawings of ideas. He or she might also photograph samples and have models made of these. The designer is also expected to choose fabrics and colors for each costume. After doing so, the costume designer brings the ideas to the director, who must approve them or ask for changes. After the director approves the sketches, the designer must have the costumes constructed. The designer might have the construction done by an outside company or by his or her assistants. After construction, the costumes must be fitted to each actor and actress.

For television shows and films in which the action takes place in a contemporary setting—where characters wear everyday street clothes—the designer goes to clothing stores to choose the necessary clothes. Sometimes the designer visits theses stores with the actors or actresses to help them choose the clothing. This clothing can be purchased or borrowed from the store. In shows or films that require extras, these actors and actresses might be instructed to wear their own clothing. The costume designer checks and approves clothing that the extras provide.

Other responsibilities of costume designers might include the following:

- Finding costumes at theatrical costume supply houses or in studio stock
- Altering or redesigning costumes
- Supervising assistants in costume alteration, fitting, changes, and repairs

EMPLOYMENT OPPORTUNITIES

Employment opportunities for costume designers working in television and film are most often located in Hollywood, Los Angeles, and New York City. Other opportunities exist in television stations and television and film production companies throughout the country. Costume designers might either freelance or work on staff at organizations such as the following:

- Independent film production companies
- Networks
- Motion picture studios
- Independent costume design companies
- Independent television production companies

EARNINGS

In most situations, costume designers have minimum earnings negotiated by one of the unions representing costume designers in the television and film industries. These unions include the United Scenic Artists (USA) union, the International Alliance of Theatrical Stage Employees (IATSE), and the Costume Designers Guild (CDG). Costume designers who work fairly consistently can earn between $22,000 and $85,000 or more, depending on the prestige and type of production as well as the designer's experience, reputation, and responsibilities. Other factors include the amount of work that the costume designer obtains during the year and whether he or she is employed on staff or freelances.

ADVANCEMENT OPPORTUNITIES

Costume designers climb the career ladder by locating more prestigious projects. They might also advance their careers by locating full-time positions with television or film production companies. Those who freelance might find more consistent work as their reputations grow.

EDUCATION AND TRAINING

There are no formal educational requirements to become a costume designer. However, a bachelor's degree in costume design or fashion is helpful. Courses and workshops in fashion design, costuming, drawing, sketching, theater arts, design, history, sewing, and staging are also useful.

Experience and Qualifications

Costume designers working in television and film usually must have had experience. They can obtain such experience through internships and apprenticeships in the costume departments of television and film production companies. Designers can acquire other experience in the costume department of theater productions. Some costume designers also have worked as dressers or wardrobe assistants.

Costume designers must be creative and have a sense of style. They should also have the ability to sew, sketch, and draw.

FOR ADDITIONAL INFORMATION: To learn more about careers in this field, contact the United Scenic Artists (USA), the Costume Designer's Guild (CDG), or the Motion Picture Costumers (MPC).

Tips

- Apprenticeships offer hands-on experience and on-the-job training for careers in this field. Locate apprenticeships by contacting independent television and film production companies as well as theaters.
- Seek other apprenticeships that might be available with costume designers, wardrobe assistants, or dressers in theater, television, or film.
- Get experience by designing costumes for local school and community theater groups.
- Get your foot in the door by locating a job as a production assistant in the area of costume design.
- Read industry trade papers to look for low-budget productions. Such productions often do not have enough financial backing to hire people with a great deal of experience. Contact these production companies to see whether they have any openings for work in costume design.
- Do not turn down any opportunity to get experience, even if the compensation is low or nonexistent. Remember that any production that you work on will be useful on your resume.
- Put together a portfolio of sketches. Try to have a varied collection illustrating your skill at designing for various situations.

MAKEUP ARTIST—TELEVISION/FILM

JOB DESCRIPTION: *Use makeup to develop and create the appearance and physical personality of actors and actresses; with the use of makeup, improve or alter the appearance of actors or actresses.*

EARNINGS: *$25,000 to $100,000+ per year.*

RECOMMENDED EDUCATION AND TRAINING: *Training requirements vary.*

SKILLS AND PERSONALITY TRAITS: *Creativity; proficiency in television and film makeup design and application.*

EXPERIENCE AND QUALIFICATIONS: *Experience working with makeup in theatrical, film, and television settings.*

Job Description and Responsibilities

Makeup artists working in television and film help convey the personality of characters. They use makeup to improve, enhance, or alter the appearance of the actors and actresses.

Responsibilities of makeup artists in this medium are varied. Because of the bright lighting in both television and film, actors and actresses can looked "washed out." Such lighting can exaggerate any flaws or imperfections in the performers' appearance. Makeup artists working with news anchors or talk show hosts, for example, often try to make them look more natural under the bright lights. Makeup artists working in other facets of television or in films might be expected to create different appearances for characters. For example, an actor might need makeup to convey that his character has scars or black eyes. Sometimes makeup artists are asked to help characters appear older or younger. Others might need to use makeup to change the entire look of actors and actresses. They might create elaborate makeup for specialized productions such as science fiction shows and fantasy films. Makeup artists often create the illusion of blood or wounds on characters. They might apply makeup to the face, arms, legs, or any other exposed portion of the character's body. Makeup artists often analyze characters, do research, and confer with the director and the actors to create just the right look for a specific character.

Makeup artists apply makeup before scenes are shot. Television and film production often starts early in the morning, so the makeup artist usually must be at work quite early. For films and television shows, makeup artists must be capable of re-creating makeup so that the appearance of characters remains consistent throughout lengthy or out-of-sequence filming. Artists can do so with the help of photographs. The artist works with the costume designers and production hairstylist to coordinate colors of makeup with the character's costumes, hair color, and style.

Other responsibilities of makeup artists in television and film might include the following:

- Doing touch-ups for actors and actresses during filming
- Keeping necessary makeup and supplies stocked
- Making changes in makeup

EMPLOYMENT OPPORTUNITIES

The most opportunities for makeup artists working in this medium exist in New York City, Los Angeles, and Hollywood. However, opportunities are also available in other areas of the country where television stations or film production companies are located. Makeup artists might work on staff or freelance for the following organizations:

- Independent television stations
- Cable stations
- Entertainment and variety shows
- Sitcoms, dramas, and soap operas
- Television movies
- Video companies
- Motion pictures and films
- Producers of commercials
- Independent television production companies
- Networks, local independent, or cable newscasts

EARNINGS

Earnings for makeup artists working in television and film vary greatly depending on an artist's experience, expertise, responsibilities, and professional reputation. Other factors include the specific type of production as well as the amount of work performed annually. Makeup artists might be paid weekly salaries or be compensated by the performance. The International Alliance of Theatrical Stage Employees (IATSE) or the National Association of Broadcast Employees and Technicians (NABET) may negotiate minimum earnings for makeup artists working in television and film.

Makeup artists can earn between $500 and $3,000 per week or more. Some makeup artists working on major films earn $3,000 per day.

ADVANCEMENT OPPORTUNITIES

Advancement opportunities for makeup artists depend on several factors, including talent, creativity, determination, and luck. Some makeup artists climb the career ladder by working on larger or more prestigious projects. Others find advancement by obtaining more consistent work. A good position to strive for in this field is that of the department head or key makeup artist in a prestigious production company.

EDUCATION AND TRAINING

Training and educational requirements for makeup artists vary. Some individuals are self-taught. Others have learned through apprenticeships. A college degree in television, film, or theater arts is often helpful in learning skills. College also provides experiences that artists might not otherwise have had the opportunity in which to participate. Several makeup schools specialize in teaching television, film, and theatrical makeup. Courses, workshops, and seminars are also offered in this field.

EXPERIENCE AND QUALIFICATIONS

Makeup artists working in television and film must obtain as much hands-on experience as possible. You can do so through apprenticeships, internships, volunteer opportunities, and experience in local or cable television, with student films, or in theater-related situations.

Artists working in unionized situations might be required to join IATSE. To become a member, a theatrical makeup artist must usually take and pass a practical exam demonstrating competence with various theatrical makeup techniques. Makeup artists should excel in the design and application of television and film makeup. In some areas of the country, makeup artists must hold state licenses. You can obtain such a license by attending a licensed school of cosmetology and taking and passing a written and practical state exam.

FOR ADDITIONAL INFORMATION: If you are interested in learning more about a career as a theatrical makeup artist, you should contact the International Association of Theatrical Stage Employees (IATSE), Makeup and Hairstylist Local 798, Makeup and Hairstylist Local 706, the National Hairdressers and Cosmetologists Association (NHCA), and the Cosmetologists Association.

TIPS

- Contact makeup artists, production companies, studios, television stations, and so on to see whether they have any openings for assistants. Television and film directories will have their names, addresses and phone numbers.

- Get experience by volunteering to handle the makeup requirements for fashion shows, local community theater, school, or college productions.

- Look for apprenticeships and internships with theaters and with opera and ballet companies.

- Seek other apprenticeship and internship programs that might be available with television stations, film production companies, studios, and so on.

- Try to find seminars and workshops in film and television makeup. Production companies and studios often offer such workshops. They are valuable for learning new skills and making important industry contacts.

- Don't forget to read the trade papers to find valuable information that might be useful to your career in this field.

- Read books on the subject of television and film makeup to get new ideas and learn new techniques.

- Look for low-budget productions, student films, college television stations, and such to find opportunities to handle their makeup requirements. Remember to get copies of the productions that you have worked on to back up experience claims on your resume.

SET DESIGNER—TELEVISION/FILM/VIDEO

JOB DESCRIPTION: *Develop and design scenery and sets for television, films, and videos.*

EARNINGS: *$18,000 to $95,000+ per year.*

RECOMMENDED EDUCATION AND TRAINING: *A bachelor's degree in theater arts, art and design, or television production is preferred.*

SKILLS AND PERSONALITY TRAITS: *Artistic ability; creativity; the ability to carry an idea from concept through fruition.*

EXPERIENCE AND QUALIFICATIONS: *Experience requirements vary.*

JOB DESCRIPTION AND RESPONSIBILITIES

Set designers working in television and film are responsible for developing and designing the sets and scenery for these productions. They work with others in the production company to come up with well-designed sets.

Set designers usually begin in the pre-production period. The set designer is expected to meet with the director and the producer to learn what their ideas are. The set designer might also meet and work with the lighting designers, costume designers, property masters, set dressers, and carpenters for the production. He or she will also read the script to determine the physical sets that must be designed. For shows set in specific time periods, the set designer must do research to make sure that the details of each set are accurate for the particular time period. Set designers might also be asked to develop sets for science fiction or surrealistic productions.

After developing ideas for the sets, the set designer must translate them into reality. The set designer must draft sketches and create miniature models of each set.

Productions often require more than one set, so the designer must create floor plans to show where to place each specific set as well as any necessary cameras, lights, or additional equipment that each set requires. The floor plans show exactly where to place everything on the set. After set designs have been approved, the set designer oversees the set construction.

Other responsibilities of set designers in this medium might include the following:

- Keeping track of sets, scenery, backdrops, and props in inventory
- Making sure that sets work for each scene in a production

EMPLOYMENT OPPORTUNITIES

Employment opportunities for set designers are most often located in Hollywood, Los Angeles, and New York City. Other opportunities exist in television stations and with television and film production companies throughout the country. Set designers might either freelance or work on staff at organizations such as the following:

- Film production companies
- Commercial production companies
- Independent television production companies
- Video production companies
- Independent television stations
- Local television stations
- Cable television stations
- Networks

EARNINGS

In most situations, either the United Scenic Artists (USA) union or the International Alliance of Theatrical Stage Employees (IATSE) negotiates minimum earnings for set designers. Set designers earn between $18,000 and $95,000 or more annually depending on the prestige and type of the production as well as their experience, reputation, and responsibilities. Other factors include the amount of work that set designers do during the year, whether they are employed or freelance, and so on. Designers who work on staff at a production company have more secure incomes than freelancers.

ADVANCEMENT OPPORTUNITIES

Set designers can advance their careers by locating full-time positions on staff with television or film production companies. Freelancers can also find more consistent work. Some designers climb the career ladder by designing sets for more prestigious projects in television and film.

EDUCATION AND TRAINING

A bachelor's degree in theater arts, art and design, television or film production, or a related field is recommended. Although a degree is not essential for all jobs in this area, a college background offers opportunities to obtain experience, make contacts, and hone skills that might not otherwise be available. Courses, seminars, and workshops in television and film production, graphic arts, drafting, drawing, stagecraft, and architecture are also helpful.

EXPERIENCE AND QUALIFICATIONS

Although experience is usually required for set designers, the degree of experience varies from job to job. The more prestigious the production, the more experience needed.

Set designers can obtain experience working as assistant set designers in television, film, or theater. They might also go through internship or apprenticeship programs.

To work in any unionized situation, set designers must usually become members of the United Scenic Artists (USA). To join the USA, you must pass an exam and an interview. Successful set designers must be creative and artistic. The ability to conceptualize and translate ideas into reality is essential.

FOR ADDITIONAL INFORMATION: To learn more about careers in this field, contact the United Scenic Artists (USA) and the Set Designers and Model Makers (SDMM).

TIPS

- Apprenticeships offer hands-on experience and on-the-job training for careers in this field. Locate apprenticeships by contacting independent television and film production companies as well as theaters.
- Get experience by designing sets for local school and community theater groups.
- Contact local television or cable stations to see whether they have any openings. It is often easier to break in on a small scale, get experience, and move forward with your career.
- Read industry trade papers to look for low-budget productions. Such productions often do not have enough financial backing to hire set designers with much experience.
- Do not turn down any opportunity to get experience, even if the compensation is low or nonexistent. Remember that any production that you work on will be useful for listing on your resume.
- Consider getting more experience and making useful contacts in the industry by becoming a production assistant. Contact

television, film, video, and commercial production companies to see whether they have any openings.

ANIMATOR

JOB DESCRIPTION: *Draw a series of pictures either by hand or with computers to create animated cartoons.*

EARNINGS: *$18,000 to $55,000+ per year.*

RECOMMENDED EDUCATION AND TRAINING: *Educational requirements vary.*

SKILLS AND PERSONALITY TRAITS: *Drawing skills; computer skills; creativity; imagination.*

EXPERIENCE AND QUALIFICATIONS: *Drawing, sketching, and using computers.*

JOB DESCRIPTION AND RESPONSIBILITIES

Animators are visual artists responsible for drawing the animated cartoons seen on television and in the movies. The Walt Disney Corporation is probably the most prominent name associated with animation. Animators might draw by hand or might create drawings with the aid of computers. In some situations, animators might work as a team, with each animator having an area of specialization. An animator might be responsible for drawing characters, scenes, or sequences. The team or a specific animator might then be responsible for assembling the various pieces into one cartoon.

Animators are responsible for rendering a series of sequential drawings of characters or other subject matter. These renderings are then photographed and projected at a speed that animates or puts the drawings into motion. Animators are expected to create the sketches of characters in the cartoon. They might also develop color patterns and paint background layouts that are used to dramatize action for animated cartoon scenes.

Other responsibilities of animators might include the following:

- Labeling each section of a rendering with the color to be used
- Preparing sketches to illustrate special effects such as wind, rain, or fire

EMPLOYMENT OPPORTUNITIES

Animators might work in the television or motion picture industries. Many opportunities also exist in animating commercials. Animators can find employment in metropolitan cities hosting television or motion picture studios or advertising agencies producing animated commercials. Such opportunites are most plentiful in Hollywood, Los Angeles, New York City, Orlando, Boston. Chicago, and Atlanta.

EARNINGS

Animators working full time have annual earnings ranging from $18,000 to $55,000 or more. Factors affecting earnings include the specific employer as well as the animator's experience, responsibilities, and professional reputation.

ADVANCEMENT OPPORTUNITIES

Animators advance their careers by obtaining experience and then being assigned to more prestigious projects. Some animators locate similar jobs in larger companies. Others move into administrative positions.

EDUCATION AND TRAINING

Although many positions do not require formal education or training, a college degree is helpful. A bachelor's degree in graphic design or fine arts or art school training can provide valuable experiences and opportunities. Classes in computer skills and computer animation are also quite helpful.

EXPERIENCE AND QUALIFICATIONS

Many positions in this field require a portfolio to demonstrate talent and skills. Aspiring animators can obtain experience though internships with established animators. Animators must be artistic, creative people with drawing and sketching skills. Computer skills, especially in the area of computer animation, are also necessary.

FOR ADDITIONAL INFORMATION: Learn more about this career from the American Institute of Graphic Arts (AIGA) and the Society of Illustrators (SOI).

TIPS

- Contact the human resources departments of the major employers—Disney Corporation, Warner Brothers, and Hanna-Barbera—to learn if they have any openings. (See appendix for addresses and phone numbers.)
- You might also contact these companies to ask about internships.
- Enter animation competitions. They will help you gain exposure.

CHAPTER 10

Careers for Artists in Advertising and Graphic Design

In today's society, it is difficult not to be affected by advertising. We are bombarded every day by advertisements. We see them on television, in newspapers, and in magazines. We hear them on the radio. We see billboards along the highway, along with trucks driving down the highway touting company names. Advertising is a multi-billion dollar industry.

A great many artistic people are needed to create advertisements. Space restrictions make it impossible for this chapter to discuss all possible opportunities. This chapter covers the following jobs:

Advertising Art Director/Creative Director—Corporate and Agencies
Graphic Designer—Corporate/Industry
Computer Graphic Artist
Commercial Artist—Agency
Retail Outlet Art Director
Mechanical Artist—Agency
Lettering Artist
Pasteup Artist

If you are interested in a career in advertising, you should also review entries in other chapters of this book. Chapter 5, "Careers for Writers in Advertising, Public Relations, Marketing, and Communications," discusses related opportunities.

ADVERTISING ART DIRECTOR/CREATIVE DIRECTOR— CORPORATE AND AGENCIES

JOB DESCRIPTION: *Design the graphics, layout, artwork, and so on, for print and broadcast advertisements.*

EARNINGS: *$22,000 to $75,000+ per year.*

RECOMMENDED EDUCATION AND TRAINING: *Educational requirements vary.*

SKILLS AND PERSONALITY TRAITS: *Creativity; artistic ability; supervisory skills; an understanding of the advertising industry; drawing, graphics, layout, and typography skills.*

EXPERIENCE AND QUALIFICATIONS: *Prior experience in graphic or commercial art; a portfolio is always required.*

JOB DESCRIPTION AND RESPONSIBILITIES

Advertising art directors are responsible for creating ads for newspapers, magazines, billboards, direct mail, packaging, posters, television, and other media. Specific responsibilities vary depending on the situation and the job.

Art directors work with copywriters, graphic artists, illustrators, account executives, and various other professionals to achieve the finished product. In some cases, the art director is totally responsible for an ad from the development of the initial visual concept to the finished advertisement seen by consumers. Agency art directors work with others in the firm to create effective and visually attractive advertisements for clients. Those in the corporate world team up with graphic designers to develop the art, graphics, and layout of company logos, packaging, promotional or sales materials, brochures, leaflets, or booklets.

Other responsibilities of advertising art directors and creative directors might include the following:

- Reviewing portfolios of freelance photographers, illustrators, artists, directors, and producers
- Supervising assistants, artists, and designers
- Designing commercial logos or trademarks

EMPLOYMENT OPPORTUNITIES

Although art directors can find employment throughout the country, the most opportunities are located in major cities. Employment settings might include the following:

- Advertising agencies
- Direct marketing agencies
- Book publishers
- Public relations firms
- Corporations in any industry
- Record companies

EARNINGS

Earnings for art directors range from $22,000 to $75,000 or more, depending on the specific type of job, geographic location, and the company's size and prestige. Earnings also depend on the individual's experience, responsibilities, and professional reputation.

ADVANCEMENT OPPORTUNITIES

Advertising art directors can choose many paths for career advancement. The path that most choose is to locate a similar job in a larger, more prestigious corporation, agency, or organization. This path usually leads to increased responsibilities and earnings.

EDUCATION AND TRAINING

Educational requirements vary. Some positions require art school training while others mandate a college degree in fine arts or commercial art. Other possible college majors include communications or advertising with an art minor. Because creativity is such an important qualification, some companies might also accept an applicant who has a good portfolio. Classes, workshops, and seminars in advertising and art are helpful for honing skills and making important contacts.

EXPERIENCE AND QUALIFICATIONS

Some employers might require prior experience as a graphic or commercial artist. Some successful candidates have had experience as assistant advertising art directors.

A portfolio is necessary for this type of position. Such a portfolio should demonstrate creativity, commercial art ability, and art skills.

FOR ADDITIONAL INFORMATION: You can find additional information regarding careers in this field by contacting the American Advertising Federation (AAF), the Art Directors Club, Inc. (ADC), the Society of Illustrators (SOI), the Graphic Artists Guild (GAG), and the American Institute of Graphic Arts (AIGA).

TIPS

- Look for jobs in the newspaper classified section. The jobs are often advertised under such headings as "Art Director," "Creative Director," and "Advertising Agencies."
- Look in trade journals for advertised job openings.
- Develop an excellent, creative portfolio demonstrating your best work. Make the portfolio diverse to showcase your talents.
- Look for internships in advertising agencies, corporations, and so on. These are excellent for getting your foot in the door, honing skills, and making contacts.
- Join relevant trade associations and attend meetings. These are other great ways to make contacts.

GRAPHIC DESIGNER—CORPORATE/INDUSTRY

JOB DESCRIPTION: *Design and develop graphics for corporate publications and packaging.*

EARNINGS: *$18,000 to $45,000+ per year.*

RECOMMENDED EDUCATION AND TRAINING: *Educational requirements vary.*

SKILLS AND PERSONALITY TRAITS: *Creativity; knowledge of pasteup, mechanicals, color, and photography; artistic ability; drawing and illustration skills.*

EXPERIENCE AND QUALIFICATIONS: *Experience requirements vary.*

JOB DESCRIPTION AND RESPONSIBILITIES

Most companies consider it essential to create a distinctive and identifiable graphic image. Corporate and industry graphic designers are responsible for handling this task. Graphic designers must develop creative, innovative, and memorable graphics to be used for a variety of purposes. Corporate graphic designers might develop graphic designs for logos, stationery, envelopes, order forms, labels, and so on. Graphic designers might handle the designs for company publications and packaging as well.

Specific responsibilities of the graphic designer depend on the corporation for which he or she works. Some might design the packages in which the company sells its products. Others might design point-of-purchase displays, signs, display racks, and shelving presented in stores. Designers who work for book publishers might design the book jackets as well as the books' interiors. Graphic designers working for record labels design the CD and cassette covers. A graphic designer's work is not necessarily seen only on paper. He or she might also be responsible for designing the logos and messages that you see on the sides of corporate trucks that travel up and down the highways. Corporate graphic designers must always keep the company's image prominently identified. Therefore, the designer must keep the design of all product names, graphics, logos, and product packages closely tied together. In this way, customers relate the visual image to the company.

Other responsibilities of corporate graphic designers might include the following:

- Developing designs for brochures, booklets, pamphlets, posters, and billboards
- Developing the art used in advertisements
- Acting as corporate art director

EMPLOYMENT OPPORTUNITIES

Employment opportunities for aspiring graphic designers can be located throughout the country. Graphic designers might work in a variety of industries, including the following:

- Manufacturers of assorted consumer-oriented products
- Food companies
- Book publishers
- Record companies
- Trade associations

EARNINGS

Earnings for corporate or industry graphic designers range from $18,000 to $45,000 or more annually, depending on the company's size, location, and prestige as well as the designer's experience, expertise, responsibilities, and professional reputation.

ADVANCEMENT OPPORTUNITIES

Advancement depends to a great extent on the designer's talent and creativity. Some corporate graphic designers move up the career ladder by locating similar positions in larger or more prestigious corporations. Other graphic designers climb the career ladder by becoming the assistant art director in the corporation's advertising department. Some graphic designers also strike out on their own and freelance.

EDUCATION AND TRAINING

Educational requirements vary from job to job. Most corporations prefer or require graphic designers to hold a college degree, although some will hire talented desigers with art school training. Good majors include fine arts or commercial art. Other majors might include advertising, communications, or marketing with courses in commercial and graphic art and computer graphics. Seminars, workshops, and classes in these areas are also helpful.

EXPERIENCE AND QUALIFICATIONS

Like the educational requirements, the experience requirements for graphic designers vary. The ability to demonstrate talent and creativity can often override a lack of experience. Employers usually require a portfolio for this job.

Corporate graphic designers should be creative and imaginative and understand advertising, pasteup, mechanicals, typography, color, and photography. They should also be skilled at drawing and sketching.

FOR ADDITIONAL INFORMATION: If you are interested in a career as a computer graphic artist, you can obtain more information by contacting the American Advertising Federation (AAF), the Society of Illustrators (SOI), and the American Institute of Graphic Arts (AIGA).

TIPS

- Check the classified section of newspapers for advertised jobs under such headings as "Graphic Designer" or "Corporate Graphic Designer."
- If you don't have the experience, try to demonstrate to potential employers that you have the skills and talent. You can do so by presenting a portfolio of your work demonstrating your skills, creativity, and imagination.
- Look for internships in the design department at large corporations. These are an excellent way to obtain on-the-job experience and training and to make important contacts.
- Get experience and samples for your portfolio by doing some freelance assignments.
- Send your resume with a short cover letter to corporations in any of the industries in which you have an interest. Ask whether they have any openings and request an opportunity to show your portfolio.

COMPUTER GRAPHIC ARTIST

JOB DESCRIPTION: *Lay out ads with computers; design graphics and type for advertisements and promotional material with computer assistance.*

EARNINGS: *$17,000 to $44,000+ per year.*

RECOMMENDED EDUCATION AND TRAINING: *Training requirements vary.*

SKILLS AND PERSONALITY TRAITS: *Computer capability; knowledge of a variety of software; artistic ability; creativity.*

EXPERIENCE AND QUALIFICATIONS: *Computer graphics experience is usually required.*

JOB DESCRIPTION AND RESPONSIBILITIES

Computer graphic artists work with a variety of computers, hardware, and software programs to create graphics and layouts. Computer graphic artists work with a keyboard, electric stylus, mouse, or scanner rather than more traditional instruments such as a pen and ink.

Responsibilities of computer graphic artists vary depending on the specific employment situation in which they work. As a rule, these individuals are expected to create the art, graphics, and type designs for advertisements. They might also be responsible for laying out ads and other promotional materials on the computer. Computer graphic artists might choose fonts for headlines and body copy from a multitude of computer fonts available. They might design new or special fonts with the computer. Font design could take a great deal of time if done by hand, but with the assistance of computer generation, a computer graphic artist can design new fonts in moments. The computer graphic artist can handle a vast array of projects by utilizing a variety of computer software. These projects might include producing computer-generated graphs, charts, diagrams, video presentations, cartoons, and page layouts.

Computer graphic artists might be expected to design original graphics or art for advertisements, marketing, or promotional materials. Those working on ads might be responsible for graphics, body copy, headline type, or all three. After designing graphically pleasing ads, logos, page layouts, or other materials, computer graphic artists, like all graphic artists, must usually obtain approval from the client or art director for whom they work.

Other responsibilities of computer graphic artists might include the following:

- Functioning as a typesetter or typographer
- Making changes on graphics, layouts, and so on, at the request of clients or art directors

- Meeting with clients to discuss their ideas for ads, sales pieces, or other marketing materials

EMPLOYMENT OPPORTUNITIES

Employment opportunities for aspiring computer graphic artists can be located throughout the country. Most jobs in advertising or public relations agencies are available in cities where the most agencies are located, such as New York, Atlanta, Chicago, Los Angeles, Detroit, Boston, and Dallas. Employment settings might include the following:

- Advertising agencies
- Public relations firms
- Newspapers
- Self-employment

- Marketing agencies
- Direct response agencies
- Periodicals

EARNINGS

Earnings for computer graphic artists range from $17,000 to $44,000 or more annually depending on the agency's size and location as well as the artist's experience, expertise, responsibilities, and professional reputation.

ADVANCEMENT OPPORTUNITIES

Advancement depends to a great extent on the artist's talent and creativity. Some computer graphic artists move up the career ladder by locating similar positions in larger or more prestigious agencies or settings. Other artists climb the career ladder by striking out on their own, building a customer base, and freelancing.

EDUCATION AND TRAINING

Educational requirements vary from job to job. Most agencies require the computer graphic artist to hold a college degree. Good majors include fine arts or commercial art. Other majors might include advertising, communications, or marketing with courses in commercial and graphic art and computer graphics. Seminars, workshops, and classes in these areas are also helpful.

EXPERIENCE AND QUALIFICATIONS

Experience requirements, like educational requirements, vary. Smaller agencies and newspapers often hire computer graphic artists directly out of college. Larger agencies usually require some sort of experience. An artist can obtain such experience through jobs at smaller agencies or through internships.

The ability to demonstrate creativity is always necessary in this field. Many positions require a portfolio of samples. Computer graphic artists must be creative and imaginative and have excellent computer skills. An understanding of advertising, pasteups, mechanicals, typography, color, and photography is necessary.

FOR ADDITIONAL INFORMATION: If you are interested in a career as a computer graphic artist, you can obtain more information by contacting the American Advertising Federation (AAF), the Society of Illustrators (SOI), and the American Institute of Graphic Arts (AIGA).

Tips

- Check the newspaper's classified section for jobs advertised under such headings as "Advertising," "Agencies," "Computer Graphic Artist," "Artists," and "Computers."
- Also look for positions advertised in trade publications.
- Look for internships at advertising agencies. You often can find such experience through college intern programs.
- Get experience and samples for your portfolio by doing some freelance assignments.
- Send your resume with a short cover letter to advertising, marketing, direct response, and public relations agencies to inquire about openings.
- Get a job at a smaller agency, obtain experience, and move on to a better job.
- Take seminars, workshops, and classes in desktop publishing, software programs, layout, art, design, graphics, and advertising. These classes are useful for honing skills and making important contacts.

COMMERCIAL ARTIST—AGENCY

JOB DESCRIPTION: *Develop illustrations for advertisements; prepare storyboards; lay out advertisements.*

EARNINGS: *$18,000 to $45,000+ per year.*

RECOMMENDED EDUCATION AND TRAINING: *Educational requirements vary.*

SKILLS AND PERSONALITY TRAITS: *Creativity; artistic ability; drawing skills; illustration skills; knowledge of layout, typography, color, and photography; understanding of the advertising industry.*

EXPERIENCE AND QUALIFICATIONS: *Experience in an art department or advertising industry might be necessary.*

JOB DESCRIPTION AND RESPONSIBILITIES

Commercial artists work in the art division of an advertising agency's creative department. They are responsible for developing creative ways to illustrate what the account executive and client want to show in either a print ad or audio-visual commercial.

Commercial artists work with others in the agency so that they can collaborate to come up with the most appealing ads possible. The commercial artist meets with the account executive to learn as much as possible about the advertising campaign and the product or service being advertised. The commercial artist must also find out what type of copy is being used in the ad. The artist can obtain this information from either the account executive or the copywriter.

The commercial artist works under the direction of the art director, who is responsible for guiding the artist on the concept of the ad or ads. Depending on the agency, the commercial artist might have several responsibilities regarding ads. He or she might be expected to illustrate the ad, create the ad's layout, or both. As part of this job, the commercial artist must consider the type of art or pictures to use in the ad as well as where to place each in relation to ad copy. Commercial artists are expected to create detailed drawings depicting the ad's completed appearance. They are constantly doing drafts of layouts, sketches, and more to make sure that the ads are as eye-catching as possible. Commercial artists might also be responsible for selecting the size and style of typeface that they believe will be most effective in the ad. Similarly, the commercial artist must select the most appropriate, eye-catching, and appealing colors to use in ads.

Commercial artists working on audio-visual commercials, such as those used on television, must develop storyboards. Storyboards resemble comic strips. They illustrate what will happen in every frame of the television commercial. Agencies also use storyboards to pitch a new ad idea or advertising campaign to a client. Commercial artists must constantly obtain approval from the art director, account executive, and the client. If any one of these does not like an idea, the commercial artist must revise the work until the idea or concept is accepted.

Other responsibilities of commercial artists working in advertising agencies might include the following:

- Designing commercial logos or trademarks
- Creating artwork for new packages, merchandising, promotional materials, booklets, or manuals
- Revising advertisements prepared by other artists

EMPLOYMENT OPPORTUNITIES

Talented, creative commercial artists can find employment in agencies throughout the country. The most jobs are available in cities where most of the larger agencies are located. These include New York City, Los Angeles, Dallas, Atlanta, Chicago, Cleveland, and Minneapolis.

EARNINGS

Commercial artists working in agencies earn between $18,000 and $45,000 annually depending on the artist's experience, expertise, and talent as well as his or her agency's size, location, and prestige.

ADVANCEMENT OPPORTUNITIES

Advancement opportunities are based largely on talent. Creative, talented commercial artists can find similar positions in larger or more prestigious agencies, resulting in increased earnings.

EDUCATION AND TRAINING

Training and educational requirements vary from agency to agency. Competition for most agency jobs is usually fierce, and formal training in this area can be helpful in landing a job. A bachelor's degree with a major in art, art school training, or even a few commercial art and advertising courses can be beneficial.

EXPERIENCE AND QUALIFICATIONS

Commercial artists who are interested in working in agencies usually must have had some type of experience in advertising layout or illustration. Artists must have a total understanding of advertising.

Commercial artists must be creative and artistic. Drawing and illustration skills are necessary. Artists also need a knowledge of pasteup, mechanicals, typography, color, and photography.

FOR ADDITIONAL INFORMATION: Aspiring commercial artists can obtain more career information by contacting the American Advertising Federation (AAF), the Art Directors Club, Inc. (ADC), or the Society of Illustrators (SOI).

TIPS

- Look in the newspaper's classified section for jobs advertised under such headings as "Commercial Artist," "Artist," Advertising," and "Agencies."
- Develop a good, creative portfolio showing your best work. Make it diversified, if you can, to show your various talents.
- Send your resume and a cover letter to agencies to see whether they have openings available. Make sure that your letter mentions that you have a portfolio available for review.
- Look for internships at advertising agencies. You can also find internships through college intern programs.

RETAIL OUTLET ART DIRECTOR

JOB DESCRIPTION: *Develop advertisements for retail outlets; design and create ads, sales flyers, and marketing and promotional material.*

EARNINGS: *$18,000 to $45,000+ per year.*

RECOMMENDED EDUCATION AND TRAINING: *Educational requirements vary.*

SKILLS AND PERSONALITY TRAITS: *Creativity; understanding of retail advertising; layout, pasteup, and graphic skills.*

EXPERIENCE AND QUALIFICATIONS: *Experience working in an advertising or art department is helpful.*

JOB DESCRIPTION AND RESPONSIBILITIES

Art directors in retail outlets have the ultimate responsibility for developing, designing, and creating ads, sales flyers, and other promotional materials for retail outlets. Depending on the retail outlet's size and structure, art directors might work under an advertising director or might also handle the duties of an advertising director. No matter what the situation, the result must be to develop the most creative, appealing, and eye-catching ads and promotional material possible.

In large retail situations, the art director is responsible not only for coming up with the advertising concepts and designing of ads but for supervising a staff as well. The staff might include sketch, mechanical, graphic, and layout artists. In some settings, the art director might also work with outside or freelance people in creating ads. In small stores, the art director might be the only person in the entire advertising department. In these cases, the art director is expected to handle the duties of sketch artists, graphic artists, layout and mechanical artists, and lettering artists. In smaller outlets, the owners often offer their advice or suggestions to the art director. He or she, in turn, might then be responsible for developing, creating, and often placing the ads. Retail outlets often utilize store posters and flyers for advertising weekly specials and special sales. The art director must develop and design these. When handling this task, the art director might work with outside printers. In some cases, the art director is additionally responsible for negotiating prices or soliciting bids for printing these flyers and sales promotion pieces.

Another responsibility of the retail art director is developing, designing, and creating advertising show cards and counter signs. These are the pieces standing on store counters, placed in windows, or suspended from the ceiling to advertise new products, specials, or price breaks. The art director must design promotional material for the retail store. In some outlets, the art director might simply handle the material's design. In others, he or she must develop the ideas, write the promotional copy, and create the artwork. Art directors in retail stores must be sure that everything used to advertise, market, and promote the store retains a unified identity and image. Logos, the store name, ad colors, and so on must be the same or be well coordinated. Customers must be led to think of the store automatically every time that they see an advertisement.

An art director must obtain approval from the store owner, marketing director, or advertising director, depending on the store's structure. If one of these persons does not like an idea, the art director is expected to revise the work until each of them accepts the idea or concept.

Other responsibilities of art directors working in retail outlets might include the following:

- Designing commercial logos or trademarks
- Creating artwork for packaging, merchandising, promotional materials, and so on

EMPLOYMENT OPPORTUNITIES

The current trend is toward in-house advertising departments. People interested in working as art directors in retail outlets can find employment throughout the country. The bulk of opportunities may be found in cities where there are more large retail stores. Employment settings might include the advertising departments of the following:

- Small department stores
- Supermarkets
- National retail chains
- Manufacturer's outlets

- Large department stores
- Regional retail chains
- Catalogers
- Malls

EARNINGS

Art directors working in retail outlets have annual earnings ranging from $18,000 to $45,000 or more depending on the art director's experience, responsibilities, and expertise. Other variables include the retail outlet's size, prestige, and location. Usually, earnings are lower in smaller cities.

ADVANCEMENT OPPORTUNITIES

Art directors working in retail outlets can take several paths to career advancement. Many art directors climb the career ladder by locating similar positions in larger or more prestigious retail stores. This path leads to increased responsibilities and earnings. Another possibility for career advancement is to find a similar position in a large corporation or an advertising agency.

EDUCATION AND TRAINING

As a rule, larger department stores and chains require or prefer their art directors to hold a four-year college degree in either fine arts or commercial art. Smaller stores might not have this requirement. These employers might accept an applicant who has had some art school training or even one who is self-taught if that applicant can demonstrate the required skills. Courses, workshops, and seminars in various aspects of advertising are helpful.

EXPERIENCE AND QUALIFICATIONS

Experience requirements vary in this area. Smaller stores might not require a great deal of experience for art directors, whereas larger department stores and chains usually prefer or require prior experience working in some aspect of advertising or in the art department in any industry.

The art director of a retail outlet must be creative and artistic. He or she must be able to sketch, draw, paste up, lay out, and put together mechanicals for ads. The art director must also have a basic knowledge of advertising.

FOR ADDITIONAL INFORMATION: If you are interested in a career as an art director for a retail store, you can obtain more career information by contacting the American Advertising Federation (AAF), the Art Directors Club, Inc. (ADC), the Society of Illustrators (SOI), the Graphic Artists Guild (GAG), or the American Institute of Graphic Arts (AIGA).

TIPS

- Look in the newspaper classified section for jobs advertised under such headings as "Art Director," "Artist," Advertising," and "Retail."

- Develop a good creative portfolio illustrating your best work. Make it diversified to showcase your talents.

- Send your resume and a cover letter to retail stores to see whether they have openings. Be sure that your letter mentions that you have a portfolio available for review.

- Look for internships in retail outlets or advertising agencies.

- Ask the manager of a local store of a retail chain where to obtain more information about internships and training programs. You can also find internships through college intern programs.

- Join relevant trade associations and attend meetings. These are great places to make contacts.

MECHANICAL ARTIST—AGENCY

JOB DESCRIPTION: *Create mechanicals for advertisements; paste up ads.*

EARNINGS: *$15,000 to $28,000+ per year.*

RECOMMENDED EDUCATION AND TRAINING: *Educational requirements vary.*

SKILLS AND PERSONALITY TRAITS: *The ability to work well with hands; neatness; accuracy; the ability to follow instructions.*

EXPERIENCE AND QUALIFICATIONS: *Experience requirements vary.*

JOB DESCRIPTION AND RESPONSIBILITIES

Mechanical artists working in advertising agencies are usually located in the art division of the agency's creative department. They are responsible for pasting up a guide for the engraver of print advertisements created by the agency.

These guides are called *mechanicals*. They are exact copies, in black and white, of the printed ad. Printers and engravers use mechanicals to reproduce ads on metal engravings or in the photo offset process.

Mechanical artists do not have to use any of their creative ability doing this job. They are given a sketch called a *comprehensive* to show the way that the ad is to look when completed. The mechanical artist is responsible for pasting all the ad's components on a white illustration board. These components might include photographs, art work, logos, borders, and type. After completing the pasteup, the mechanical artist must make a photostat or "stat" of the artwork and photos. Stats are photographic reproductions used in creating ad layouts to scale art, graphics, and type to the correct size. Engravers use stats to make the ads. Mechanical artists must work very neatly, precisely, and accurately. They must place everything wherever the artist or art director has requested.

Other responsibilities of mechanical artists working in advertising agencies might include the following:

- Preparing color overlaying and separations for color advertisements
- Performing tasks of pasteup artists

EMPLOYMENT OPPORTUNITIES

Mechanical artists can find employment in agencies throughout the country. Most jobs are in the cities where most of the larger agencies are located. These include New York, Los Angeles, Dallas, Atlanta, Chicago, Cleveland, and Minneapolis.

EARNINGS

Mechanical artists working in agencies earn between $15,000 and $28,000 annually depending on the artist's experience and responsibilities as well as the agency's size, location, and prestige.

ADVANCEMENT OPPORTUNITIES

Mechanical artists can choose from several paths toward career advancement, depending on their skills and talent. Artists who are experienced and talented in producing mechanicals can locate positions in design studios handling the creation of mechanicals. Some mechanical artists climb the career ladder by becoming lettering artists, sketch artists, or graphic artists. Others become assistant art directors.

EDUCATION AND TRAINING

Training and educational requirements vary from agency to agency. Many agencies require all employees working in the art department to have a college degree. Good choices are a bachelor of fine arts or a four-year degree in commercial art. Some agencies might hire people who have had art school training and can demonstrate creative skills.

EXPERIENCE AND QUALIFICATIONS

In some agencies, the position of mechanical artist is an entry-level job. In others, the candidate must have had some experience working in an agency art department. You can often obtain such experience by working as a paste-up artist.

Mechanical artists need to work well with their hands. The ability to work neatly, accurately, and in a timely fashion is mandatory. The ability to follow instructions precisely is essential.

FOR ADDITIONAL INFORMATION: If you are interested in a career as a mechanical artist, you can obtain more career information by contacting the American Advertising Federation (AAF), the Art Directors Club, Inc. (ADC), the Graphic Artists Guild (GAG), the American Institute of Graphic Arts (AIGA), or the Society of Illustrators (SOI).

TIPS

- Look in the newspaper classified section for jobs advertised under such headings as "Mechanical Artist," "Artist," "Advertising," and "Agencies."

- Develop a good, creative portfolio illustrating your best work. Make it diversified to show your various talents. Although you might not need creativity for this job, a portfolio demonstrating your creativity will show employers that you have talent.

- Send your resume and a cover letter to agencies to see whether they have openings. Make sure that your letter mentions that you have a portfolio available for review.

- Look for internships at advertising agencies. You can also find such internships through college intern programs.

- Join professional trade associations. Many have student memberships. These are useful for making contacts in the advertising industry.

LETTERING ARTIST

JOB DESCRIPTION: *Produce and choose letters and type styles for headlines and logos used in advertisements.*

EARNINGS: *$15,000 to $35,000+ per year.*

RECOMMENDED EDUCATION AND TRAINING: *Training requirements vary.*

SKILLS AND PERSONALITY TRAITS: *The ability to hand letter; drawing and illustration skills; a sense of style, design, and color; computer capability; creativity.*

EXPERIENCE AND QUALIFICATIONS: *Experience requirements vary.*

JOB DESCRIPTION AND RESPONSIBILITIES

Lettering artists are responsible for producing the letters or typefaces used in headlines, logos, and advertisements. Artists might work with computers, electronics, or press type to produce lettering. They might also do hand lettering. To do hand lettering, the lettering artist must have a great deal of talent, as well as a fair amount of creativity and patience. The artist can do hand lettering with an array of ink, paint, pens, and brushes. Lettering created by hand is original and likely to attract more attention than computer-generated lettering.

Hand lettering is exacting work. The artist must use different types of strokes with pens, brushes, and pencils until he or she achieves the desired effect. In most cases, the artist must produce the type in various sizes as well. The lettering artist uses a variety of tools such as rules, triangles, arcs, and T-squares to assist in the production of the finished letters. In addition to working on single letters, the lettering artist must be able to produce script and connecting letters. The artist must also produce letters in a variety of styles such as bold and italics. One of the most sought-after talents of lettering artists is that of calligraphy. This style of lettering produces a flowing, decorative type.

Usually, the lettering artist works together with art directors as well as with the graphic, mechanical, and commercial artists who are developing ads. Together they determine the best typefaces, sizes, and styles to use in ads. As there are hundreds of different typefaces, fonts, and styles, this determination can be quite a job.

Other responsibilities of lettering artists might include the following:

- Getting approval from clients regarding typefaces and styles
- Producing final letters for ads or headlines in ink or paint form
- Pasting letters and words in correct place on ads

EMPLOYMENT OPPORTUNITIES

Employment opportunities for lettering artists are available throughout the country. Most opportunities are in metropolitan areas where there are many advertising agencies. These areas include such cities as New York, Chicago, Los Angeles, Atlanta, and Detroit. Letting artists might work in the following settings:

- Advertising agencies
- Advertising departments of corporations
- Advertising departments of large retail outlets
- Newspapers
- Freelance

EARNINGS

Lettering artists earn between $15,000 and $35,000 or more annually depending on the artist's skills, experience, and responsibilities. Other variables include the prestige, size, and location of the agency or other specific employment setting.

ADVANCEMENT OPPORTUNITIES

Lettering artists can advance their careers by locating similar jobs in larger or more prestigious agencies. Most artists, however, climb the career ladder by becoming sketch, graphic, or commercial artists, depending on their talents and desires.

EDUCATION AND TRAINING

Educational requirements for lettering artists vary from job to job. A high school diploma is usually the minimum requirement for applicants. For some positions, employers prefer or require candidates to hold a four-year art degree or training in commercial art. Also useful are additional courses and workshops in calligraphy and decorative lettering offered by many schools, art societies, colleges, and craft co-ops.

EXPERIENCE AND QUALIFICATIONS

Different positions require different degrees of experience. Some employers do not require any experience at all, as long as the applicant can do the job. Others require a greater degree of experience. Some employers might require a portfolio of work.

Letting artists must be able to work neatly, accurately, and quickly. A knowledge of various typefaces is vital. Lettering artists must also have artistic ability. Computer ability is essential.

FOR ADDITIONAL INFORMATION: If you are interested in learning more about a career as a lettering artist, you should contact the Society of Illustrators (SOI), the American Institute of Graphic Arts (AIGA), or local or statewide calligraphy societies.

TIPS

- Keep a portfolio of lettering work that you have done. Such a portfolio can be helpful in obtaining a job. For the best presentation, make the portfolio creative and diversified.
- Look in the newspaper classified section for jobs advertised under such headings as "Lettering Artist," "Artist," and "Advertising Agency."
- Get experience working on school or local newspapers. Such positions offer you hands-on experience working with different kinds of type.
- Obtain other experience by working at a summer or part-time job for a printer.
- Find and take classes in hand lettering and calligraphy. These arts can make you quite marketable.

PASTEUP ARTIST

JOB DESCRIPTION: *Paste and mount artwork; cut mats and posterboard.*

EARNINGS: *$14,000 to $17,000 per year.*

RECOMMENDED EDUCATION AND TRAINING: *Educational requirements vary.*

SKILLS AND PERSONALITY TRAITS: *The ability to work well with hands; neatness; accuracy.*

EXPERIENCE AND QUALIFICATIONS: *No experience necessary.*

JOB DESCRIPTION AND RESPONSIBILITIES

Pasteup artists usually work in the art departments of ad agencies. Pasteup artist is an entry-level position. The pasteup artist's main responsibility is assisting others in the art department handle things that they are too busy to do. This job requires little, if any, creativity. The pasteup artist is told exactly what to do and how it should be done.

The pasteup artist might work with mechanical artists, lettering artists, sketch artists, graphic artists, and art directors in the agency. Large agencies might assign the pasteup artist to assist one or two individuals. In smaller agencies, the pasteup artist might be responsible for helping anyone in the department who needs assistance. The role of the pasteup artist in the studio, or "bullpen" as it may be called, is often compared to that of an office secretary. Responsibilities can run the gamut from assisting with art work to making coffee, typing a short memo, or answering the telephone.

One of the responsibilities of the pasteup artist is to paste up art work that others in the department have put together. He or she is also expected to mount onto mounting or posterboard drawings, advertisements, storyboards, and so on. The pasteup artist uses special tools and knives to cut posterboard for the artwork produced in the studio. He or she also must measure and properly size drawings. Pasteup artists must be able to follow instructions. The art studios of advertising agencies are busy places, so the pasteup artist must work neatly, accurately, and in a timely fashion.

Other responsibilities of pasteup artists might include the following:

- Bringing finished artwork to other departments and getting preliminary sketches and ideas sheets from others in the office
- Handling office errands
- Collating booklets, pamphlets, and leaflets that the art department has designed

EMPLOYMENT OPPORTUNITIES

Employment opportunities for pasteup artists can be located throughout the country. However, most jobs are in cities where most of the larger agencies are located. These include New York City, Los Angeles, Dallas, Atlanta, Chicago, Cleveland, and Minneapolis.

EARNINGS

Earnings for pasteup artists are usually low, ranging from $14,000 to $17,000 annually. The reason that people search for these jobs is that, although the pay is low, the job often gives them an entry into advertising agencies and experience in the art department.

ADVANCEMENT OPPORTUNITIES

As noted previously, pasteup artist is an entry-level position. Artists who are creative and aggressive can climb the career ladder in several ways. Some pasteup artists do sketches, lettering, or sample ad layouts and show them to the art director. Then when a position opens up, the art director might recommend promotion. Other pasteup artists get experience and move to other agencies as lettering artists, sketch artists, or commercial artists, depending on their skills and interests.

EDUCATION AND TRAINING

Educational and training requirements vary from job to job. Although employers might require no formal training for this particular position, a background in commercial art or a college degree with a major in art is beneficial for moving up the career ladder. Some agencies also prefer or require every individual in the organization to hold a college degree.

EXPERIENCE AND QUALIFICATIONS

Experience is usually not necessary for this job. Pasteup artists should be able to work neatly and precisely with their hands. Knowledge of mounting techniques or the use of cutting knives is helpful but not necessary.

FOR ADDITIONAL INFORMATION: If you are interested in a career in this field, you can get more information by contacting the American Advertising Federation (AAF), the Art Directors Club, Inc. (ADC), or the Society of Illustrators (SOI).

TIPS

- Look in the newspaper classified section for jobs advertised under such headings as "Advertising," "Agencies," "Pasteup Artists," or "Artist."
- Send your resume and a cover letter to agencies to see whether they have openings. Ask the agencies to keep your resume on file if there are no current openings.
- Look for internships at advertising agencies. You might also find such internships through college intern programs.
- Join trade associations to meet others in the field and make important contacts.

CHAPTER 11

Careers for Artists in Fine Arts and Crafts

Fine artists and craftspeople create to satisfy their own need for self-expression. They paint, sketch, and draw. They create beautiful sculptures, pottery, woodwork, fabrics, crafts, and jewelry. There is virtually no limit to what fine artists and craftspeople can accomplish.

Artists and craftspeople might display their work in museums, collections, art galleries, or private homes. Most important, they also sell their work.

Space restrictions make it impossible for this chapter to discuss all possible opportunities. This chapter covers the following careers:

Painter
Sculptor
Potter

Stained Glass Artist
Craftsperson

PAINTER

JOB DESCRIPTION: *Create artwork with oils, watercolors, acrylics, or a combination of media.*

EARNINGS: *Impossible to determine due to the nature of the work.*

RECOMMENDED EDUCATION AND TRAINING: *No formal educational or training requirements.*

SKILLS AND PERSONALITY TRAITS: *Artistic ability; creativity; painting skills; self-motivation; sales ability.*

EXPERIENCE AND QUALIFICATIONS: *No experience required.*

Job Description and Responsibilities

Painters are visual artists. They communicate ideas, thoughts, and feelings using brushes to apply oils, watercolors, acrylics, or a combination of media. Painters work in a two-dimensional plane. They use techniques of shading, perspective, and color mixing in their work. There is no limit to the subject matter that painters select and create. They might paint realistic scenes or create abstract designs. As artists hone their skills, their own special styles often evolve.

Other responsibilities of painters might include the following:

- Purchasing art supplies
- Locating places to sell paintings
- Pricing paintings

Employment Opportunities

Painters can work anywhere in the country, or even the world. They often work independently, choosing whatever subject matter suits them—a portrait, landscape, still life, pets, or other animals. Painters can display and sell their work in the following settings:

- Stores
- Commercial art galleries
- Museums
- Art shows
- Collectors

Earnings

As in most other fine arts careers, determining the earnings of painters is almost impossible. Earnings depend on the number and prices of paintings sold. Prices depend on the painter's popularity and reputation. Painters who sell directly to collectors, stores, galleries, or museums must set their own prices. Commercial galleries can also sell artists' work on consignment, determining in advance the proportion of the sale price that each is to receive. In some cases, artists have agents who sell their work for them.

Advancement Opportunities

Painters advance their careers by establishing a reputation for a particular style in their medium. They then receive more recognition for their work, professionally and monetarily.

Education and Training

Painters in the fine arts are not required to have had any formal training. However, basic training is helpful for honing skills. For some, a simple art class might suffice. For others, a bachelor's or master's degree in fine arts is useful.

EXPERIENCE AND QUALIFICATIONS

Although no experience is needed to become a painter, usually the more experience an artist has, the better his or her skills will be developed. Painters should be artistic, creative people with a need to express themselves.

FOR ADDITIONAL INFORMATION: If you are interested in a career in the fine arts, you should contact the American Artists Professional League (AAPL) and the American Society of Artists (ASA).

TIPS

- Join local art societies to bring you together with others in the field. Many art societies also have galleries that they rent out to their members for showings.

- Contact banks, hospitals, and other public institutions to see whether they might consider displaying your work.

SCULPTOR

JOB DESCRIPTION: *Create three-dimensional artwork using a variety of materials.*

EARNINGS: *Impossible to determine due to the nature of the work.*

RECOMMENDED EDUCATION AND TRAINING: *No formal educational or training requirements.*

SKILLS AND PERSONALITY TRAITS: *Artistic ability; creativity; imagination; enjoyment at working with hands; sculpting skills; knowledge of various media; self-motivation; sales ability.*

EXPERIENCE AND QUALIFICATIONS: *Experience requirements vary.*

JOB DESCRIPTION AND RESPONSIBILITIES

Sculptors are visual artists who create three-dimensional artwork. *Three-dimensional* means that the work is not flat like a piece of paper. The sculptor builds up or shapes the work in some manner. Sculptors work in various media. These can include clay, glass, fabric, wire, plastic, metal, wood, or stone, or a combination of one or more. A sculptor might mold, join, or carve materials to create sculptures.

The subject matter of sculptors is limitless. Sculptures might be large or small depending on the particular artist and what he or she is trying to create. They might be realistic, such as a bust of person, or might be an abstract design.

Other responsibilities of sculptors might include the following:

- Locating places to sell the items that they have created
- Pricing artwork
- Purchasing art supplies

EMPLOYMENT OPPORTUNITIES

Sculptors can create in any location. Sometimes they work at home. At other times, they work in studios. Sculptors can display and sell their work in the following settings:

- Stores
- Art shows
- Collections
- Craft shows
- Commercial art galleries
- Museums

EARNINGS

As in most other fine arts careers, determining the earnings of sculptors is almost impossible. Earnings depend on the number and prices of sculptures sold. Prices depend on the artist's popularity and reputation. Sculptors who sell directly to collectors, stores, galleries, or museums must set their own prices. Commercial galleries can also sell artists' work on consignment, determining ahead of time what percentage of the sale price the sculptor will receive. In some cases, sculptors have agents who sell their work for them.

ADVANCEMENT OPPORTUNITIES

Sculptors and other fine artists advance their careers by establishing professional reputations in their media. Sculptors then receive more professional and popular recognition for their work and increased earnings.

EDUCATION AND TRAINING

Sculptors are not required to have had any formal training. Basic training is often useful for learning and honing skills. Sculptors can obtain such training through art classes in sculpting. A bachelor's or master's degree in fine arts can also be useful.

EXPERIENCE AND QUALIFICATIONS

Sculptors develop their craft through experience. They should be artistic and creative and enjoy working with their hands. The need to express themselves often helps motivate sculptors.

FOR ADDITIONAL INFORMATION: If you are interested in a career in the fine arts, you should contact the American Artists Professional League (AAPL) and the American Society of Artists (ASA).

TIPS

- Consider entering one or more of your pieces in an art competition.
- Join local art societies to bring you together with others in the field. Many art societies also have galleries that they rent to their members for showings.
- Contact banks, hospitals, libraries, and other public institutions to see whether they might consider displaying your work.

POTTER

JOB DESCRIPTION: *Create vases, urns, pitchers and other decorative and functional pieces with clay.*

EARNINGS: *Impossible to determine.*

RECOMMENDED EDUCATION AND TRAINING: *No formal education or training requirements.*

SKILLS AND PERSONALITY TRAITS: *Artistic ability; creativity; enjoyment at working with hands.*

EXPERIENCE AND QUALIFICATIONS: *Prior experience working in clay is helpful.*

JOB DESCRIPTION AND RESPONSIBILITIES

Potters are craftspeople who work with clay and glazes to create decorative and functional art objects. To succeed, potters must create unique, well-made items. A potter might create a line of products ranging from very inexpensive to high-priced. Potters make pieces such as bowls, urns, pitchers, vases, cups, plates, and saucers.

They might also make decorative wall hangings or smaller items such as jewelry or boxes. Potters often conceptualize their ideas and then find ways to bring them to life in clay.

Some potters work with a ball of clay on an electric or manual potter's wheel. They press their thumbs down into the center of the revolving clay to form a hollow area, press on the inside and outside of the clay cylinder, and shape the clay to the desired form and size. They then smooth the surface of the finished piece using rubber scrapers, hands, or wet sponges. Potters might glaze their work in natural colors or paint them before or after firing. Some potters mold clay into shapes instead of using a potter's wheel to create pieces.

After potters create their products, they must find a way to market and sell their wares successfully. Some sell their crafts locally, on a small scale. Others sell on a much larger scale at craft shows, fairs, and exhibitions throughout the country. Potters might wholesale their work to retail outlets or sell them on a consignment basis or through mail order. Some potters sell their creations to stores, shops, and galleries or are commissioned by people to create special pieces.

Other responsibilities of potters might include the following:

- Consulting with clients regarding commissioned work
- Keeping accurate records of business expenses and revenues
- Setting up business books and handling bookkeeping duties
- Filing the required taxes

EMPLOYMENT OPPORTUNITIES

Potters might work full or part time. They can design and create at home or in studios. Potters might display and sell their work in the following settings:

- Stores
- Art shows
- Collections
- Street fairs
- Home sales
- Mail order
- Craft shows
- Commercial art galleries
- Museums
- Flea markets
- Retail outlets

EARNINGS

As in most other fine arts and crafts careers, determining the earnings of potters is almost impossible. Earnings depend on the number and prices of pieces sold. Prices depend on the potter's popularity and reputation. Potters who sell directly to collectors, stores, galleries, or museums must set their own prices. Commercial galleries might also sell artists' work on consignment, determining in advance the percentage of the sale price of each piece that the potter will receive. In some cases, potters have agents who sell their work for them.

ADVANCEMENT OPPORTUNITIES

Potters advance their careers by creating and selling a unique line of items and by obtaining professional recognition in their medium. Some successful potters build their reputation and have their work displayed and sold in galleries or to collectors.

EDUCATION AND TRAINING

Potters are not required to have had any formal training. Basic training is often useful for learning and honing skills. Potters can obtain such training through art or craft classes in clay and pottery. A bachelor's or master's degree in fine arts can also be useful.

EXPERIENCE AND QUALIFICATIONS

Experience creating pottery helps potters hone skills to ensure that their work is acceptable and that they can sell enough work in this craft to earn a living. Potters must know the necessary techniques for crafting pottery. They should be creative, artistic, and imaginative. Business and marketing skills are also necessary for selling the potter's work.

FOR ADDITIONAL INFORMATION: If you are interested in a career in the fine arts, you can obtain additional information by contacting the American Artists Professional League (AAPL), the American Society of Artists (ASA), and the American Craft Council (ACC).

TIPS

- Take classes and workshops in pottery to hone skills and make contacts with others who have similar interests.
- Consider entering one or more of your pieces in an art competition.
- Join local art societies to bring you together with others in the field.
- Many art societies also have galleries that they rent out to their members for showings.
- Contact banks, hospitals, and other public institutions to see whether they might consider displaying your work.
- Remember to contact your state sales tax department to see what regulations are necessary to go into business in your location.
- Visit craft shows and fairs to get ideas on displaying your work.
- To help limit operational and selling expenses when first starting your business, consider craft shows in your area.
- As your business expands, look for larger shows in other marketing areas.

STAINED GLASS ARTIST

JOB DESCRIPTION: *Design and create stained glass designs and artwork.*

EARNINGS: *Impossible to determine.*

RECOMMENDED EDUCATION AND TRAINING: *No formal education or training is required.*

SKILLS AND PERSONALITY TRAITS: *Artistic ability; creativity; enjoyment at working with hands; a sense of color and balance.*

EXPERIENCE AND QUALIFICATIONS: *Prior experience working in stained glass is helpful.*

JOB DESCRIPTION AND RESPONSIBILITIES

Stained glass artists are craftspeople who work with glass and leading to create art objects and other decorative pieces. They create stained glass designs and artwork for display and profit. To succeed, stained glass artists must create unique, well-made items that are either novel or necessary. Artists in this field usually create a line of products ranging from very inexpensive to high-priced. In this manner, they can attract a variety of buyers. Stained glass artists might design large stained glass pieces such as windows, mirrors, and wall hangings. They might also craft smaller items such as jewelry, boxes, or sun catchers. Stained glass artists conceptualize their ideas and then find ways to bring them to fruition in glass. After coming up with an idea, they must cut the glass, paint or stain it, assemble pieces, and lead and solder the whole object.

After creating their products, stained glass artists must find a way to market and sell their wares successfully. Some sell their crafts locally on a small scale. Others sell on a much larger scale at craft shows, fairs, and exhibitions throughout the country. Some artists wholesale their work to retail outlets. Others sell them on a consignment basis or through mail order. Successful stained glass artists might sell to stores, shops, and galleries or be commissioned to create special-order, custom pieces.

Other responsibilities of stained glass artists might include the following:

- Consulting with clients regarding commissioned work
- Keeping accurate records of business expenses and revenues
- Setting up business books and handling bookkeeping duties
- Filing required taxes

EMPLOYMENT OPPORTUNITIES

Stained glass artists might work full- or part-time. Artists can create in any location. Some design and create stained glass pieces at home, whereas others create in studios. Stained glass artists might display and sell their work in the following settings:

- Stores
- Art shows
- Collections
- Street fairs
- Home sales
- Mail order
- Craft shows
- Commercial art galleries
- Museums
- Flea markets
- Retail outlets

EARNINGS

As in most other fine arts and crafts careers, determining the earnings of stained glass artists is almost impossible. Earnings depend on the number and prices of pieces sold. Prices depend on the artist's popularity and reputation. Artists who sell directly to collectors, stores, galleries, or museums must set their own prices. Commercial galleries might also sell an artist's work on consignment, determining in advance the percentage of the sale price that each party will receive. In some cases, stained glass artists have agents who sell their work for them. Stained glass artists might also sell their work at craft shows or other types of outlets. Earnings in these cases depend on the prices and number of pieces sold.

ADVANCEMENT OPPORTUNITIES

Some stained glass artists move up the career ladder by creating and selling a unique line of items. Others can advance their careers by obtaining professional recognition in their medium and having their work displayed and sold in galleries or to collectors.

EDUCATION AND TRAINING

Stained glass artists are not required to have had any formal training. Basic training is often useful for learning and honing skills. Artists can obtain such training by taking art or craft classes in stained glass. A bachelor's or master's degree in fine arts can also be useful.

EXPERIENCE AND QUALIFICATIONS

Experience creating stained glass items will help aspiring artists hone skills. Stained glass artists must have a knowledge of glass cutting, painting, leading, and soldering techniques. Artists in this line of work should be creative, artistic, and imaginative. Business and marketing skills are also necessary for selling the stained glass pieces.

FOR ADDITIONAL INFORMATION: If you are interested in a career in fine arts, you can obtain additional information by contacting the American Artists Professional League (AAPL), the American Society of Artists (ASA), and the American Craft Council (ACC).

TIPS

- Take classes and workshops in stained glass to hone skills and make contacts with others who have similar interests.
- Consider entering one or more of your pieces in an art competition.
- Join local art societies to bring you together with others in the field. Many art societies also have galleries that they rent out to their members for showings.
- Contact banks, hospitals, and other public institutions to see whether they might consider displaying your work.
- Remember to contact your state sales tax department to see what regulations you must meet to go into business in your area.
- Visit craft shows and fairs to get ideas on displaying your work.
- To help limit operational and selling expenses when first starting your business, consider craft shows in your area.
- As your business expands, look for larger shows in other areas.

CRAFTSPERSON

JOB DESCRIPTION: *Develop, design, and make crafts or artwork.*

EARNINGS: *Impossible to determine due to the nature of the job.*

RECOMMENDED EDUCATION AND TRAINING: *No formal training is required.*

SKILLS AND PERSONALITY TRAITS: *Creativity; artistic ability; business aptitude.*

EXPERIENCE AND QUALIFICATIONS: *Sales experience is helpful; most states require a certificate of authority to collect sales tax.*

JOB DESCRIPTION AND RESPONSIBILITIES

Craftspeople develop, design, and make crafts. They sell their work for profit. Craftspeople might work with a variety of materials. These include fabric, clay, metal, wood, plastic, glass, paint, and paper. Craftspeople might create jewelry, dolls, quilts, clothes, accessories, housewares, sculpture, wall hangings, or a multitude of items.

To succeed, craftspeople must create unique, well-made items that are either novel or necessary. These artists usually create a line of products ranging from inexpensive to high-priced. In this manner, they can attract a variety of buyers. After creating their products, craftspeople must find a way to market and sell their wares successfully. Some sell their crafts on a small scale. They might sell to friends, relatives, and colleagues with whom they work. Others sell on a much larger scale at craft shows, fairs, and exhibitions throughout the country. Some craftspeople wholesale their crafts to retail outlets. Others sell them on a consignment basis or through mail order. Some craftspeople open up their own craft stores, shops, or galleries.

Craftspeople must attend to a variety of business functions. For example, they must make sure that they comply with any local, state, and federal laws and regulations. They must find the best prices on materials, supplies, and equipment. Craftspeople are also expected to price their crafts so must keep abreast of competition and the marketplace.

Other responsibilities of craftspeople might include the following:

- Keeping accurate records of business expenses and revenues
- Setting up business books and handling bookkeeping duties
- Filing required taxes

EMPLOYMENT OPPORTUNITIES

The crafting business has turned into an alluring home business. This is because craftspeople can start up a business with very little money while doing something that they enjoy. Crafting is an ideal business for those who need to earn an extra income, for retired persons, and for those craftspeople who want to be near their children while working. Craftspeople might create almost any type of product. The ability to sell the product depends on the public's response to it. Craftspeople might sell in a variety of settings, including the following:

- Craft shows put on by schools, churches, synagogues, hospitals, and other not-for-profit organizations
- Craft shows, fairs, and exhibitions put on by professional promoters
- Street fairs
- Flea markets
- Home sales
- Retail outlets
- Mail order

EARNINGS

Because of the nature of the job, determining the earnings of craftspeople is impossible. Earnings depend, to a great extent, on the type of crafts that the craftsperson creates. Earnings also depend on the sales ability and marketing skills of the craftsperson and the amount of time that he or she puts into the business.

ADVANCEMENT OPPORTUNITIES

Craftspeople advance their careers by obtaining large wholesale orders or by creating and marketing higher-priced crafts. Some craftspeople climb the craft career ladder by being invited to participate in more prestigious, juried craft shows.

EDUCATION AND TRAINING

There are no formal educational requirements to become a craftsperson. Many people, however, take classes and workshops in various areas of crafts to learn new techniques and to hone skills. Classes in marketing, business, and sales are also useful.

EXPERIENCE AND QUALIFICATIONS

Craftspeople might be required to have a certificate of authority to collect sales tax in states in which they sell products. You can usually obtain such a certificate by contacting the department of taxation in each state in which you are selling. Craftspeople should be creative, artistic people with good marketing and business skills.

FOR ADDITIONAL INFORMATION: Craftspeople can learn more about this field by contacting their local art and craft guilds and the American Craft Council (ACC).

TIPS

- Visit craft shows and fairs to get ideas on displaying your work.
- Take classes and workshops in your craft field to hone skills and to make contacts with others who have similar interests.
- Take classes in marketing and small business management.
- Remember to contact your state sales tax department to see what regulations you must follow to go into business in your area.
- To help limit operational and selling expenses when first starting your business, consider craft shows in your area.
- As your business expands, look for larger shows in other areas.

CHAPTER 12

Careers for Artists in Teaching

Much of our individual success is based on education, training, and continued learning experiences. To many, teaching their love of art to others is the best possible job.

Artists might teach art classes in public, private, or parochial schools as well as at colleges and universities and in a wide variety of other settings. Art teachers might instruct classes for persons of all ages—from young children to senior citizens.

Space restrictions make it impossible for this chapter to discuss all possible opportunities. This chapter covers the following careers:

Elementary School Art Teacher
Secondary School Art Teacher
Craft Instructor

ELEMENTARY SCHOOL ART TEACHER

JOB DESCRIPTION: *Teach elementary students art skills; develop ideas for classes.*

EARNINGS: *$20,000 to $55,000+ per year.*

RECOMMENDED EDUCATION AND TRAINING: *Bachelor's degree in art education; some schools require additional education for permanent certification.*

SKILLS AND PERSONALITY TRAITS: *Enjoy working with children; teaching ability; communications skills; art skills; patience; creativity; organization.*

EXPERIENCE AND QUALIFICATIONS: *Student teaching and certification are usually required.*

JOB DESCRIPTION AND RESPONSIBILITIES

Elementary school art teachers teach art skills to elementary school children. Duties vary depending on the specific school and the ages and grades that the teacher teaches.

Planning activities for kindergarten children is quite different from planning art activities for third or fourth grade students. For example, very young children might learn about color and shapes. Older children might learn about working in various media such as paper, clay, and paint.

Art teachers, like all other teachers, usually follow guidelines regarding what they teach students. The school, the state, or the district in which the teacher works might set these guidelines.

Art teachers find ways to teach art skills that children will find fun. In this way, they hope to develop in the students a lifelong interest in art. Good elementary art teachers are creative and enthusiastic. They come up with unique ways of teaching so that children are motivated. For example, a teacher might have the class make holiday gifts using various media.

Art teachers learn a great many teaching methods during their semesters as student teachers. Student teaching gives aspiring art teachers a chance to obtain hands-on training while still under supervision.

Art teachers are usually evaluated after a certain number of years in which they work in a specific school system. If the school feels that a teacher is effective, he or she can receive tenure. *Tenure* means that the school system cannot fire the teacher under normal circumstances.

Other responsibilities of elementary school art teachers might include the following:

- Meeting with parents to discuss their children's talent
- Planning activities for classroom work
- Ordering art materials
- Working on extracurricular art activities in the school

EMPLOYMENT OPPORTUNITIES

Elementary school art teachers can find employment opportunities throughout the country. Some, however, might have to relocate to obtain a job.

Potential employment settings include the following:

- Public schools
- Parochial schools
- Private schools

EARNINGS

Elementary school art teachers earn between $20,000 and $55,000 or more annually, depending on the school's type, size, location, and prestige as well as the teacher's education, experience, and responsibilities.

ADVANCEMENT OPPORTUNITIES

Elementary school art teachers can advance their careers in several ways. School teachers receive salary increments as they obtain more experience and education. Some teachers find similar positions in larger or more prestigious school districts. Others advance by becoming department heads.

EDUCATION AND TRAINING

The minimum requirement is a bachelor's degree in education or art education. Usually education students must take a semester of student teaching while still in school.

Many school districts require their teachers to have or to obtain a master's degree.

EXPERIENCE AND QUALIFICATIONS

Elementary school art teachers usually must be certified or licensed in the state in which they work.

Art teachers must enjoy working with young people. The ability to teach is mandatory. Art skills in various media are also necessary. Elementary school art teachers must be creative, innovative, and imaginative.

FOR ADDITIONAL INFORMATION: If you are interested in seeking a career in this field, you can get additional information from the National Educators Association (NEA) or the National Federation of Teachers (NFT).

TIPS

- Look in the newspaper classified section for positions advertised under such headings as "Teacher," "Art Teacher," "Elementary School Teacher," or "Education."
- Check your college placement office for notices of teacher openings at schools.
- Remember to get letters of recommendation from several of your professors at school as well as from your student teaching supervisor.
- Try to get positions in summer school. They are often easier to obtain and can help you get your foot in the door.

SECONDARY SCHOOL ART TEACHER

JOB DESCRIPTION: *Teach secondary students art skills; develop ideas for classes.*

EARNINGS: *$20,000 to $55,000+ per year.*

RECOMMENDED EDUCATION AND TRAINING: *A bachelor's degree in education or art education; some schools require additional education for permanent certification.*

SKILLS AND PERSONALITY TRAITS: *Enjoy working with young people; teaching ability; communications skills; art skills; patience; creativity; organization.*

EXPERIENCE AND QUALIFICATIONS: *Student teaching and certification are usually required.*

JOB DESCRIPTION AND RESPONSBILITIES

Secondary school art teachers teach art skills to junior high school or high school students. Specific duties vary depending on the school and the size of the art department.

Although teachers usually follow a mandated curriculum, they are required to develop activities for each class and to decide how to teach each subject. They must plan interesting, inspiring lessons to make learning a positive experience.

Most art classes in secondary schools involve students' learning art techniques and then trying them in hands-on activities. Students might learn to use oil paints, water colors, pastels, and other media. They might then create pictures using the various media. In many schools, the art teacher is responsible for coordinating student art shows with work that students have created using art skills learned in the classroom.

Art teachers learn many teaching methods for classroom use during their student teaching. Aspiring teachers undergo student teaching programs while still in college. Such programs give the student teachers a chance to obtain hands-on training under supervision.

Art teachers are usually evaluated after a certain number of years of work in a specific school system. If the school feels that the teacher is good, he or she might receive tenure. With tenure, the teacher cannot be fired from the school system under normal circumstances.

Other responsibilities of secondary school art teachers might include the following:

- Attending parent-teacher conferences
- Grading work
- Nurturing special talent in students
- Ordering art materials
- Working on extracurricular art activities in the school

EMPLOYMENT OPPORTUNITIES

Secondary school art teachers can find employment opportunities throughout the country. Some, however, might have to relocate to obtain a job.

Employment settings include the following:

- Public schools
- Private schools
- Parochial schools

EARNINGS

Secondary school art teachers earn between $20,000 and $55,000 or more annually depending on the school's type, size, location, and prestige as well as the teacher's education, experience, and responsibilities.

ADVANCEMENT OPPORTUNITIES

Secondary school art teachers can advance their careers in several ways. Teachers receive salary increments as they obtain more experience and education. Some teachers find similar positions in larger or more prestigious school districts. Others advance by becoming department heads.

EDUCATION AND TRAINING

The minimum requirement is a bachelor's degree in education or art education. Usually education students must take a semester of student teaching while still in school.

Many school districts require teachers to have or to obtain a master's degree.

EXPERIENCE AND QUALIFICATIONS

Secondary school art teachers usually must be certified or licensed in the state in which they work.

Art teachers must enjoy working with young people. The ability to teach is mandatory. Art skills in various media are also necessary. Secondary school art teachers must be creative, innovative, and imaginative.

FOR ADDITIONAL INFORMATION: If you are interested in seeking a career in this field, you can obtain additional information from the National Educators Association (NEA) or the National Federation of Teachers (NFT).

TIPS

- Look in the newspaper classified section for positions advertised under such headings as "Teacher," "Art Teacher," "Secondary School Teacher," or "Education."

- Check your college placement office for notices of teacher openings at schools.
- Remember to get letters of recommendation from several of your professors at school as well as from your student teaching supervisor.
- Seek positions in summer school. These positions are often easier to obtain and can help you get your foot in the door.

CRAFT INSTRUCTOR

JOB DESCRIPTION: *Teach craft skills to others.*

EARNINGS: *Difficult to determine due to the nature of the job.*

RECOMMENDED EDUCATION AND TRAINING: *No formal education is required.*

SKILLS AND PERSONALITY TRAITS: *Teaching ability; artistic skill; creativity; enjoyment at working with others; communication skills; patience.*

EXPERIENCE AND QUALIFICATIONS: *Experience requirements vary.*

JOB DESCRIPTION AND RESPONSBILITIES

Crafts are becoming a big industry. People enjoy buying handcrafted items and many more try their hand at creating crafts themselves. Craft instructors teach a wide variety of arts and crafts classes. The crafts taught include toling, woodworking, stenciling, soft sculpture, pottery, jewelry making, sculpting, painting, basket making, and floral arrangement.

Many people take classes, courses, seminars, or workshops not only to learn new skills, but to enhance their quality of life. Others want to pursue a new hobby or learn more about a craft so that they can start their own home businesses.

Craft classes can be any length. Some are limited to a single hour; others continue on a weekly basis for a specified amount of time. The instructors determine how much time is needed to teach a particular craft subject.

Craft instructors must develop the course that they teach. They must prepare an outline to define for both themselves and their potential students what the course will cover. They must be experts in their specific areas.

Other responsibilities of craft instructors might include the following:

- Ordering materials
- Finding potential students
- Answering students' questions

EMPLOYMENT OPPORTUNITIES

Craft instructors can find employment opportunities throughout the country. They might work full- or part-time. Possible employment settings include:

- Continuing education programs
- Craft stores
- Fabric and notion stores
- Community colleges
- Self-employment

EARNINGS

Determining the earnings of craft instructors is difficult. Some might be paid an hourly wage or be compensated by the number of students in the class. Sometimes instructors are paid a flat fee for teaching a class. Hourly rates range from $6 to $25 or more depending on the specific employment setting.

ADVANCEMENT OPPORTUNITIES

Craft instructors can advance their careers by finding similar positions teaching in larger or more prestigious locations. They might also develop followings and be compensated with higher rates for each class.

EDUCATION AND TRAINING

There are no formal educational or training requirements for craft instructors. They should know as much as possible about their specific crafts.

EXPERIENCE AND QUALIFICATIONS

Craft instructors must be able to teach others skills with which they are familiar. They should be articulate and have good communication skills.

FOR ADDITIONAL INFORMATION: For more information about this career, contact the American Craft Council (ACC) as well as local art and craft guilds.

TIPS

- Check the newspaper classified section for positions advertised under such headings as "Craft Instructor," "Crafts," "Instructor," and "Craft Teacher."
- Speak to managers of variety stores selling craft material to see if they might be interested in having you teach one or more courses.
- Consider setting up your own home-instruction craft business.

CHAPTER 13

Miscellaneous Careers for Artists

Careers in art cover a broad spectrum. This chapter discusses several careers that do not fit into the specific categories defined in previous chapters of this book.

This chapter covers the following careers:

Medical Illustrator
Conservator—Museum
Art Therapist
Fashion Illustrator

Photographer
Fashion Copyist
Police Sketch Artist

MEDICAL ILLUSTRATOR

JOB DESCRIPTION: *Illustrate human anatomy and surgical procedures with drawings.*

EARNINGS: *$20,000 to $75,000+ per year.*

RECOMMENDED EDUCATION AND TRAINING: *Educational requirements vary.*

SKILLS AND PERSONALITY TRAITS: *Drawing and illustration skills; artistic ability; full knowledge of human and animal anatomy.*

EXPERIENCE AND QUALIFICATIONS: *Experience is required; a portfolio is necessary.*

JOB DESCRIPTION AND RESPONSIBILITIES

Medical illustrators are technical artists. They combine their artistic skills with a knowledge of biological sciences. Medical illustrators are responsible for drawing illustrations of various medical subject matter. Medical illustrators might be required to do line drawings or full-color renderings of medical illustrations. These illustrations might be used in medical publications, journals, or textbooks. Some medical illustrators do drawings for audiovisual presentations used in teaching. Medical illustrators also prepare drawings used in court to demonstrate various exhibits in medical trials. Medical illustrators do their work in a variety of media. In addition to doing hand drawings and sketches, medical illustrators also use computers.

Other responsibilities of medical illustrators might include the following:

- Performing research to understand an illustration assignment
- Collaborating with physicians to illustrate medical techniques
- Observing medical procedures prior to illustrating them

EMPLOYMENT OPPORTUNITIES

Medical illustrators might freelance or be employed in several settings, including the following:

- Large teaching hospitals
- Medical schools, universities, and other large educational institutions
- Publishers of medical books
- Attorneys

EARNINGS

Earnings for medical illustrators range from $20,000 to $75,000 or more. Factors affecting earnings include the illustrator's experience, responsibilities, and talent. Other variables include whether the illustrator is employed full time and, if not, how much freelance work he or she obtains each year.

ADVANCEMENT OPPORTUNITIES

Medical illustrators can advance their careers by locating positions in larger or more prestigious institutions. Some illustrators climb the career ladder by obtaining more freelance opportunities illustrating medical books and teaching texts.

EDUCATION AND TRAINING

Educational requirements for medical illustrators vary. Employers usually prefer a master's degree in medical illustration. For some positions, however, employers accept a bachelor's degree combining art and pre-med courses.

EXPERIENCE AND QUALIFICATIONS

Medical illustrators usually must show a portfolio of their work before being hired. They must have drawing and illustration skills as well as artistic ability. Medical illustrators must have a thorough knowledge of living organisms, of surgical and medical procedures, and of human and animal anatomy.

FOR ADDITIONAL INFORMATION: Aspiring medical illustrators can learn more about this career by contacting the Association of Medical Illustrators (AMI).

TIPS

- Check your college placement office for openings. Only a few schools offer this type of degree, so employers looking for a medical illustrator often contact the colleges directly.
- Consider sending your resume and a cover letter to medical publishers, teaching hospitals, and so on.
- Check medical publishers for freelance opportunities.
- Look in the classified section of newspapers for jobs advertised under such headings as "Medical Illustrator," "Medical Artist," "Technical Illustrator," or "Illustrator."
- Start now developing a portfolio of your work illustrating your skills. As noted previously, employers usually require candidates to submit a portfolio.

CONSERVATOR—MUSEUM

JOB DESCRIPTION: *Oversee, manage, examine, and preserve works of art; document status of art work; restore art work.*

EARNINGS: *$25,000 to $60,000+ per year.*

RECOMMENDED EDUCATION AND TRAINING: *Bachelor's degree in art history; graduate degree in conservation.*

SKILLS AND PERSONALITY TRAITS: *Painting and drawing skills; artistic skills; technical and science skills; writing skills.*

EXPERIENCE AND QUALIFICATIONS: *An apprenticeship or work experience is usually required.*

JOB DESCRIPTION AND RESPONSIBILTIES

Art museums purchase, collect, and exhibit works of art. Conservators are responsible for overseeing, managing, and preserving these works of art.

Conservators might have a variety of responsibilities. When art comes into the museum, conservators are expected to uncrate it. They might then photograph the art to document the piece and its condition on arrival. Conservators then examine each piece of art to determine its status. They might be expected to clean the work in a prescribed manner. In some cases, the art work has deteriorated. Conservators might take various steps to restore the work of art to its original status. These steps might include structural repair or retouching.

Art work is often quite fragile and must be kept under specific types of conditions. The conservator must make sure that each piece is kept at the proper humidity, the correct temperature, and under the correct lighting. These factors might differ depending on the types of artwork involved. An exhibit of watercolors differs in treatment from photographs or sculptures. The conservator is responsible for ensuring that works of art are properly stored and maintained. Many museums lend collections of artwork. Conservators might be responsible for determining which of a museum's pieces are fit for travel.

Other responsibilities of conservators might include the following:

- Writing reports on art objects to substantiate the condition of pieces
- Determining conditions under which artwork can be exhibited
- Working with specialists in specific types of art objects

EMPLOYMENT OPPORTUNITIES

Opportunities for conservators are greatest in culturally active cities that have many art museums. These include New York City, Los Angeles, Washington, DC, Boston, Chicago, Seattle, and Atlanta.

EARNINGS

Earnings for conservators range from $25,000 to $60,000 or more depending on the conservator's experience, training, responsibilities, and professional reputation. Other factors affecting earnings include the specific employment setting and its geographic location.

ADVANCEMENT OPPORTUNITIES

Conservators can advance their careers by obtaining experience and being promoted to supervisory positions. Others climb the career ladder by locating similar positions in more prestigious facilities.

EDUCATION AND TRAINING

You need a great deal of education to become a conservator. Employers usually look for applicants who hold an undergraduate degree in science or art and a master's degree in conservation. In the United States, there are only a few graduate programs in this field. To gain entry into one of these programs, you must have a background in studio art, art history, and chemistry. The graduate program lasts from three to four years including an internship. An alternative method of entering this profession is through an apprenticeship program. These are available through museums, not-for-profit organizations, and private-practice conservators. Aspiring conservators entering the field through such programs must also take courses in art history, studio art, and chemistry.

EXPERIENCE AND QUALIFICATIONS

To gain employment, an aspiring conservator must usually have a substantial amount of practical work experience. Some people obtain this experience through an apprenticeship program. Others work in museums while completing their formal education.

Conservators should enjoy working around objects of art. They need to have artistic ability as well as technical and scientific skills. Those working in museums should also have good writing skills and strong interpersonal skills so that they can get along with others in the museum.

FOR ADDITIONAL INFORMATION: If you are interested in a career as a conservator, you can get additional information by contacting the American Institute for Conservation of Historic and Artistic Works (AICHAW).

TIPS

- Take continuing education programs to keep up with developments in the field. Programs are often available through archival, historical, and curatorial associations.
- Get the best education possible. In this field, the most qualified candidates are the most marketable ones.
- Look in the classified section of newspapers published in areas where there are art museums. Look for positions advertised under such headings as "Conservator," "Art," "Museum," and "Art Museums."
- Also check trade journals for advertised jobs.
- Prepare to relocate to find a position.
- Be sure to contact your college's placement office to see whether it has any information about openings in this field.

ART THERAPIST

JOB DESCRIPTION: *Use art to treat disabilities in patients; develop courses of action for patients.*

EARNINGS: *$18,000 to $45,000+ per year.*

RECOMMENDED EDUCATION AND TRAINING: *A bachelor's degree in art therapy; a master's degree might be required.*

SKILLS AND PERSONALITY TRAITS: *Art skills; creativity; sensitivity; compassion; emotional stability.*

EXPERIENCE AND QUALIFICATIONS: *An apprenticeship in art therapy.*

JOB DESCRIPTION AND RESPONSIBILITIES

Art therapists use art activities to treat patients. Patients who might be helped by art include those with physical, mental, or emotional disabilities. Art therapists work with ill and injured patients to help restore health. Often, art therapy helps break through to a patient when no other therapy or treatment has worked. Art therapy can help patients build their confidence, bring back memories from the past, or develop a sense of accomplishment. Expressing feelings creatively often helps patients feel better about themselves and their problems.

Art therapists begin by assessing the patient's needs. They are then expected to develop a course of action using a variety of art activities. They must determine the type of art to use with each patient. Art therapists use their art skills to assist patients in communicating their feelings. Therapists might use painting, drawing, coloring, crafting, or sculpting to help patients feel better about themselves. In some cases, an art therapist might work with a patient on a one-to-one basis. In other cases, the therapist works with a group of patients together.

Other responsibilities of art therapists might include the following:

- Meeting with the patient's family
- Conferring with the patient's health-care team
- Ordering materials

EMPLOYMENT OPPORTUNITIES

Art therapists can find jobs throughout the country. They might work full or part time. Art therapists might work in the following settings:

- Hospitals
- Schools
- Health-care facilities
- Rehabilitation centers

- Nursing homes
- Private practice

- Extended care facilities
- Independent expressive arts therapy centers

EARNINGS

Annual earnings for art therapists range from $18,000 to $45,000 or more. Factors affecting earnings include the therapist's experience, education, and responsibilities. Other variables include the specific job setting and geographic location as well as the facility's size and prestige.

ADVANCEMENT OPPORTUNITIES

Art therapists can advance their careers by obtaining experience and locating similar positions at larger or more prestigious facilities. Therapists can also obtain additional training and climb the career ladder by moving into supervisory positions. Some art therapists strike out on their own and open private practices.

EDUCATION AND TRAINING

A bachelor's degree in art therapy is the minimum required for this position. Art therapy programs include courses in fine arts as well as in theory and practice of art therapy and behavioral and social sciences. Some employers might require a master's degree.

EXPERIENCE AND QUALIFICATIONS

Art therapists are required to obtain experience through an internship taken as part of the art therapy degree. Art therapists must have a knowledge of a multitude of art activities. They should be creative and imaginative. It is critical that art therapists have the ability to work with those who are physically, mentally, or emotionally disabled.

FOR ADDITIONAL INFORMATION: To learn more about career opportunities in this field, contact the American Art Therapy Association (AATA).

TIPS

- Check whether your college placement office knows of openings.
- Send your resume and a cover letter to hospitals, long-term care facilities, and schools to see whether they have openings.
- Get experience by volunteering to give art classes at skilled nursing

- Get experience by volunteering to give art classes at skilled nursing units of hospitals and health-care facilities.
- Look in the classified section of newspapers for jobs advertised under such headings as "Art Therapist," "Health Care," "Therapist," "Education," "Long Term Care," and "Schools."

FASHION ILLUSTRATOR

JOB DESCRIPTION: *Draw illustrations of women's, men's, and children's clothing and accessories.*

EARNINGS: *$20,000 to $65,000+ per year.*

RECOMMENDED EDUCATION AND TRAINING: *Educational requirements vary.*

SKILLS AND PERSONALITY TRAITS: *Drawing and illustration skills; artistic ability.*

EXPERIENCE AND QUALIFICATIONS: *Experience is required; a portfolio is necessary.*

JOB DESCRIPTION AND RESPONSIBILITIES

Fashion illustrators are visual artists. They draw illustrations of women's, men's, and children's clothing and accessories. Fashion illustrators might also render drawings of complementary articles and backgrounds. Fashion illustrators use a variety of media to do their work. In addition to doing hand drawings and sketches, some use computers to create illustrations. Fashion illustrators might be required to do line drawings or full-color renderings of fashions. These illustrations might be used in newspapers, magazines, or other visual media. Illustrations might also be used in design houses and advertisements.

Other responsibilities of fashion illustrators might include the following:

- Attending fashion shows to illustrate new trends in clothing
- Collaborating with fashion designers to illustrate apparel

EMPLOYMENT OPPORTUNITIES

Fashion illustrators might freelance or be employed in a number of settings, such as the following:

- Design houses
- Magazines
- Newspapers
- Advertising agencies

EARNINGS

Earnings for fashion illustrators range from $20,000 to $65,000 or more. Factors affecting earnings include the illustrator's experience, responsibilities, and talent, and whether the illustrator works full time or freelances. The amount of work that a freelance illustrator can obtain also influences earnings.

ADVANCEMENT OPPORTUNUTIES

Fashion illustrators can advance their careers by locating positions in larger or more prestigious companies. Some illustrators climb the career ladder by obtaining more freelance opportunities.

EDUCATION AND TRAINING

Educational requirements for fashion illustrators vary from job to job. Two- and four-year programs in fashion design and fashion illustration are available in colleges and universities throughout the country. Vocational, technical, and trade schools also offer programs in fashion illustration.

EXPERIENCE AND QUALIFICATIONS

Employers usually require candidates to show a portfolio of their work. The portfolio demonstrates the fashion illustrator's talent and skill. Fashion illustrators must have drawing and illustration skills as well as artistic ability. An understanding of the fashion industry is useful.

FOR ADDITIONAL INFORMATION: Aspiring fashion illustrators can learn more about this career by contacting the Society of Illustrators (SOI), The Fashion Association (TFA), the Council of Fashion Designers of America (CFDA), the American Apparel Manufacturers Association (AAMA), and the National Association of Schools of Art and Design (NASAD).

TIPS

- Check your college placement office for openings. Few schools offer this type of degree, so employers looking for a fashion illustrator often contact the colleges directly.
- Consider sending your resume and a cover letter to design houses, manufacturing firms, department stores, newspapers, magazines, and advertising agencies.

- Look in the classified section of newspapers for jobs advertised under such headings as "Fashion Illustrator," "Fashion Artist," or "Illustrator."
- Start now developing a portfolio of your work demonstrating your skills.

PHOTOGRAPHER

JOB DESCRIPTION: *Take photographs of various subjects.*

EARNINGS: *Impossible to determine due to the nature of the job.*

RECOMMENDED EDUCATION AND TRAINING: *Requirements vary.*

SKILLS AND PERSONALITY TRAITS: *Artistic ability; manual dexterity; technical understanding of photographic techniques.*

EXPERIENCE AND QUALIFICATIONS: *Experience requirements vary.*

JOB DESCRIPTION AND RESPONSIBILITIES

Photographers take pictures with still cameras. They use color or black-and-white film and a wide variety of photographic accessories. Responsibilities vary depending on the type of photography required.

Some photographers specialize in commercial photography. This might include taking pictures at weddings, bar mitzvahs, or other events. Commercial photographers might also specialize in portrait photography. These photographers take photos of individuals or groups of people or pets. Photographers often work in their own studios. Other photographers specialize in photojournalism, taking pictures for newspapers, magazines, or other types of publications.

Other photographers take artistic photos, using photography as an art medium. This type of photography emphasizes self-expression and creativity. Good photographers do not just point a camera at a subject and shoot a picture, but compose pictures by choosing the subject and achieving desired effects through careful presentation. Photographers often use technical accessories to create specific effects. They use lights, lenses, special film, and unusual camera settings to achieve different visual results.

Other responsibilities of photographers might include the following:

- Scheduling appointments to photograph subjects
- Developing and printing their own photographs
- Handling business functions if self-employed

EMPLOYMENT OPPORTUNITIES

Photographers can find employment opportunities throughout the country. Photographers might specialize in the following areas:

- Photojournalism
- Commercial photography
- Industrial photography
- Art photography
- Portrait photography
- Editorial photography
- Scientific photography

EARNINGS

Earnings for photographers are difficult to determine due to the nature of the job. Many photographers are self-employed. Earnings depend on the type and amount of work as well as on geographic location and professional reputation. Full-time photojournalists can earn between $18,000 and $65,000 or more annually. Photographers working in other fields might have similar salaries.

ADVANCEMENT OPPORTUNITIES

Advancement for photographers depends to a great extent on individual talent. Photographers who work for others might climb the career ladder by striking out and starting their own businesses. Others find positions as photographers in larger companies or are offered more prestigious photography assignments.

EDUCATION AND TRAINING

Some photographers are self-taught. For many positions, a basic course in photography can be useful. Basic courses are often offered in vocational or technical schools, trade schools, community colleges, four-year colleges and universities, and private trade and technical schools. Although most colleges do not offer majors in photography, a college degree can be useful. Good majors include liberal arts, communications, or journalism.

EXPERIENCE AND QUALIFICATIONS

Experience requirements for photographers vary. Some employers might hire an applicant if he or she can demonstrate the ability to take good photographs. Others might require a portfolio.

Photographers must be artistic, creative, and imaginative. The ability to enable subjects to relax in front of the camera is also essential. Self-employed photographers also need business skills.

FOR ADDITIONAL INFORMATION: Aspiring photographers can obtain additional career information by contacting the Professional Photographers of America, Inc. (PPA), the American Society of Media Photographers (ASMP), and the Eastman Kodak Information Center.

TIPS

- Look in the newspaper classified section for positions advertised under such headings as "Photographer," "Photojournalist," "Commercial Photographer," and "Photography Studio."
- Get experience by taking pictures for your school newspaper.
- Check local weeklies for advertised openings for part-time or freelance photographers.
- Put together a portfolio of your photographs to bring to interviews.

FASHION COPYIST

JOB DESCRIPTION: *Gathers information on trends in fashion; sketches garments of competitors.*

EARNINGS: *$20,000 to $55,000+ per year.*

RECOMMENDED EDUCATION AND TRAINING: *Educational requirements vary.*

SKILLS AND PERSONALITY TRAITS: *Drawing and illustration skills; artistic ability.*

EXPERIENCE AND QUALIFICATIONS: *Experience is required; a portfolio is necessary.*

JOB DESCRIPTION AND RESPONSIBILITIES

Fashion copyists gather information about the current trends in fashion and garment styling. They look at the styles of garments of competitors and then sketch them. The copyists' employer might then use the sketches to create copies or duplicate types of styles. Fashion copyists might visit stores, boutiques, design houses, fashion shows, or public events and functions to see what people are wearing. As part of their research, fashion copyists might also go through fashion magazines to review style trends, consumer preferences, and price ranges of apparel and accessories. Fashion copyists might research women's, men's, and children's clothing and accessories.

Fashion copyists can do their work in a variety of media. These include pen and ink, pencil, markers, or even crayons. They must show both color and detail. In addition to doing hand drawings and sketches, copyists also use computers to create illustrations. Fashion copyists might be required to produce line drawings or full-color renderings of fashions.

Other responsibilities of fashion copyists might include the following:

- Making actual copies of garments by ripping apart clothing to make patterns or pinning fabric to sample garments
- Designing original garments incorporating features of observed garments

EMPLOYMENT OPPORTUNITIES

Fashion copyists can find employment throughout the country. Opportunities are best in large metropolitan areas where most apparel manufacturers are located. Fashion copyists might freelance or be self-employed, or be on staff in a number of settings, including the following:

- Apparel manufacturers
- Dressmaking companies
- Department stores
- Theatrical wardrobe rooms
- Custom dress shops
- Design studios
- Pattern houses

EARNINGS

Earnings for fashion copyists range from $20,000 to $55,000 or more. Factors affecting earnings include the copyist's talent, training, experience, responsibilities, and professional reputation. Other variables include the employer's size, type, and prestige.

ADVANCEMENT OPPORTUNITIES

Fashion copyists can advance their careers by locating positions in larger or more prestigious companies. Some copyists climb the career ladder by becoming full-fledged fashion designers.

EDUCATION AND TRAINING

Educational requirements for fashion copyists vary from job to job. Two- and four-year programs in fashion design and fashion illustration are available in colleges and universities throughout the country. Vocational, technical, and trade schools also often offer programs in both fashion design and fashion illustration.

EXPERIENCE AND QUALIFICATIONS

Employers might seek various degrees of experience for fashion copyists. Some employers might require that candidates show portfolios. Portfolios illustrate appropriate talents and skills. Fashion copyists must have drawing and illustration skills as well as artistic ability. Some employers might require the ability to sew. Copyists also need an understanding of textiles, fabrics, and ornamentation and a sense of style and trends.

FOR ADDITIONAL INFORMATION: Aspiring fashion copyists can learn more about this career by contacting the Society of Illustrators (SOI), the American Apparel Manufacturers Association (AAMA), The Fashion Association (TFA), and the Council of Fashion Designers of America (CFDA).

TIPS

- Look for apprenticeships and internships to get hands-on experience and on-the-job training. You can often find apprenticeships by contacting apparel manufacturers, theaters, production companies, colleges, universities, or costume designers.

- Put together a portfolio of sketches to bring to interviews. Try to have a varied collection demonstrating your skill at designing for various situations.

- Take classes, workshops, and seminars in fashion design and fashion illustration. These are excellent ways to hone skills, get new ideas, and make important contacts.

- Make sure that you register with your school's job placement office.

- Look in trade journals or the classified section of newspapers for job openings advertised under such headings as "Fashion Copyist," "Fashion," or "Pattern Houses."

- Send your resume with a short cover letter to custom dress stores, design studios, clothing manufacturers, and dressmaking companies.

POLICE SKETCH ARTIST

JOB DESCRIPTION: *Sketch suspects and crime scenes for law enforcement agencies.*

EARNINGS: *$20,000 to $55,000+ per year.*

RECOMMENDED EDUCATION AND TRAINING: *Educational and training requirements vary.*

SKILLS AND PERSONALITY TRAITS: *Drawing and illustration skills; artistic ability.*

EXPERIENCE AND QUALIFICATIONS: *Sketching experience might be required; a portfolio is often necessary.*

JOB DESCRIPTION AND RESPONSIBILITIES

Few crimes are committed directly in front of a photographer with a camera at the ready to take a picture of suspects. In the absence of photographs of the criminal in action, police sketch artists are responsible for creating sketches of alleged crime suspects. Police artists do their work in a number of media, including pen and ink, pencil, markers, or even crayons to show color and detail.

In addition to doing hand drawings and sketches, police sketch artists often use computers to put together composites of suspects. Police sketch artists might be required to do line drawings or full-color renderings of suspects. Their sketches might be used in newspapers, magazines, posters, television, or other media to help police and the public locate and identify criminal suspects.

The police sketch artist must question witnesses to obtain information on the physical characteristics of suspects. The artist might ask about a suspect's height, weight, and body type as well as facial features and hair color and style. Police sketch artists might have to do a series of revisions as more witnesses add new details of a suspect's appearance.

Other responsibilities of police sketch artists might include the following:

- Rendering drawings of crime scenes
- Collaborating with police officers to revise sketches

EMPLOYMENT OPPORTUNITIES

Although police sketch artists can find positions throughout the country, most opportunities are in metropolitan cities that have large law enforcement agencies and high crime rates. Police sketch artists might freelance or be employed full or part time by local police agencies, state police agencies, or federal law enforcement agencies.

EARNINGS

Earnings for police sketch artists range from $20,000 to $60,000 or more. Factors affecting earnings include the artist's experience, responsibilities, and talent and the amount of work that he or she does each year.

ADVANCEMENT OPPORTUNITIES

Police sketch artists can advance their careers by locating full-time positions and by seeking jobs in larger law enforcement agencies.

EDUCATION AND TRAINING

Educational requirements for police sketch artists vary. Employers often accept demonstrated talent in lieu of formal education. Some talented sketch artists are self-taught. Others have fine arts degrees from colleges or universities or art schools. Vocational, technical, and trade schools throughout the country offer programs and courses in illustration and sketching.

EXPERIENCE AND QUALIFICATIONS

Some employers might require candidates to show portfolios of their work to demonstrate their talent and skill. Police sketch artists must have the artistic ability to draw and sketch people and scenes accurately on the basis of verbal descriptions of witnesses.

FOR ADDITIONAL INFORMATION: Aspiring police sketch artists can learn more about this career by contacting the Society of Illustrators (SOI), the National Association of Schools of Art and Design (NASAD), or law enforcement agencies.

TIPS

- Contact local law enforcement agencies to see whether they have openings.
- Consider part-time or freelance opportunities with several agencies if no full-time jobs exist.
- Look in the classified sections of newspapers for jobs advertised under such headings as "Police Artist," "Police Sketch Artist," or "Law Enforcement Agency Artist."
- Start now developing a portfolio of your work to demonstrate your skills.

APPENDIX

Trade Associations, Unions & Other Organizations

The following is a listing of trade associations, unions, and organizations mentioned in the "For Additional Information" section of each job entry. There are also a number of other associations that might be useful in obtaining information on the careers discussed in this book. Names, addresses, and phone numbers are included so that contact can be made with any of the organizations for information regarding membership, career guidance, scholarships, or internships. Many of the organizations have branch offices located throughout the country. Organization headquarters will usually provide the phone number and address of the closest local branch.

Advertising Club of New York (ACNY)
235 Park Avenue South, 5th Floor
New York, NY 10003
212-533-8080

American Advertising Federation (AAF)
1101 Vermont Avenue NW, Suite 500
Washington, DC 20005
202-898-0089

American Apparel Manufacturers Association (AAMA)
2500 Wilson Boulevard
Arlington, VA 22201
703-524-1864

American Art Therapy Association (AATA)
1202 Allanson Road
Mundelein, IL 60060
708-949-6064

American Artists Professional League (AAPL)
47 Fifth Avenue
New York, NY 10003
212-645-1345

American Association of University Professors and National Education Association (AAUPNEA)
1-12 14th Street NW, Suite 500
Washington, DC 20005
202-737-5900

American Craft Council (ACC)
72 Spring Street
New York, NY 10012
212-274-0630

American Federation of Television and Radio Artists (AFTRA)
260 Madison Avenue
New York, NY 10016
212-532-0800

265

American Film Institute (AFI)
John F. Kennedy Center for the
Performing Arts
Washington, DC 20566
202-828-4000

**American Institute For Conservation
of Historic and Artistic Works
(AICHAW)**
1717 K Street NW, Suite 301
Washington, DC 20006
202-452-9545

**American Institute of Graphic Arts
(AIGA)**
164 Fifth Avenue
New York, NY 10010
212-807-1990

**American Marketing Association
(AMA)**
250 South Wacker Drive
Chicago, IL 60606
312-280-6000

**American Newspaper Publishers
Association Foundation (ANPAF)**
The Newspaper Center
11600 Sunrise Center
Reston, VA 22091
703-648-1000

American Publicist Guild (APG)
13415 Ventura Boulevard
Sherman Oaks, CA 91423
213-995-3329

**American Society For Interior
Designers (ASID)**
608 Massachusetts Avenue NE
Washington, DC 20002
202-546-3480

American Society of Artists (ASA)
P.O. Box 1326
Palatine, IL 60078
312-751-2500

**American Society of Composers,
Authors, and Publishers (ASCAP)**
1 Lincoln Plaza
New York, NY 10023
212-595-3050

**American Society of Journalists and
Authors (ASJA)**
1501 Broadway
New York, NY 10036
212-997-0947

**American Society of Magazine
Editors (ASME)**
913 Third Avenue
New York, NY 10022
212-872-3700

**American Society of Media
Photographers (ASMP)**
14 Washington Road, Suite 502
Princeton Junction, NJ 08550
609-799-8300

**American Theatre Critics
Associations (ATCA)**
The Tennessean
2200 Hemingway Drive
Nashville, TN 37215
615-665-0595

**American Women in Radio and
Television (AWRT)**
1650 Tyson Boulevard
Mclean, VA 22102
703-506-3290

Art Directors Club, Inc. (ADC)
250 Park Avenue South
New York, NY 10003
212-674-0500

Associated Press (AP)
50 Rockefeller Plaza
New York, NY 10020
212-621-1500

Association for Computing
Machinery (ACM)
1515 Broadway
New York, NY 10036
212-869-7400

Association of Authors'
Representatives (AAR)
10 Astor Place
New York, NY 10003
212-353-3709

Association of Computer Programmers and Analysts (ACPA)
9 Forrest Drive
Plainview, NY 11803
516-938-8223

Association of Entertainers (AE)
P.O. Box 1393
Washington, DC 20013
202-546-1919

Association of House Democratic
Press Assistants (AHDPA)
House of Representatives
2459 Rayburn Building
Washington, DC 20515
202-225-1554

Association of Medical Illustrators
(AMI)
1819 Peachtree Street NE, Suite 620
Atlanta, GA 30309
404-350-7900

Association of Theatrical Press
Agents and Managers (ATPAM)
165 West 46th Street
New York, NY 10036
212-719-3666

Authors Guild (AG)
330 West 42nd Street
New York, NY 10036
212-563-5904

Broadcast Music, Inc. (BMI)
320 West 57th Street
New York, NY 10019
212-586-2000

Broadcast Promotion and Marketing
Executives (BPME)
6255 Sunset Boulevard, Suite 624
Los Angeles, CA 90028
213-465-3777

Business/Professional Advertising
Association (B/PAA)
21 Kilmer Road
Edison, NJ 08899

Community College Journalism
Association (CCJA)
4619 Larchwood Lane
Philadelphia, PA 19143
215-898-8918

Cosmetologists Association
1811 Monroe
Dearborn, MI 48124
313-563-0360

Costume Designer's Guild (CDG)
13949 Ventura Boulevard
Sherman Oaks, CA 91423
818-905-1557

Council of Fashion Designers of
America (CFDA)
1412 Broadway
New York, NY 10018
212-502-1821

Direct Mail/Marketing Association
(DM/MA)
1120 Avenue of the Americas
New York, NY 10036
212-768-7277

Direct Marketing Association (DMA)
1120 Avenue of the Americas
New York, NY 10036
212-768-7277

Direct Marketing Creative Guild (DMCG)
c/o Richard Sachinis
Graphic Experience
341 Madison Avenue
New York, NY 10017
212-867-0806

The Disney Corporation
500 South Buena Vista Street
Burbank, CA 91521
818-558-2868

Dow Jones Newspaper Fund
P.O. Box 300
Princeton, NJ 08543
609-452-2820

Dramatist Guild (DG)
234 West 44th Street
New York, NY 10036
212-398-9366

Eastman Kodak Information Center
343 State Street
Rochester, NY 14650
716-724-4000

Editorial Freelancers Association (EFA)
71 West 23rd Street, Suite 1504
New York, NY 10010
212-929-5400

Foundation for Interior Design Education Research (IDER)
60 Monroe Center NW, Suite 300
Grand Rapids, MI 49503
616-459-0400

Graphic Artists Guild (GAG)
11 West 20th Street
New York, NY 10011
212-463-7730

Hanna-Barbera
3400 Caunaga Boulevard
Hollywood, CA 90068
213-851-5000

Hollywood Comedy Club (HCC)
c/o Jimmy Val Gray
649 North Rossmore Avenue
Los Angeles, CA 90004
213-467-4772

International Alliance of Theatrical Stage Employees (IATSE)
Local 33 IATSE
1720 West Magnolia Boulevard
Burbank, CA 91506
818-841-9233

International Association of Business Communicators (IABC)
1 Hallidie Plaza, Suite 600
San Francisco, CA 94102
415-433-3400

International Brotherhood of Electrical Workers (IBEW)
1125 15th Street NW
Washington, DC 20005
202-833-7300

International Society of Weekly Newspaper Editors (ISWNE)
Department of Journalism
Brookings, SD 57007
605-688-4171

Investigative Reporters and Editors (IRE)
Box 838
Columbia, MO 62505
314-882-2042

Mail Advertising Service Association (MASA)
1421 Prince Street, Suite 200
Alexandria, VA 22314
703-836-9200

Makeup and Hairstylist Local 706
11519 Chandler Boulevard
North Hollywood, CA 91601
818-984-1700

Makeup and Hairstylist Local 798
31 West 21st Street
New York, NY 10010
212-627-0660

Marketing Research Association (MRA)
2189 Silas Deane Highway, Suite 5
Rocky Hill, CT 06067
203-257-4008

Microcomputer Software Association (MSA)
c/o ADAPSO
1616 North Fort Meyer Drive, Suite 1300
Arlington, VA 22209
703-522-5055

Motion Picture Costumers (MPC)
Local 705, IATSE, MPMO
1427 North La Brea Avenue
Hollywood, CA 90028
213-851-0220

Music Critics Association (MCA)
7 Pine Court
Westfield, NJ 07090
908-233-8468

National Academy of Recording Arts and Sciences (NARAS)
303 North Glen Oaks Boulevard
Burbank, CA 91502
213-849-1313

National Association of Broadcast Employees and Technicians (NABET)
501 3rd Street NW
Washington, DC 20001
202-434-1254

National Association of Broadcasters (NAB)
1771 N Street NW
Washington, DC 20036
202-429-5300

National Association of Government Communicators (NAGC)
669 South Washington Street
Alexandria, VA 22314
703-519-3902

National Association of Schools of Art and Design (NASAD)
11250 Roger Bacon Drive
Reston, VA 22090
703-437-0700

National Association of Science Writers, Inc. (NASW)
P.O. Box 294
Greenlawn, NY 11740
516-757-5664

National Cable Television Association, Inc. (NCTA)
1724 Massachusetts Avenue NW
Washington, DC 20036
202-775-3550

National Council For Interior Design (NCID)
50 Main Street
White Plains, NY 10606
914-948-9100

National Critics Institute (NCI)
c/o Ernest Schier
Eugene O'Neil Theater Center
234 West 44th Street
New York, NY 10036
212-382-2790

**National Educators Association
(NEA)**
1201 16th Street NW
Washington, DC 20036
202-833-4000

**National Entertainment Journalists
Association (NEJA)**
P.O. Box 24021
Nashville, TN 37202
615-256-4048

**National Federation of Press Women
(NFPW)**
Box 99
Blue Springs, MO 64015
816-229-1666

**National Federation of Teachers
(NFT)**
555 New Jersey Avenue NW
Washington, DC 20036
202-879-4400

**National Hairdressers and Cosme-
tologists Association (NHCA)**
3510 Olive Street
St. Louis, MO 63103
314-534-7980

**National Newspaper Association
(NNA)**
1525 Wilson Boulevard, Suite 550
Arlington, VA 22209
703-907-7900

**National Sportscasters and Sports-
writers Association (NSSA)**
Box 559
Salisbury, NC 28144
704-633-4275

New Dramatist
424 West 44th Street
New York, NY 10036
212-757-6960

**New York Drama Critics Circle
(NYDCC)**
c/o Michael Huchware
Associated Press
50 Rockefeller Plaza
New York, NY 10020
212-621-1841

**Newspaper Association of America
Foundation (NAAF)**
1921 Gallows Road
Vienna, VA 22182
703-902-1600

Newspaper Guild (NG)
8611 Second Avenue
Silver Springs, MD 20912
301-585-2990

One Club
3 West 18th Street
New York, NY 10011
212-255-7070

Opera America (OA)
777 14th Street NW, Suite 520
Washington, DC 20005
202-347-9262

Outer Critics Circle (OCC)
c/o Marjorie Gunner
1010 West 57th Street
New York, NY 10019
212-765-8557

**Professional Photographers of
America, Inc. (PPA)**
1090 Executive Way
Des Plaines, IL 60018

Public Relations Society of America (PRSA)
33 Irving Place
New York, NY 10003
212-460-1474

Publishers' Publicity Association, Inc. (PPA)
866 Third Avenue
New York, NY 10022
212-702-6759

Radio Advertising Bureau (RAB)
304 Park Avenue South
New York, NY 10010
212-387-2100

Radio Television News Directors Association (RTNDA)
1000 Connecticut Avenue NW,
Suite 615
Washington, DC 20006
202-659-6510

Republican Communications Associations (RCA)
Longworth Building, Box 550
Washington, DC 20515
202-225-2476

Reuters
1700 Broadway
New York, NY 10019
212-603-3300

Romance Writers of America (RWA)
13700 Veterans Memorial Drive,
Suite 315
Houston, TX 77014
713-440-6885

Sales and Marketing Executive International (SMEI)
Statler Office Tower, Suite 977
Cleveland, OH 44115
216-771-6650

SESAC, Inc. (Society of European Songwriters, Authors, and Composers)
10 Columbus Circle
New York, NY 10019
212-586-3450

Set Designers and Model Makers (SDMM)
Local 847, IATSE
14724 Ventura Boulevard, PH-B
Sherman Oaks, CA 91403
818-784-6555

Society for Technical Communications (STC)
901 North Stuart Street, Suite 904
Arlington, VA 22203
703-522-4114

Society of American Florists (SAF)
1601 Duke Street
Alexandria, VA 22314
703-836-8700

Society of Illustrators (SOI)
128 East 63rd Street
New York, NY 10021
212-838-2560

Society of Professional Journalists (SPJ)
16 South Jackson
Greencastle, IN 46135
317-653-3333

Songwriters Guild (SG)
276 Fifth Avenue
New York, NY 10001
212-686-6820

The Fashion Association (TFA)
475 Park Avenue South
New York, NY 10016
212-683-5665

Touring Entertainment Industry Association (TEIA)
1203 Lake Street
Fort Worth, TX 76102
817-338-9444

United Scenic Artists (USA)
575 Eighth Avenue
New York, NY 10018
212-736-4498

Warner Brothers
4000 Warner Boulevard
Burbank, CA 91522
818-954-6000

Women in Animation/New York (WIA)
330 West 45th Street
New York, NY 10036
212-765-2727

Women in Communications, Inc. (WIĆ)
6900 Newman Road
Clifton, VA 20124
703-803-3728

Women's National Book Association (WNBA)
160 Fifth Avenue, Room 604
New York, NY 10010
212-675-7805

Writers Guild of America East (WGA)
555 West 57th Street
New York, NY 10019
212-767-7800

Writers Guild of America West (WGA)
8955 Beverly Boulevard
West Hollywood, CA 94008
213-550-1000

INDEX